Money of the World:
Coins That Made History

MONEY
of the
WORLD
Coins That
Made History

Ira Goldberg and Larry Goldberg, Editors

Whitman Publishing, LLC
Atlanta, Georgia

MONEY OF THE WORLD
Coins That Made History

www.whitman**books**.com

© 2007 Whitman Publishing, LLC
3101 Clairmont Road · Suite C • Atlanta GA 30329

ISBN: 0-7948-2062X
Printed in China

Disclaimer: Expert opinion should be sought in any significant numismatic purchase. This book is presented as a history. No warranty or representation of any kind is made concerning the completeness of the information presented. The editors are professional numismatists who regularly buy, sell, and sometimes hold certain of the items discussed in this book.

About the front cover: The silver tetradrachm of Rhodes (coin 6, described on pages 8 and 10) bears a remarkable portrait of the sun-god Helios, and dates to the fourth century B.C. The 1479 gold coin is a 7 ducats of Holy Roman Emperor Maximilian I (coin 79, described on pages 130 and 131), showing his beloved first wife, Mary. The 1703 Queen Anne VIGO 5 guineas (coin 105, described on page 176) is the largest multiple of gold guineas from the era of England's rise to prominence as a mercantilist sea power. The 1771 "Greenland dollar" (coin 156, described on pages 265 and 266) models the famous Pillar design of Spanish coins of the 18th century, even though it was minted by King Christian VII of Denmark.

These coins, and many more, tell their fascinating stories in *Money of the World: Coins That Made History*.

For a complete catalog of numismatic reference books, supplies, and storage products, visit Whitman Publishing online at www.whitman**books**.com.

OCG™ collecting guide   WCG™ valuations guide

Contents

Money of the World

Preface

The inspiration for this book began more than 40 years ago, near the end of my teens, when I read a book published in England by John Porteous, *Coins in History*. I was fascinated by the relationship of coinage to money and the historical importance of the role coins played. The book weaves a story of history through coinage that captivated and inspired me, and created a passion that has motivated me throughout my professional career.

The important private collection presented in this volume illustrates the history of Western Civilization through significant coins of the realm. In assembling this collection, the goal was not completion of any series, but rather to demonstrate the organic nature of money and the circumstances that shape it. Each coin had to meet certain criteria before it could be added to the collection:

1. A coin must have been struck for commerce; thus neither patterns nor commemorative issues were sought.
2. A coin had to capture both the beauty and the art of the period.
3. Only the largest circulating size or denomination of a coin was collected; therefore, dollars or talers, and frequently multiples of gold, are showcased, excluding the smaller denominations.
4. The coin had to be of superb quality, not just "the best you can get" or "it does not exist any better."
5. Above all, the coin had to have a story to tell.

In other words, the collection is composed of large and beautiful coins with interesting stories, which, as coins of the realm, were also meant to be spent as money.

For much of Western Civilization, from the earliest Greek coins of the seventh century B.C. until the end of the 19th century, a nation's wealth and influence could be measured through its coinage. (Only during the last 100 years or so have coins become merely tokens for commerce, with little impact on a nation's trade.) The Greeks certainly understood this importance. The rise and fall of Athens, the power and influence of ancient Persia, the conquests of Alexander the Great and the breakup of his empire, can all be traced through coinage and its evolution (or debasement).

The might of Rome is certainly reflected in its coinage. Virtually every Roman emperor boldly stamped his likeness on the money of the day, even as Rome's once-pure silver coin was becoming a mere piece of silver-plated bronze. After the fall of Rome, throughout the Byzantine period, many coinages waned and barter as a form of trade once more resumed. Western Civilization took a step backwards. During the so-called Dark Ages free thinking, along with the arts and sciences, registered steep declines. All of these events can be traced through the coinage of the period. For more than 400 years, few gold coins were struck. Generally, the largest silver coins were a denier, dinero, grosso or silver penny, and the like.

The sciences and arts re-emerged with the Renaissance and trade guilds were formed. Gold once more came to the fore in commercial coinage, and wealth increased throughout Europe. Nations were expanding, exploration and colonization flourished, and a nation's coinage served not only as "coin of the realm" but often as coin of the commercial world as well.

The shift in a country's coinage from regional commerce to the present-day reality of a world commodity truly begins with the monies of Spain, Portugal, and England. The acquisition and exploitation of the Western Hemisphere by these three countries is played out during the 16th, 17th, and 18th centuries. The vast bullion wealth that flowed from the Latin American colonies to the mother countries and the rest of Europe was economically disruptive in the beginning. Soon, though, it was absorbed and utilized throughout the European continent, creating new and important banking, manufacturing, and exporting centers—all with abundant coinages that often employed new forms and art. With this huge influx of bullion assets, Spain was on the cusp of becoming the world's first superpower in a millennium. The failure of its Armada to conquer England in 1588 started Spain's gradual decline and provided England with the momentum to supersede Spain as the world's most powerful nation.

Napoleon was in power for only the first decade and a half of the 19th century, but his influence on Western Civilization and its coinage lasted far beyond his lifetime. Initially feared by Europe's aristocracy as a bringer of revolution, Napoleon would eventually try to establish his own royal dynasty. His numismatic legacy lay in introducing Europe to the system of decimalization. Napoleon implemented his numismatic policy by installing his many siblings and relations as heads of state in the countries France occupied. This gave rise to a fascinating situation in which many of the countries had dual currencies, one maintaining the local traditional coin, and the other slanted to free exchange with France.

On the other side of the world, the American experiment in self-government quickly manifested a sophisticated currency on par with that seen in Europe, such as our early Bust dollars,

1794–1803, and our first gold eagles and half eagles of 1795. As leaders of a new country on the world stage, presidents learned quickly the craft of mixing one's coinage—as an image and symbol of country—with diplomacy. Coinage and image were likewise taken to heart by the newly independent countries of Latin America. Primitive revolutionary monies evolved in a short time to currencies fully at home on the world markets.

And then there is the art. . . .

The best art, combined with craftsmanship and precious material, can be literally transcending. Lay on a velvet tray a Syracuse dekadrachm by the master artist Cimon, or feel the heft and texture of an Egyptian gold octodrachm depicting the beautiful Queen Arsinoe. Marvel at the realistic boldness of a Roman emperor as depicted on a first-century gold aureus. And even the intricate, linear beauty of a hammer-struck medieval coin, such as an English gold noble or a French mouton d'or, can be moving. Relish and admire the artist's painstaking details lavished on a mining scene or city-view taler. Hold in your hand and slowly turn a finely toned German New Guinea Bird of Paradise five marks, and watch the bird change colors. . . then behold an American 1907 Roman Numeral High Relief $20 gold piece. . . just see what happens to your pulse!

It is my hope that the publication of this work will spark the interest and imagination of the next generation of numismatists, just as John Porteous' *Coins in History* inspired and motivated me more than 40 years ago.

Ira Goldberg
Beverly Hills, California

Like that of my father before me, my career began at the age of 10 at Superior Stamp and Coin, the company founded by my grandfather, Isadore Goldberg, in 1931. My father, Harold, began to help around the store from the time it opened. Then, in 1952, it was my turn. I swept floors, cleaned the counters, and soaked thousands of stamps off covers. It truly was work.

Soon I found that I liked coins a lot better than stamps. A few years later, I was joined by my cousin, Ira Goldberg. We started learning everything there was to know about U.S., foreign, and ancient coins. We were not allowed to collect coins—only to sell them. My dad said that everything in the store was for sale, including the safes.

In the early 1960s, we bought a very large foreign coin collection from Abner Kreisberg. There were thousands of choice-quality, silver-crown-size coins. This collection got us started in the foreign coin business and put us on the map. It also made me want to collect foreign coins, but my dad said, "Do not collect what you are selling."

Taking my father's advice, we concentrated on selling. During the 1970s, '80s, and '90s, we were the premier vendors and auctioneers of notable collections such as those belonging to Buddy Ebsen, Ed Trompeter, Irving Goodman, Dr. Benson, and Edwards Huntington Metcalf, often setting world-record prices. These highlight sales included not only U.S. coins, but world and ancient coins as well.

In 2001, one of our clients started selling his U.S. coin collection. Ira and I were auctioning the Irving Goodman collection of crowns of the world at that time, and we approached our client about assembling a world-class collection of ancient and foreign coins of historical significance equal to or better than the Goodman collection. We formed a five-year plan involving the creation of the collection. Our client gave us the go-ahead.

Ira and I are very proud of the collection that we have assembled. We have personally selected each and every coin. Because of our experience building so many important collections, we were able to tap into the abundant connections and resources that we have built up over the past four decades. With an unlimited checkbook behind us, we knew exactly where to go to find the key pieces that are the stars of this collection. We also knew who was ready to sell and who could be persuaded to sell. Every week we examined as many as 10 different catalogs from all over the globe, selecting only the finest numismatic pieces. For us as dealers, this was both a dream come true and an unparalleled adventure. There is nothing more invigorating than competing personally in the international arena for that special prize.

Our ultimate goal was to present a special numismatic reference book showcasing this spectacular collection, and share it with dealers, collectors, and the public. In finding and collecting the treasures contained in this book, we experienced the pride of true collectors—vindication for all those years of not being allowed to collect! For this we thank our special client who encouraged us to carry out this important project that we now call the Millennia Collection.

Larry Goldberg
Beverly Hills, California

Acknowledgments

We would like to express our gratitude to the following writers who contributed to this work. We are thrilled that they accepted our invitation to contribute to the special numismatic book that we long envisioned over our professional careers.

Considerable time and effort went into choosing these writers. Each is an expert in his or her field. Each was given a précis of what we proposed to do and was provided with photographs of the coins to be featured. The task was to use their numismatic knowledge to weave the story behind each coin. We feel that they did an exceptional job.

We also want to thank Lyle Engleson for taking the outstanding photographs that enrich the text.

Finally, we would like to thank the people at Whitman Publishing for taking on this project and for being as excited about it as we are.

Richard G. Doty (*chapter 6*, "An Age of Revolution"), has been working in numismatics for more than 30 years. He is the author or editor of ten books and has written more than 250 articles, mostly on numismatics—from ancient coinage to technology to American currency. He serves as senior curator of numismatics at the Smithsonian Institution (National Museum of American History, Behring Center).

Robert Wilson Hoge (*chapter 3*, "Coins of the Middle Ages"), is a curator at the American Numismatic Society in New York. He is the author of several hundred articles on numismatics and other topics, and was a representative in the International Partnerships among Museums Program of the International Council of Museums. Hoge was director of the Sanford Museum and Planetarium from 1976 to 1981. From 1981 to 2001, as curator of the American Numismatic Association, he was in charge of the ANA's Money Museum, serving also as manager of the association's Authentication Bureau, and as a columnist and contributing editor for *The Numismatist*. He has taught and lectured on anthropology, numismatics, and other subjects.

Ana Lonngi de Vagi (*chapters 7 and 8*, "Latin American Colonial Coinage" and "Coins of the Latin American Republics") is a specialist in the history and coinage of Mexico and Latin America, and is a former member of the curatorial staff at the numismatic department of the Banco de México. She earned a degree in Latin American Studies at the National Autonomous University of Mexico and studied at the National School of Music in Mexico City and the State University of Milan, Italy. While at the Banco de México she co-authored the book *La Distribución de Moneda en México*. She continues to conduct numismatic research based upon original documents in archives in Mexico and Spain.

Bruce Lorich (*chapter 4*, "Coins of the European Renaissance") is a writer, cataloger, and dealer who has been involved in almost every area of numismatics since the early 1970s. Dozens of his articles about rare coins have appeared in print for more than 30 years, and lately online. He has cataloged almost every U.S. and world coin rarity for auction, and is an expert on British coins.

Michael J. Shubin (*chapter 5*, "1600–1750: The Age of Reason?"), after receiving his schooling in Fine Arts, ended up spending half of his working career involved in numismatics, antiquities, and antiques, serving in such capacities as cataloger, researcher, consultant, and appraiser. His interests are those of a generalist, with a preference for the ancient.

David L. Vagi (*chapters 1 and 2,* "Ancient Greek Coinage" and "Ancient Roman Coinage") began his career as a staff writer for *Coin World* and later worked as a numismatist for leading commercial firms and the international auction house Christie's. He remains active as an independent dealer, researcher, writer and editor, and as a consultant to publishers, museums, and auction houses in North America and Europe. He is a longtime instructor at the American Numismatic Association's annual Summer Seminar, an active columnist, and author of the award-winning, two-volume *Coinage and History of the Roman Empire*.

CHAPTER ONE

ANCIENT GREEK COINAGE

David L. Vagi

In the most general terms we may say the first coins of the Western World were struck between about 650 and 600 B.C., and that they were most likely produced in the regions of Ionia or Lydia in modern Turkey. But beyond that, little can be said with precision.

The earliest coins were hardly objects we would recognize today as coins: they were lumps of electrum (an alloy of gold and silver), generally without inscriptions or a design, or with crude ornamentation such as striations. Importantly, though, they were struck with dies, their weights adhered to a standard, and there were subdivisions of that standard, indicating a system of denominations.

It took several generations of use before the production of coinage became widespread. We are fortunate that this collection contains an example (coin 1) of one of the very first royal coinages, a gold stater of the type introduced by Lydian king Croesus (c. 561–546 B.C.), a man who was famous in his time, as now, for his wealth.

Coin 1: gold stater of Lydia

This coin is old enough to illustrate all of the important aspects of early "Greek" coinage. First, it has a design on only one side, the obverse, in this case bearing a confronted lion and bull—familiar royal symbols in the ancient cultures of the Near East. By contrast, the reverse consists of deep impressions made by two incuse punches with rough surfaces. These had no artistic content and were simply a means by which the coin could be struck efficiently.

It is interesting to note that the two segments of the reverse punch are of unequal size. This is not always the case on early coins, and there can be no doubt it was tailored to the obverse die, on which the lion occupies more of the die design than the bull. Not only did this mean the planchets had to be somewhat egg shaped, but the dies—both obverse and reverse—also had to meet that requirement.

As mentioned, coinage originated in Asia Minor in regions that today are part of western Turkey. The commercial contacts between the indigenous peoples of Asia Minor, the Persians, and Greeks were significant because the Greeks had founded numerous colonies in Asia Minor in the centuries prior to the advent of coinage. Thus, it was inevitable that through these colonies the invention of coinage would become known in mainland Greece.

Even so, the Greeks did not strike their own coins until some 50 to 100 years after coinage was developed. Though it was slow to be intro-

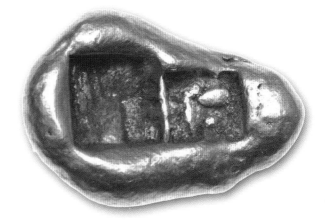

Coin 1: gold stater of Lydia

This coin is one of the type introduced by the wealthy King Croesus of Lydia. While preparing for war with Cyrus the Great of Persia, Croesus consulted the oracle at Delphi. He was told that if he crossed the Halys River, a great empire would be toppled. The famous king did not know it, but the toppled empire would be his own.

duced in Greece, once coin production began it spread rapidly: within two generations coins were being struck at several cities on the mainland, as well as on some Cycladic islands. Within a century of that, coins were being struck in virtually every Greek city of note.

Historians generally agree that the first coins of Greece were produced on the island of Aegina, not far from Athens. Its main coinage for two centuries or more was a silver stater depicting on its obverse a sea turtle or a land tortoise, cut in very high relief. Like most early Greek coins, the reverse die had no design, but served only as a utilitarian punch.

The Aeginetan stater (**coin 2**) in this collection was struck c. 480–457 B.C., about a century after the first coins were struck on the island. In that time the quality of the dies and striking had improved considerably and the incuse punch on the reverse had been transformed from a varying number of deep-cut segments to five shallow segments with thick bars of separation. On the later issues, letters and symbols would appear in the fields on the obverse and within the sunken fields of the incuse punch.

When admiring the extraordinarily high relief of this coin one can appreciate why it was struck on a short, thick planchet. Had a thinner or broader planchet been used the obverse die could not have been filled with sufficient metal to reveal all of the fine details.

The specimen in this collection is remarkable for its centering, and even for the amount of metal in the fields that surround the sea turtle. For as much pride as the artists may have taken in cutting of the dies, the production of coinage at Aegina was crude. They were never intended as objects of art to the degree we appreciate them today, and so long as their weight and purity were correct, and the strike marginally complete, these coins were released into circulation.

Another early Greek coin (**coin 3**) in this collection was produced at Corinth, a city at the base of the isthmus that connects central Greece with the Peloponnese. The attractive design of the winged horse Pegasus reflects a mythological episode in which a Corinthian nobleman named Belerophon sought the help of Pegasus to slay the Chimera, a fire-breathing monster that had become a menace.

This is one of the city's earliest issues, from late in the sixth century B.C. Its style is fully archaic, for Pegasus is shown with a curled wing

Coin 2: silver stater of Aegina

Coin 3: silver stater of Corinth

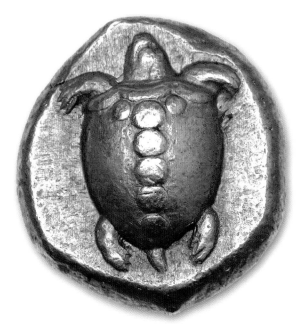

Coin 2: silver stater of Aegina
The turtle had religious signifigance to the ancient Greeks; it was a creature sacred to the goddess Aphrodite.

Coin 3: silver stater of Corinth
The winged horse Pegasus was born of the blood of Medusa, a snake-haired monster slain by Perseus.

rather than with the straight wing of most of the later issues of the classical period. We are fortunate that this coin was struck with fresh dies, for most of the surviving examples of these early Corinthian staters were struck with dies that had lost their fine detail due to over-use.

Though the coins of Corinth are well known to collectors, the earliest issues were not struck on the same large scale as were the tetradrachms of Athens or the staters of Aegina. Also, their planchets were broad and thin, rather than thick and globular, which was uncharacteristic of Greek coinages of the sixth century B.C.

Greek Cities and Kingdoms

Once beyond its origins in the archaic period (c. 760–479 B.C.), coinage proliferated greatly throughout the Greek world and beyond. It became recognized as a convenient and reliable medium of exchange for transactions ranging from acquiring one's daily bread to paying thousands of mercenaries on a military expedition. Thus, most every free city of sufficient size began to strike its own coins.

The largest production of Greek coinage occurred during the classical (c. 479–350/336 B.C.) and the Hellenistic (c. 350/336–30 B.C.) periods, and it continued on a large scale during the Roman period (c. 30 B.C.–A.D. 297), during which Greece and all of its former territories came under Roman rule.

Any discussion of the height of Greek coinage must begin with Athens, the most important of all Greek cities. Its principal coinage, silver tetradrachms (four-drachm coins) bearing the helmeted head of Athena and a standing owl, are the most familiar numismatic image of ancient Greece. In their day they were a common sight from Sicily and Italy in the West, to Egypt, the Arabian Peninsula, and Afghanistan in the East. If any coinage was the "international currency" of the ancient Greek world before the age of kings, it was the so-called owl of Athens.

This collection contains a tetradrachm (**coin 4**) from the height of production at Athens, from about 449 to 420 B.C. Though the basic design of this coin had not changed for a hundred years, by now it had lost its archaic vigor and achieved an appearance consistent with the classical period of art.

Because the dies used at Athens to strike coins bore designs that usually were broader than the surfaces of the coins themselves, it is highly

Coin 4: silver tetradrachm of Athens

Coin 4: silver tetradrachm of Athens The issues of Athens are perhaps the best known of all ancient coinages. This is not surprising considering the fame of Athens and the broad circulation of its coins. On both sides the designs are cut in high relief, though the field of the reverse is deeply set within an incuse square created by the shape of the die.

unusual to find a tetradrachm with a nearly full crest on Athena's helmet. Not only does this coin display far more of the crest than is commonly observed, but also it is exceptionally well preserved.

Athens was fortunate that it controlled enormously productive silver mines at nearby Laurium. In large part we can attribute the great prosperity of Athens to this virtually inexhaustible source of wealth.

The large silver coins of the major city-states were struck mainly for local, regional, and international trade, and some of them were struck consistently over long periods of time. We find a notable exception to this model at Olympia, the sanctuary and site of the Olympic Games that were held every four years. Careful study has shown that Olympic staters were produced only on the occasions of the games to support the temporary economy that was generated.

The Games were the most important event on the Greek calendar. They drew participants from throughout the Greek world, and their victors became international heroes. This collection contains one of the finest surviving examples of the Olympic Games coinage—a silver stater thought to have been produced for the 87th Olympiad of c. 432 B.C. **(coin 5)**. It shows an eagle (a bird sacred to Zeus, chief deity of the sanctuary) with its prey, and a seated Nike (symbolic of victory), both of which are appropriate themes for the Olympics.

This coin is unusually fine for Olympic staters, for in general they seem to have been hammered out very quickly to meet the periodic demand. The surviving examples show that some of the most skilled die-cutters were employed, yet the production standards were poor. Off-center strikings are very common, and the masterful dies were routinely used beyond their ideal lifetime, until they were extremely worn or broken.

As we have already mentioned, the Greeks had established colonies in Asia Minor, notably along the Aegean coast and on the islands just off shore. Up until the time of Alexander the Great these cities were either under Persian domination or at risk of being so. Nonetheless, they remained prosperous, and gave the Greeks a foothold on the Asiatic mainland.

One of the most prolific issuers of Greek coins in Asia Minor was Rhodes, a city on the island of the same name. Its artists were quite skilled, as they routinely achieved one of the most difficult feats for a die engraver—producing a full-facing head in high relief. This collection has

Coin 5: silver stater of Olympia

Coin 5: silver stater of Olympia
Coins of the Olympic Games were often kept as souvenirs by those who visited from throughout the Greek world. The sanctuary at Olympia and the games were supported in part with revenue earned by the exchange of foreign coins for Olympic coins, which were the only ones accepted at the games.

a truly remarkable silver tetradrachm of Rhodes **(coin 6)** depicting the facing head of the sun-god Helios, which was struck at the beginning of the fourth century B.C.

Much can be learned about Greek coins by studying the reverse of this coin. First, above the rose, there is a Greek inscription POΔION which is rendered in the genitive plural, and translates to "(coin) of the Rhodians." The rose—a punning allusion to the name of the city (Rhodes)—is accompanied by the Greek letter Φ and a laurel wreath. Usually symbols and letters like these represented city magistrates or the official(s) responsible for coinage, or they were administrative symbols of a less personal nature. Occasionally they represented the signatures of artists.

In addition to producing substantial coinages in central Greece and Asia Minor, the Greeks (or semi-Greeks) also were active coiners in Northern Greece—notably in the regions of Macedon, Thrace, and the Greek Chalcidice. There were important silver mines in the North, and the local inhabitants converted much of their output into coinage, often into uncommonly large silver coins. The minting authorities included Greeks who had established cities in the North, and, to the interior, various tribes and kingdoms.

One of the most substantial coinages of Northern Greece came from the island of Thasos, located off the Thracian mainland. Though renowned for its high-quality wine, the Thasians also controlled productive mines on their island and on the mainland.

For about 150 years during the archaic and classical periods they produced silver staters that showed a nymph being abducted or being seduced by a satyr (a mythological part-human creature from the retinue of Dionysus, god of wine). This collection has a magnificent example of the "seduction" type **(coin 7)**, which is of highly refined, classical style.

The Greeks had always cherished their independence, especially at the level of the city-state. However, the tide of history swept that ideal aside on numerous occasions when kings or cities (notably Athens as head of the Delian League) gained extraordinary power over their neighbors, or when a group of cities banded together to form a league for their common defense.

The death-blow to the independent city-state, though, was delivered

Coin 6: silver tetradrachm of Rhodes

Coin 7: silver stater of Thasos

Coin 6: silver tetradrachm of Rhodes
The Greek sun-god Helios is here shown as a
calm youth with windswept hair and wide-
staring eyes.

Coin 7: silver stater of Thasos
The wilder side of Greek culture is
revealed in scenes such as this, in
which a satyr seduces a nymph.

in the second half of the fourth century B.C., when the Macedonian Kingdom came into prominence under King Philip II (359–336 B.C.) and his son Alexander III, "the Great" (336–323 B.C.). Alexander was able to finish the Greek unification that his father had envisioned, and before he died, he had conquered not only Greece, but also Egypt and most of the Near East up to the border of India. In doing so, Alexander destroyed the mighty Persian Empire.

The unprecedented success of the Macedonians was fueled not only by the dynamic personalities of Philip and Alexander, but also by the incredible mineral wealth they controlled: gold and silver was being mined in enormous quantities, and this was of inestimable help in funding their campaign for expansion.

This collection contains spectacular examples of the two principal gold coins of these kings—one struck in the name of Philip II (**coin 8**), showing the laureate head of Apollo and a chariot scene, the other in the name of Alexander III (**coin 9**), showing the helmeted head of Athena and the standing figure of Nike. Much like the "owls" of Athens, the principal coins of the Macedonian Kingdom were a common sight from Afghanistan to Western Europe.

Both coins are exceptionally well preserved and are unusually well struck on broad planchets. The coin in Philip's name—a gold stater—weighs 8.60 grams, conforming to the standard weight that had long ago been established by Athens for a didrachm (or stater). Alexander's coin is of a significantly rarer double-denomination, a distater, and this particular example weighs 17.23 grams. It is remarkable how precise the standardized weights on ancient gold coins could be, as is demonstrated by these two coins.

Interestingly, both of these coins were struck c. 324–318 B.C., after both Philip II and Alexander III were dead. In ancient times, as now, coinage was an inherently conservative instrument, and popular coin designs were often perpetuated by successor kings or even by independent city-states seeking a commercial advantage. Such is the case here, for both were probably struck during the reign of Alexander's successor, Philip III (323–317 B.C.).

When Alexander died at Babylon in 323 B.C. he left a vast kingdom in need of rulership. This is scarcely something Alexander would have considered at the time, for he was still a young man who had survived

Coin 8: gold stater in the name of Philip II of Macedon

Coin 9: gold distater in the name of Alexander the Great

Coin 8: gold stater in the name of Philip II of Macedon The reverse of this coin might celebrate a chariot race Philip II personally won in the Olympic Games.

Coin 9: gold distater in the name of Alexander the Great Athena here wears a triple-crested helmet of the Corinthian style, and Nike holds a wreath of victory.

Coin 10: silver tetradrachm of Demetrius

Coin 11: gold stater of Lysimachus

countless hardships. Also, years before his death he had succumbed to megalomania, and he no doubt believed he would live many decades more and conquer all of the lands he had thus far bypassed.

Theoretically his kingdom was to be inherited by his nearest family—his yet-unborn son Alexander IV, and his half-brother Arrhidaeus, who adopted the name Philip III. We are told that Philip III was feeble-minded. Considering the dynastic gap, a group of seasoned generals and noblemen filled the power vacuum left by Alexander, and in essence ruled the Macedonian Kingdom in the names of Alexander IV and Philip III.

The truth of the matter was that none of these ambitious, deserving men intended to preserve the throne for Alexander IV or Philip III. They were content for nearly two decades to rule in their names, but it was just a matter of time before both heirs were eliminated and Alexander's true successors established their own hereditary monarchies, based principally in Macedon, Thrace, Syria, and Egypt.

Perhaps the greatest of the generals to succeed Alexander was Antigonus, surnamed Monophthalmus ("the one-eyed"), who ruled much of the Near East for more than two decades. But if we had to rely on coinage alone, we would never know he existed, for he did not put his name on any of the millions of coins he struck. Instead, he used the names of Alexander or Philip, and utilized their familiar designs.

Such was not the case with Antigonus' son Demetrius, surnamed Poliorcetes ("the besieger"), who struck coins with his own name and his own original designs. This collection contains one such coin—a silver tetradrachm (coin 10) bearing a portrait of Demetrius. He presents himself not only as a king, but as an associate of the gods, for he wears the horn of a bull, an animal sacred to the sea-god Poseidon (who is depicted on the reverse). Since Demetrius' strength had always been his navy, it was an appropriate connection to make.

Another of Alexander's immediate successors was Lysimachus, who initially took control of Thrace, but who over time expanded his territories to include Macedon and a large part of Asia Minor. Like his contemporaries, Lysimachus initially struck coins bearing the name and the types of Alexander, but he eventually introduced his own coin types. This collection contains a fine example of his most familiar type (coin 11), which he struck in both gold and silver. This particular coin, a gold stater, was struck in Macedon near the end of Lysimachus' life, by which

Coin 10: silver tetradrachm of Demetrius The standard formula for royal Hellenistic coins is a portrait on the obverse and a deity on the reverse.

Coin 11: gold stater of Lysimachus The head of Alexander the Great, wearing the horn of Zeus-Ammon, appears on this coin of Lysimachus.

time Alexander had been dead for about four decades. Lysimachus demonstrated more humility than most of his contemporaries, for he never struck a coin with his own portrait. Instead, we see here an idealized portrait of Alexander himself, who had achieved divine status even in his lifetime. The reverse shows the goddess Athena, seated in triumph as she holds a small figure of Nike, the ancient goddess of victory, who crowns the name of Lysimachus.

The modesty of Lysimachus was not shared by Ptolemy I, who soon after Alexander's death assumed control of Egypt. There he established a hereditary dynasty that proved to be the longest lasting of them all, enduring more than three centuries until the nation fell to the Romans after its last Greek monarch—the famous Queen Cleopatra VII—committed suicide in 30 B.C.

The coins of the Ptolemies seldom bore the images of reigning monarchs. Instead they most often had the portrait of Ptolemy I, the first king of the dynasty, or the portrait of a deity, especially Zeus-Ammon. On certain issues, though—notably on gold coins—the portraits of other members of the dynasty appear.

Coin 12: gold octodrachm of Berenice II

We have in this collection a gold octodrachm (an eight-drachm coin) of Berenice II, the cousin-wife of Ptolemy III, the third king in Ptolemy's hereditary line **(coin 12)**. The Ptolemies often portrayed royal women on their coinage, with their recurring royal Greek names Berenice, Arsinoe, and Cleopatra inscribed on the reverse.

This magnificent coin demonstrates the typical simplicity of royal Greek coins, which usually show the portrait of a ruler without an accompanying inscription on the obverse. As will be seen in the next chapter, even though the Romans adopted the Greek idea of royal portraits they did not copy this particular aspect; the portraits of Roman emperors tended to be enclosed within an identifying inscription. In contrast, the Greeks usually identified the issuer with an inscription on the reverse. Here it is extremely simple: Sometimes they were more elaborate, such as with the later issues of the Seleucid kings of Syria, most of whom added to their names and titles an epithet such as *Epiphanes* (God Manifest), or *Soter* (Savior).

Like the other royal Greek portrait coins in this collection, this coin of Berenice II was struck early enough in the Hellenistic period that its dies were cut in high relief and in fine style. As time marched on,

**Coin 12: gold octodrachm of
Berenice II** The Greeks who ruled
Egypt often struck large gold coins, for
they had that metal in relative abundance.

though, the beautifully idealized images of the Greek monarchs lost their vigor, and eventually were transformed into generic and simplistic portraits that bore little individuality.

The Western Greeks

Centuries before the age of coinage, the Greeks had experienced the need to colonize. Their population had expanded and there was comparatively little opportunity for the youth, who often became mercenaries in order to earn a living.

They colonized in all directions: northward to Macedon and Thrace (and even the Crimea), eastward and southward into Asia Minor, and, as the next few coins testify, westward to Italy and Sicily and beyond.

Within a generation or two of coins being struck in Greece, they were being struck in their colonies in the West—in Sicily, and in southern Italy (called *Magna Graecia*: "greater Greece"). The earliest coins of these two regions took on very different forms.

This collection contains a magnificent silver stater of Caulonia (**coin 13**) that exemplifies the type of coinage that initially was preferred in Magna Graecia. The coin immediately stands out from other ancient coins in this collection because of the interrelationship between its obverse and reverse: the obverse design is in relief, and the reverse is incuse, closely following the contours of the obverse. This was not only an artistic feat, but it required careful attention to the technical aspects of coin production.

Another aspect worth noting on this stater is the vigorous archaic style. The overall composition is realistic, but the details are presented in unrealistic ways, such as Apollo's eye and chest, which are shown fully facing when in a naturalistic composition they would be shown in profile.

Not far from Caulonia, at the tip of the "toe" of the Italian peninsula, was Rhegium, another colony of the Greeks. Here we see an extraordinary silver tetradrachm of Rhegium (**coin 14**). It was struck some two centuries after the Caulonia stater just described, and thus is of a very different style and fabric. It also honors the god Apollo, though not as a muscular standing figure, but in the form of a rather effeminate portrait. The reverse shows a facing lion's scalp, a design that on coinage is recognized as the badge of the city, much like the rose of the coin of Rhodes

Coin 13: silver stater of Caulonia

Coin 14: silver tetradrachm of Rhegium

Coin 13: silver stater of Caulonia
Striking incuse-style coins had to be done with precision to protect the coins and the dies from damage.

Coin 14: silver tetradrachm of Rhegium The god Apollo is here shown with long, curly hair contained within an elaborate wreath of laurel leaves.

described earlier. On the earlier issues of this city the lion's scalp was engraved into the obverse die.

Though this was one of the last tetradrachms to be struck at Rhegium, its artistry shows that the standards at the mint had not wavered with the passage of time. It is interesting to note this tetradrachm appears to be a product of the high-classical period, while hoard evidence and a technical study of the coinage proves it was struck well into the later (and typically cruder) Hellenistic period.

Though Rhegium had several neighbor cities in Southern Italy, its closest neighbor of consequence was actually the Greek colony of Messana on the island of Sicily, directly across the treacherous Strait of Messina. Because of their proximity, Rhegium and Messana frequently interacted, and often were at odds.

This collection contains an excellent silver tetradrachm of Messana (**coin 15**) with its classic design of a mule-chariot on the obverse and a bounding hare on the reverse. Though the main types remained consistent, there is a great deal of variety within the series based on the style of the engraving, the details of the scenes, and the symbols that appear in the fields. This particular coin is from the height of the classical period, and was struck not long before the city was destroyed.

In the 480s B.C. Messana (then known by its original name, Zankle) was captured by Anaxilas, the tyrant of the aforementioned Rhegium. Anaxilas not only changed the city's name to Messana but he also radically changed its coinage. It is believed that the mule-chariot alludes to a victory Anaxilas had scored in that event at the Olympic Games, and that the hare is a reflection of the god Pan, whose worship Anaxilas is thought to have introduced to Sicily.

We now will observe the coinage of Syracuse, the chief city on the island of Sicily and, along with Rome and Carthage, one of the three most important cities in the Western Mediterranean. Though Rome would only begin to become powerful in the fourth century B.C., Carthage and Syracuse had long been important cities, and for just as long they had been enemy capitals.

We are fortunate that this collection contains three coins of Syracuse. We may begin with a silver tetradrachm (**coin 16**) from the earliest phase of coin production at this city, which shows on its obverse a four-horse chariot in profile, and on its reverse a quadripartite incuse square that incorporates a design.

Coin 15: silver tetradrachm of Messana

Coin 16: silver tetradrachm of Syracuse

Coin 15: silver tetradrachm of Messana It is believed that the mule-chariot and the hare were designs of personal interest to the tyrant Anaxilas.

Coin 16: silver tetradrachm of Syracuse This tetradrachm of Syracuse bears all of the stylistic and technical hallmarks of an archaic Greek coin.

Despite the fact that this exact composition did not last long, these early coins of Syracuse set a trend that would last for more than two centuries on Syracusan coinage: a chariot on the obverse and the head of a goddess (usually described as Arethusa or Artemis-Arethusa) on the reverse. Collectors often find it unusual that on these coins the head is on the reverse and the chariot on the obverse, but a technical study of the coins reveals this is the case.

The style and fabric of the early coins of Syracuse differ greatly from the previously described stater of Caulonia (which was typical of the earliest coinages from Southern Italy). Early Syracusan coins clearly were inspired by products from the mints in mainland Greece and Northern Greece, and from the artistry of Attic vase paintings.

The ingenious aspect of this tetradrachm, however, is the incorporation of the head of the goddess within a circle at the center of the utilitarian, swastika-like incuse punch of the reverse die.

The stiff, formal chariot scene on this early tetradrachm underwent a slow evolution at Syracuse, and in its various permutations it came to influence other coinages in Sicily. In this case the four horses are shown in close profile, with the heads and necks of the two pair of horses purposely separated so as to give depth and dimension to the design which otherwise might not be discernible.

The most practical way to determine there are four horses is to examine their legs, among which there is significant overlapping. On the later coinages of Syracuse the difficulty of representing all four horses was resolved by changing the angle at which the scene was displayed.

We may now observe two of the most famous silver coins of Syracuse, which serve to illustrate that transformation. Both are of a most unusual denomination for Greek coinage—a decadrachm (a ten-drachm coin). Compared to the standard large silver Greek coin, the tetradrachm of 17.2 grams, the decadrachm of about 43 grams was enormous. Only on very rare occasions were heavier silver coins produced in the Greek world.

Silver decadrachms were struck at Syracuse in three varieties; by the Greek king Alexander the Great in two varieties; and in one type each at Athens and Acragas (another city on Sicily). Because of their size and rarity, it has long been believed that decadrachms were struck as commemoratives. Though it is clear from a variety of evidence that they were used

Coin 17: silver decadrachm of Syracuse (by Cimon) The signature of Cimon, the artist who originated this design, appears in three places on this example.

Coin 18: silver decadrachm of Syracuse (by Euainetos) Unlike on most Greek coins, the head is on the reverse of many archaic and classical Syracusan coins.

Coin 17: silver decadrachm of Syracuse (by Cimon) (shown enlarged on page 23)

Coin 18: silver decadrachm of Syracuse (by Euainetos) (shown enlarged on page 23)

as circulating coins, each of these issues must have been initiated under special circumstances.

The first decadrachm of Syracuse was struck about 470–465 B.C. Only a handful of specimens survive from that first emission. Some three or four generations later two issues of decadrachms began more or less contemporaneously, and they were struck over longer periods. Because they were more substantial issues their designs became influential in Sicily and throughout the Greek world.

The first of these (**coin 17**) was designed by the artist Cimon, whose decadrachms were produced from about 405 B.C. to 400 B.C., and the second (**coin 18**) was introduced soon after by the artist Euainetos, whose decadrachms were struck for a much longer period—perhaps more than three decades.

Cimon's series probably marked Syracuse's survival of the devastating Carthaginian invasion of Sicily in 406–405 B.C. There is good reason to think a victory prompted this coinage, for beneath the chariot scene there is a display of armor and weapons accompanied by the inscription AΘΛA, which indicates "prizes."

> *There is good reason to think a victory prompted this coinage. . . .*

As suggested earlier, these coins transform the traditional Syracusan chariot scene from a somber affair to a highly energized event. Rather than trotting, the horses are at a full gallop, and they are also shown at a slight angle, allowing the artist to represent the depth of the scene. It is interesting to note that on the Cimonian die the heads of the horses are tossing in all directions, whereas the horses are all in perfect alignment on the die of the Euainetos type.

The reverses of these decadrachms both bear an inscription (identifying the mint as Syracuse), before which the head of Artemis-Arethusa is shown surrounded by four dolphins. Syracuse had an excellent natural harbor and an abundant supply of fresh water from springs, a fortunate circumstance that it is believed is symbolized by this attractive reverse type.

The designs of both artists were impressive enough that each signed at least the initial set of his dies. Some scholars now believe that most (if not all) of the subsequent dies were engraved by their protégés at Syracuse, who in many cases included the signatures of their masters as a standard part of the design.

The dies used to strike the coin of the Cimonian type in this collection bear no fewer than three signatures. Cimon's initial K appears on the band at the forehead of the goddess, and his full signature KIMΩN appears twice: boldly on the body of the dolphin below the goddess' neck, and in small, indistinct letters on the ground line beneath the chariot.

The "Other" Greeks

Among collectors of ancient coins the definition of "Greek coins" usually includes any non-Roman coin issued by a Greek-influenced civilization that existed from Britain to the westernmost regions of India. This includes, of course, the royal Lydian coin discussed at the beginning of this chapter (for Croesus was not a Greek).

In this section we will highlight ten coins from from this collection that fall under the heading of Greek coins, but which were the creations of non-Greek civilizations.

Our survey will follow a geographical path from west to east, and will begin with the Punic colonies in the Western Mediterranean, which had been founded by Phoenicians. These colonists are often referred to generically as Carthaginians because their main base was at Carthage, on the coast of North Africa. This city not only had a superb harbor, but it also was on the spur of land that came closest to Sicily and Italy.

Carthaginians were in frequent contact with the indigenous peoples of the Western Mediterranean, and with the Greeks who, likewise, had sailed west to establish colonies. The Western Greeks became the principal enemies of the Carthaginians, going to war with them many times in the fifth, fourth, and third centuries B.C. Thereafter, once Greek power in the West began to decline, the Carthaginians found a new, more substantial enemy in the Romans.

The rivalry between the Greeks and the Carthaginians is represented by a silver tetradrachm from this collection **(coin 19)** that in its style and fabric appears to be Greek. But it is a Carthaginian coin that was modeled after Greek coinage, and its dies almost certainly were cut by a Greek artist. It was important that the coin appealed to Greek sen-

Coin 19: silver tetradrachm of the Siculo-Punic series (shown enlarged on page 27)

sibilities because it was meant to pay the largely Greek mercenary army that the Carthaginians had assembled to fight other Greeks.

The female head on the obverse is clearly modeled after the Artemis-Arethusa on the silver decadrachm of Syracuse, of the Euainetos type that was earlier described. The reverse, though rendered in fine late classical–early Hellenistic style, bears a design that betrays its Punic origins, for both the horse and the palm tree were symbols of Carthage. Here they are combined to create a pleasant design that still would seem appropriate for Greek coinage.

Interestingly, this coin was struck c. 330–325 B.C., when in the East the Macedonian king Alexander the Great had defeated the Persians and was continuing to conquer lands as remote as Afghanistan. Though the conquests of Alexander were monumental, the West remained largely unaffected, for Alexander's focus was elsewhere.

Another Punic coin in this collection **(coin 20)**, a superbly preserved gold trihemistater (1-1/2 staters), was struck about 70 years later. Its design is fundamentally the same as the earlier silver coin, though the palm tree has been eliminated and the horse is shown in a less animated posture.

But that is where the similarities end, because the artistry on this piece is decidedly non-Greek. Unlike the previous coin (which was struck in Sicily), this was struck in Carthage. The Punic style is easy to identify: the features of the goddess—in this case Tanit-Persephone—are less proportionate than those of its Greek forbearer. But therein lies the charm, for the result is an image of great power and subtlety.

Also in the West was a famous and diverse network of civilizations collectively known as the Celts. They occupied much of the lands from Britain, Gaul, and Spain to the Black Sea, though they even settled into Asia Minor. With few exceptions their domains did not extend to the shores of the Mediterranean, for these coastal regions, over time, were claimed by Greeks, Romans, and others who continued to drive the Celts northward.

The designs of Celtic coins are a mixture of original compositions and ones they borrowed from the Greeks and the Romans. Celtic coins are easily identified because of their art style, which is imaginative and distinctive. This collection contains a silver tetradrachm **(coin 21)** struck by Celts who lived along the Danube River in Eastern Europe. Among

Coin 20: gold trihemistater of Carthage

Coin 21: silver tetradrachm of the Eastern European Celts (shown enlarged on page 29)

Coin 19: silver tetradrachm of the Siculo-Punic series This elegant design seemingly was created by a Greek artist working for the Carthaginians.

Coin 20: gold trihemistater of Carthage The Punic influence can be seen readily in this coin, which was struck at Carthage rather than in Sicily.

their trading partners were the Greeks in Macedon and Thrace, whose coins they used on a regular basis.

Thus, we find in this collection a Celtic invention based upon the designs on the coinage of the Macedonian king Philip II (359–336 B.C.): the obverse is inspired by the head of Apollo on Philip's gold staters (an example of which is seen in coin 8), and the reverse copies an equestrian scene from the reverse of Philip's silver tetradrachms. This coin was struck perhaps two centuries after Philip introduced his coinage, which demonstrates the enduring influence of the Macedonian coinage among the Celts.

We can easily determine the prototypes of these designs, but the style and the details differ substantially from the Macedonian originals. It is especially noticeable on the reverse, where the rider is only partial, the horse is shown in a highly stylized fashion, and where a gold torque—a form of Celtic jewelry that demonstrated the wealth and status of its owner—appears beneath.

A civilization that was even more remote from the Greeks was that of the Scythians of the Cimmerian Bosporus, a region north of the Black Sea comprising much of the modern Ukraine. The Scythians had long dealt with the Greeks, who desired their trade goods.

Coin 22: gold stater of Pharnaces II

We are fortunate that this collection contains a rare and interesting gold stater (**coin 22**) of Pharnaces II, who, in defiance of the Romans, ruled the Cimmerian Bosporus from 63 to 47 B.C. Though it was struck long after the Greeks had lost their independence to the Romans, its designs are derived from a long tradition of Greek coin typology.

The reverse shows one of the principal Greek gods, Apollo, reclining against a lyre and holding an olive branch over a tripod (representing his roles as a god of music and of prophecy). It also bears a date, equating 53/52 B.C., which is rendered in the traditional Greek manner in which Greek letters represented numerals. Though the regal inscription is rendered in Greek, its form is clearly influenced by long-standing Persian and Parthian traditions, for it describes Pharnaces as the "great king of kings."

The obverse is derived from the portrait-type of Alexander the Great that had originated under the aforementioned Lysimachus, one of Alexander's successors. Since the accuracy of Pharnaces' portrait was of less importance than its role in evoking a connection with Alexander, we should not be surprised to see that the image is highly stylized.

Coin 21: silver tetradrachm of the Eastern European Celts The Celts often modified Greek coin designs to suit their own artistic bent.

Coin 22: gold stater of Pharnaces II This Bosporan king was particularly defiant, revolting against his father and powerful Roman generals.

Coin 23: silver tetradrachm of Mithradates VI

Coin 24: gold daric of Persia

Pharnaces was the son of one of the ancient world's most infamous kings—Mithradates VI, who ruled much of the lands in the Black Sea region from 120 to 63 B.C. Reigns this long are uncommon in any point in world history, and the Greeks and Romans would have preferred Mithradates VI had not enjoyed such longevity. He was a fierce enemy of Rome, against whom he waged war three times. The first time, in 88 B.C., was the most shocking; he initiated the war by, in a single night, murdering some 80,000 Romans living in Asia Minor. He then invaded Greece, and for a brief time even occupied Athens.

Twenty-five years later, after having endured many conflicts with Rome, Mithradates' options were diminishing: he had been defeated by the Roman general Pompey the Great and had little choice but to seek refuge in the most remote part of his kingdom, the Cimmerian Bosporus.

From his new headquarters Mithradates envisioned yet another campaign against Rome, one in which he would lead barbarian tribes into Italy itself. But his bloodlust and desire for revenge were no longer convincing to his war-weary subjects, and in 63 B.C. he committed suicide after suffering the revolt of one of his sons, the aforementioned Pharnaces II.

The portrait on the silver tetradrachm of Mithradates VI this collection (**coin 23**) should be easily recognized, for it is essentially the same one that was later adopted by his rebellious son Pharnaces. The reverse of Mithradates' coin bears the Greek inscription "King Mithradates, Nobly Begotten" and shows a Pegasus and a star-in-crescent moon, both of which were royal badges.

Mithradates' coin (like that of Pharnaces) also bears a date reckoned in Greek letters that had numerical equivalents. In this case, the Greek letters indicate the 202nd year after the kingdom in Bithynia-Pontus was founded in October of 297 B.C. Remarkably, a second inscription comprised of the letters Iota (10) and Alpha (1) indicate the month in which this coin was struck.

With all of this information we can determine that our coin was struck in the eleventh month of "year 202" of the royal era of Bithynia-Pontus, which equates to August, 95 B.C. Precise dates such as this are unusual on Greek coins, though, as will be shown in the next chapter, Roman coins can often be attributed to very narrow timeframes.

Coin 23: silver tetradrachm of Mithradates VI The imagery of Alexander the Great is here revived by Mithradates VI, who opposed expansionist Rome.

Coin 24: gold daric of Persia
The Persian Empire, a fierce enemy of the Greeks, was finally toppled by Alexander the Great in 330 B.C.

Coin 25: large bronze coin of the Bar Kochba Revolt

Coin 26: silver tetradrachm of Eucratides I

Long before Mithradates VI reigned, the Persians ruled most of the Near East. The Persian Empire lasted from about 650 B.C. until 330 B.C., when its last king was defeated by Alexander the Great. The Greeks and the Persians were archenemies, and except for their participation in trade they were perpetually at odds.

This leads us to one of the most familiar "non-Greek" coins of antiquity—the gold darics and silver sigloi that comprised the lion's share of Persian royal coinages in western Asia Minor. Production began in the archaic period and these coins retained their archaic qualities even into the classical and early Hellenistic periods.

The obverse of both the daric and the siglos show an advancing king (or hero) ready for battle. The highly stylized figure holds a bow in his extended left hand, and with his right hand, he either draws the bow or he holds a spear or a dagger. The reverse is occupied by a utilitarian incuse punch essentially unchanged from the very earliest coinages.

This collection contains a fine example of the Persian gold daric just described (**coin 24**), pictured on the previous page. In this case the king holds a bow and a spear, a type that seems to have been issued by several Persian kings throughout most of the fifth and fourth centuries B.C. Few of the surviving examples are as attractive as this, for the Persians hammered out this massive coinage carelessly.

Coinage was also issued in Syria, Phoenicia, Samaria, and the Holy Land by indigenous peoples and by the Greeks and Romans who eventually occupied these lands. This collection contains a coin from the Holy Land (**coin 25**) struck by Jews who in A.D. 132 organized a movement and revolted against their Roman overlords. The insurgency was led by Rabbi Akiba, Eleazar the Priest, and by Simon Bar Kochba, after whom the revolt has been named.

The struggle lasted slightly more than three years and ended in utter ruin for the Jews. Despite fighting valiantly, they could not match the resources, the expertise, and the persistence of the Romans.

The rebels produced coins in silver and copper by overstriking Roman coins that they withdrew from circulation. The most impressive of these revolt coins are the "large bronzes," of which this collection contains one of the finest known specimens. It shows an amphora and a wreath, and bears the Hebrew inscriptions "Shim'on" and "Year Two of

Coin 25: large bronze coin of the Bar Kochba Revolt These Jewish revolt coins were overstruck on circulating Roman coins.

Coin 26: silver tetradrachm of Eucratides I This "heroic" bust has long been among the most admired designs of ancient Greek coinage.

the Freedom of Israel," indicating not only the purpose of the rebellion, but also the year in which it was struck, A.D. 133/134.

Moving further east we encounter some of the more remote cultures that were influenced by the Greeks. As Alexander the Great moved eastward in pursuit of the Persian king, he established Greek rule in Bactria, more or less comprising parts of modern Afghanistan and Pakistan. Though there had been advanced civilizations in this region for millennia, coinage only came to be struck there under the influence of the Greeks.

The silver tetradrachm of Eucratides I (c. 171–135 B.C.) in this collection is an excellent example of the coinage of the kings of Bactria (**coin 26**). It bears a remarkable "heroic" portrait of the king as seen from behind, wearing a crested helmet and raising a spear. Though there is no prototype for this obverse in mainstream Greek coinage, the reverse falls into a more recognizable format: a royal Greek inscription accompanying a scene from Greek mythology, in this case the Dioscuri on horseback.

Coin 27: silver tetradrachm of King Bagadates

Coin 28: gold stater of Kanishka I

Another important kingdom of the East was Persis, the Iranian homeland of the Persians who centuries earlier had founded the Achaemenid-Persian Empire that had been defeated by Alexander the Great in 330 B.C. This Persian land was never convincingly ruled by the Greeks, and it eventually became subject to the Parthian Empire, which allowed it to retain some degree of independence.

This collection contains one of the finest-known silver tetradrachms (**coin 27**) of the first king of Persis, Bagadates. His coins are difficult to acquire in any condition, and since his portrait is cut in such high relief it is remarkable to find one as sharply struck as this. In many ways this coin of King Bagadates is Greek: it has a royal portrait on its obverse and its reverse bears an identifying inscription and a scene of religious and political value. But the style and the details are non-Greek, beginning with the inscription, which is rendered in the local Aramaic script. Also, Bagadates wears a traditional satrapal headdress, and on the reverse he is shown worshipping at a fire altar, the central object of the Persian Zoroastrian religion. This unique combination of elements reveals that Greek culture had influenced the Persians, but that it had not stamped out their cultural identity.

A final "non-Greek" coin in this collection was struck in a land more remote still—India. It is a gold stater (**coin 28**) of Kanishka I, who ruled

Coin 27: silver tetradrachm of King Bagadates Coins are some of the most useful pieces of evidence for unraveling the history of Persis.

Coin 28: gold stater of Kanishka I Early Indian coins have much in common with Greek coins, yet their appearance is decidedly exotic.

the Kushan Empire from about A.D. 127 to 152. Like most royal Greek coins, the obverse is devoted to the ruler and the reverse to a deity. In this case the king is represented not by a portrait, but with a complete image of him sacrificing at an altar. The reverse is more exotic still, for it shows the multi-armed Shiva holding a thunderbolt, a flask, and a trident, and clutching the horns of a goat.

Both the Greeks and the Romans traded with the Indians, acquiring from their distant land not only raw materials and luxury goods of local extraction, but also trade goods from further east, which the Indians brokered. This coin was probably struck with gold that the Romans had sent east in their efforts to obtain spices, silk, precious stones, and a variety of other raw materials and finished goods.

CHAPTER TWO

ANCIENT ROMAN COINAGE

David L. Vagi

Coin 29: silver denarius of Julius Caesar

Coin 30: gold aureus of Brutus

Rome had existed at least seven centuries before it issued its first coin. In that respect the Romans were slow starters, for the Greeks and Persians had been issuing coins for two or three centuries before Romans abandoned their primitive system of exchange in favor of coinage.

However, within a century of their adoption of coinage, the Romans became one of the most prolific coin issuers in the Mediterranean World. Eventually, they were to become unrivaled in that regard.

The earliest coins of the Republic bore "anonymous" designs of a patriotic nature that paid tribute to socio-religious aspects of the Roman world. However, in the last century of the Republic coin types transformed from the patriotic to the personal; designs were used to promote the families of the moneyers (mint directors) more than Rome or the Republic.

Civil Wars

The Roman coins in this collection begin with a famous coin issued at a moment when the old Republican form of government was in grave danger, for Julius Caesar (who already possessed the title "dictator") was preparing to ask the senate for the title of "king." Though that was a traditional title for Greek monarchs, at this stage in Rome's history it was inconceivable.

The silver denarius of Julius Caesar in this collection (**coin 29**) was struck in January or February of 44 B.C., when Caesar was at the pinnacle of his power. The obverse bears an uncommonly well-struck portrait of this, the most famous of all Romans. Behind Caesar's head is a set of priestly implements indicating his role as a priest of the Republic, and the reverse shows Venus, the goddess from whom Julius Caesar's family rather fancifully claimed descent.

It is one of the first Roman coins ever struck with the portrait of a living man, and it understandably upset the aristocratic elements of Roman society. The leading families had for centuries exercised power through the senate, an institution Caesar had consistently opposed through his desire for personal supremacy.

The next Roman coin in this collection is of great importance. It is a gold portrait aureus of Brutus (**coin 30**), the nobleman who, with his co-conspirator Cassius, rallied a group of fellow senators to murder Julius Caesar on the Ides (15th) of March, 44 B.C. Very few of these aurei survive, and this one is not only extremely well preserved, but is struck on a large, impressive planchet.

Coin 29: silver denarius of Julius Caesar The portrait of Julius Caesar is here paired with the goddess Venus, from whom his family claimed descent.

Coin 30: gold aureus of Brutus Brutus, along with his victim the dictator Julius Caesar, broke tradition with coins bearing his own portrait.

The murder of Caesar was a defensive measure taken by the conspirators before Caesar completely overpowered the senate, the source of their power. In the short term we could say they succeeded in their mission, but after the coup the conspirators were forced to flee Italy as the followers of Caesar claimed control in Rome.

This portrait aureus was struck in Northern Greece or Western Asia Minor, the regions to which Brutus and Cassius had fled. Ever since the murder of Caesar they had been raising armies and outfitting navies in anticipation of the war they would soon wage against Caesar's followers.

On this aureus we see the portrait of Brutus within the laurel wreath of a victor. His bust is identified by the inscription BRVTVS IMP, similar to the inscription CAESAR IMP on the denarius of Caesar that was just described. In both cases IMP abbreviates "imperator," the title sometimes given to a victorious general. The reverse is equally militant, for it shows a display of armor and weapons, some of which are fashioned into a trophy. Also like Caesar's coin, Brutus' aureus bears on the reverse the name of the official responsible for its issuance.

> *One might assume Marc Antony would triumph over the younger Octavian.*

Meanwhile, in Rome there ensued a struggle for power among the followers of Caesar. The leading roles were assumed by Marc Antony, who for years had been Caesar's right-hand man, and Octavian, Caesar's great-nephew and adopted son. Despite his years of service Antony had received nothing from Caesar, whereas Octavian inherited three-fourths of his fortune and his political legacy.

But receiving money and a political legacy did not guarantee success: Octavian was only 18 years old, and had hurriedly returned from Greece, where he had been a student. One might assume the older, militarily experienced Antony, who had established a base of support in Rome itself, would triumph over Octavian. But the opposite proved true, and from the very outset Octavian was a formidable opponent.

Antony and Octavian (better known as Augustus, the name he adopted in 27 B.C.) were immediate enemies, and they waged war against one another before they decided to join forces rather than exhaust themselves fighting each other. To this end, late in 43 B.C. they created the Second Triumvirate, a formal pact in which they were joined by Lepidus, the chief priest of Rome, and they jointly opposed the senate and any other foes.

One of their first cooperative efforts was to wage war against Brutus and Cassius, the "republican" rebels in the East. Lepidus remained in the West as Antony and Octavian led their forces to Greece, where they defeated Brutus and Cassius in two pitched battles at Philippi late in 42 B.C. Antony and Octavian then parted, with Antony governing the Roman territories in the East and Octavian returning to govern in the West.

This collection contains an uncommonly fine dual-portrait aureus of Antony and Octavian (**coin 31**) struck from dies engraved by a gifted artist. The issue was meant to reflect their alliance, and the fact that Lepidus is not portrayed or referenced is a further indication that his role in the Triumvirate was thought to be inconsequential. Since this coin was issued by Antony in the East, his portrait occupies the obverse, and Octavian's appears on the reverse.

Despite their geographical separation, their triumviral pact, and even a royal marriage between Antony and Octavian's sister, the rivalry between Antony and Octavian did not diminish. In the best of times they were cold, wary allies, and in the worst of times they were openly at war.

In the meantime, though, both had regional enemies to deal with: Antony had to contend with the threat posed by the Parthians—Rome's traditional enemy in the East—and Octavian was unable to master Sextus Pompey, a rogue commander who controlled the western part of the Mediterranean Sea with his navy.

This leads us to another collection highlight: a gold aureus (**coin 32**) that portrays Sextus Pompey and his deceased father and brother, Pompey the Great and Pompey Junior. Sextus Pompey had survived the deaths of his father and brother at the hand of Julius Caesar, and after Caesar's murder had managed to find some marginal support in the senate, by which he was awarded command of Rome's western navies.

He remained a thorn in the side of Octavian until he was defeated in 36 B.C. by a fleet commanded by Octavian's principal general, Agrippa. The victory not only eliminated Sextus Pompey, but also the Triumvir Lepidus, who had chosen that moment to oppose Octavian in a poorly executed maneuver on Sicily.

Coin 31: gold aureus of Antony and Octavian (shown enlarged on page 43)

Coin 32: gold aureus of Sextus Pompey (shown enlarged on page 43)

Coin 33: silver denarius of Octavian (shown enlarged on page 45)

Coin 34: gold aureus of Tiberius (shown enlarged on page 45)

Octavian's victory was thus complete in the West, and he now focused on defeating Antony in the East. In the meantime Antony had allied himself with Cleopatra VII, the last Greek queen of the kingdom of Egypt. Hostilities rose until the old enemies clashed in Greece and Octavian's general Agrippa routed the combined forces of Antony and Cleopatra at the Battle of Actium in 31 B.C.

The last coin in this collection from this era of civil war (**coin 33**) virtually defines the end of an age: it is a silver portrait denarius of Octavian with a reverse that celebrates his capture of Egypt from Cleopatra VII. The style of the portrait is delicate and refined, and this example is not only well struck, but also magnificently preserved.

Octavian was now the unrivaled leader of the Roman world, and in 27 B.C., a year after this denarius was struck, he accepted from the senate the name Augustus ("sacred") which he used for the next 41 years that he exercised supreme power in Rome.

The Early Empire

Augustus achieved much during the 45 years between his victory over Antony and his death in A.D. 14. Not only did he make significant improvements to the Roman world, but also he gradually and systematically reduced the power of the senate, thus completing the transformation from a republic to an empire.

Augustus had been the towering figure in the Roman world for many decades, and his death represented an opportunity to restore the Republic, but that did not occur. With virtually no protest, his stepson Tiberius ascended the throne, which he would occupy until his own death in 37.

Tiberius' accession not only assured the continuance of the monarchy, but it also confirmed the hereditary aspect of the system, for Tiberius was then the senior man within the Julio-Claudian family, and it was only natural that he would succeed his adoptive father.

This collection contains a superb gold aureus of Tiberius (**coin 34**) bearing his portrait on the obverse, and on its reverse the seated image of his mother Livia shown in the guise of Pax ("peace"). Because Livia was Augustus' widow and Tiberius' mother she was an important figure both politically and dynastically. Indeed, it was through her efforts that the Julio-Claudian dynasty was firmly established, for she arranged

Coin 31: gold aureus of Antony and Octavian Dual-portrait coins such as this betrayed a fictional solidarity between the warlords Antony and Octavian.

Coin 32: gold aureus of Sextus Pompey This aureus is a miniature portrait gallery of the short-lived family dynasty founded by Pompey the Great.

numerous marriages between members of her own family, the Claudians, and the Julians, the family of Julius Caesar and Augustus.

Though the reign of Tiberius was stable, it was filled with hostility and tragedy. Like Augustus before him, Tiberius suffered a string of setbacks with the death or banishment of potential heirs, many of whom showed promise. In the end, Augustus had to pass the throne to Tiberius, whom he did not like, and Tiberius had to settle for his great-nephew Caligula, whom *he* did not like. The circumstances of all of these deaths have been rightly questioned: were they unfortunate, natural deaths, or were some of them murders?

Tiberius' first heir had been Caligula's father Germanicus. The emperor and his heir never saw eye to eye, and the public, many of the soldiers, and the lesser nobility wanted Germanicus to be emperor. Thus, when Germanicus died under mysterious circumstances in 19, there was an uproar that greatly damaged Tiberius' reputation.

Coin 35: gold aureus of Caligula

> *Caligula honored his family on coinage to remind the public of his heritage.*

It is uncertain whether Germanicus was murdered, but the people of Rome believed that Tiberius had ordered his death. In the succeeding years Germanicus' widow Agrippina Senior and their two eldest sons, Nero Caesar and Drusus Caesar, also died under terrible circumstances.

Thus, when Caligula succeeded Tiberius in 37 the core of his family was already dead, and only his three sisters survived. He extensively honored his family on coinage not only out of fond memory, but to remind the public of his heritage, for it was his only source of legitimacy as emperor. Unlike Augustus and Tiberius before him, Caligula had no experience in government or the military: he had been chosen simply because of his pedigree.

This collection contains two rare and impressive coins of Caligula, the first of which (**coin 35**) is a gold aureus bearing the portraits of Caligula and his father Germanicus. Though it was issued nearly two decades after Germanicus died, Caligula's father was still popular, especially among the legions stationed along the Rhine.

Coin 33: silver denarius of Octavian

Coin 34: gold aureus of Tiberius

Coin 35: gold aureus of Caligula

Coin 36: brass sestertius of Caligula

Coin 37: gold aureus of Claudius

The second (**coin 36**) is a brass sestertius depicting on its reverse the emperor's three sisters, who are individually named in the inscription: Agrippina, Drusilla, and Julia. This coin type is famous among collectors because the ancient sources indicate that Caligula had incestuous relationships with all three of his sisters.

They are shown in the guise of the divinities Securitas, Concordia, and Fortuna. The connections between the sisters and these divinities would have been obvious to an educated Roman based upon the objects associated with each: Agrippina sets her cornucopia upon a column; Drusilla holds a cornucopia and a patera; and Julia holds a cornucopia and a ship's rudder.

Both of these coins were struck in the first year of Caligula's reign, when the hopes of every Roman were high. With the passage of time, though, their expectations diminished. Caligula's apparent insanity emerged more strongly with each passing month, and eventually the soldiers who had sworn to protect the emperor could bear no more. Early in 41 they conspired to murder him.

The monarchy was again in jeopardy because only one Julio-Claudian male of sufficient age remained—50-year-old Claudius. Though his pedigree was outstanding, Claudius had physical problems that stemmed from childhood diseases, and which had always caused those around him to doubt his fitness to rule. His ailments had caused Claudius great ridicule throughout his life, but they also had sheltered him from public life, and thus had preserved him for this moment.

In the aftermath of Caligula's murder the praetorian guards proclaimed Claudius emperor. The soldiery welcomed him, for not only did they presume he would be easy to control, but he was also the son of Nero Claudius Drusus and the brother of Germanicus, both of whom were heroes.

The aureus of Claudius in this collection (**coin 37**) was struck in his inaugural year, and its reverse records the senate's bestowal upon him of the *corona civica*, an oak wreath awarded to those who had saved the life of a Roman citizen. Not only had this become a standard part of accession honors, but Claudius' actions during the hysterical reign of his nephew Caligula no doubt had spared the life of many a Roman.

The portrait on this aureus is particularly fine. Later issues of Claudius bear an increasingly realistic portrait, whereas this one is youthful and somewhat idealized considering he was 50 years old when the coin was struck.

Coin 36: brass sestertius of Caligula The mad emperor is here paired with the three sisters for whom he apparently held an unnatural affection.

Coin 37: gold aureus of Claudius This vigorous portrait gives no indication of the physical problems Claudius had endured since childhood.

Claudius ruled honorably and competently for some 13 years, surviving numerous plots hatched by those who resented his rise to power. He even helped lead an invasion of Britain by which that island eventually became a province of the empire. His greatest troubles, though, were within his own family; he was married four times and each union was disgraceful.

The fourth and final wife of Claudius was his niece Agrippina Junior, whom he married nearly eight years into his reign. Since she was one of the three sisters of Caligula her first appearance on imperial coinage was as a standing figure on the previously described sestertius (**coin 36**, seen enlarged on page 47).

Agrippina was ambitious on her own account and for her son from her previous marriage, a boy who came to adopt the name Nero. Her ambition had grave consequences for both Claudius and his son Britannicus, who had been born to Claudius' previous wife a few months after Claudius was hailed emperor.

Though every detail of the dynastic infighting is not known, Claudius eventually adopted Agrippina's son Nero and supported him over his own son Britannicus. The dynastic arrangement is clearly reflected on the coinage, for Britannicus is not celebrated on standard imperial coins, whereas Nero is promoted rather strongly with large quantities of gold aurei and silver denarii bearing his portrait.

When Claudius died in October, 54 (seemingly poisoned by Agrippina), he was replaced by Nero, but not without complications: Nero was still young enough that for a few months he had to tolerate his mother's meddling, and Britannicus was waiting in the wings as an alternative ruler. But all was sorted out when Britannicus was poisoned four months later and Nero subsequently removed his mother from authority, and then had her murdered.

Thus we have occasion to discuss another important aureus in this collection (**coin 38**), one that shows the confronted busts of Nero and his mother Agrippina. It was issued very early in Nero's reign, from October through December of 54, and was discontinued thereafter. Agrippina appeared on one more brief issue, after which she disappeared from imperial coinage altogether.

Like Claudius before him, Nero reigned for 13 years, but his term was undignified and was marked by what is usually described as insan-

Coin 38: gold aureus of Nero and Agrippina

Coin 38: gold aureus of Nero and Agrippina If ever there was an unhealthy family relationship, it existed between the emperor Nero and his ambitious mother Agrippina Junior. Here the pair is confronted— an unwitting reflection of a struggle for power that, on the darker side, may have helped fuel rumors that Agrippina had seduced her teenage son.

Coin 39: gold aureus of Galba

Coin 40: gold aureus of Vitellius

ity. His demise was a consequence of his extravagance, cruelty, and dereliction of duty, and, specifically, of his insensitivity toward the plight of his subjects in the provinces.

It all began when a revolt was sparked in Gaul in 68 by the governor Vindex, which prompted two other provincial officials to rebel, Clodius Macer in North Africa and Galba in Spain. Though Vindex's rebellion was easily crushed, those of Macer and Galba continued, with the latter gaining such broad support that it brought Nero's regime to an end.

Unlike his uncle Caligula, Nero was at least afforded the luxury of committing suicide rather than being murdered by his soldiers. Nero's death and his replacement by Galba did not, however, end the civil war, which raged for 21 months in 68 and 69 and which caused the senate to recognize five men as emperors in that brief time.

This collection contains two magnificent gold aurei from this famous civil war (**coins 39** and **40**). Both are of remarkably fine quality, with their strike, surfaces, centering, and style being virtually unimprovable for coins of the era. Further, both have a rich toning that suggests a pedigree to the famous "Bosco Reale" hoard unearthed in 1895 from beneath the volcanic ash laid down by the eruption of Mount Vesuvius in the year 79.

The first (**coin 39**) portrays Galba, the provincial governor whose uprising had toppled Nero's regime. Galba was quite elderly when he led his revolt, and he held the title of emperor for only about seven months before he was murdered by his soldiers.

Galba ranked among the nobility of Rome, and this aureus publicizes his ties to the Julio-Claudians. The reverse shows the standing figure of Livia, the wife of Rome's first emperor, Augustus, and the mother of its second emperor, Tiberius. Since she had been declared a goddess by her grandson Claudius, Rome's fourth emperor, she is here identified by the inscription DIVA AVGVSTA.

But Galba's old-fashioned morality was his undoing, for he demanded loyal service from his soldiers without feeling the need to bribe them. This did not please his guards, who in this age of chaos welcomed the riches promised by the nobleman Otho, whom they forced the senate to hail emperor after they murdered Galba in open view.

Otho reigned only three months before he committed suicide in the face of the advancing legions of a new rival, Vitellius, the governor of

Coin 39: gold aureus of Galba After his unexpected rise from provincial governor to emperor, Galba was murdered in public by soldiers.

Coin 40: gold aureus of Vitellius The magnificent toning on this coin was caused by ash from the eruption of Mount Vesuvius in 79.

Lower Germany. Galba had sent Vitellius to a frontier province to remove him from the capital, but that strategy had backfired when the German legions forced him to accompany them to Rome, where they hoped to be awarded the bonus they had been promised for earlier having defeated the rebellious governor Vindex.

Though Vitellius' reign was also brief, the engravers at the Rome mint produced coins for him with portraits of exceptional style. The image of Vitellius on the second aureus **(coin 40)** certainly supports the claims of the ancient historians that he could eat enormous quantities of food.

Peace Restored

Fortunately for Rome the chaos of civil war did not last much longer. About the time Vitellius entered the capital a general named Vespasian revolted in the East. Though at the time he was leading a war against rebels in Judaea, he left that task to his eldest son Titus to finish as he proceeded to Egypt to make his preparations to overthrow Vitellius.

Vespasian had succeeded by the end of 69. He associated with his regime his two sons, Titus and Domitian, and in doing so founded the Flavian Dynasty. The new emperor was a capable and honorable man who restored Rome's fortune, though not without himself suffering ridicule for his stinginess. He had little choice, for the civil war had been more costly than was imagined.

The determined character of Vespasian can be seen in the portrait on his brass sesterius in this collection **(coin 41)**. Though he was pensive and focused, he was also renowned for his dry sense of humor, which no doubt made his burden easier to bear. During his decade on the throne Vespasian relied heavily on his eldest son, Titus, who shouldered much of the day-to-day responsibilities.

Titus had become famous when he sacked Jerusalem in 70, which ended the First Revolt of the Jews (except for an isolated holdout at Masada, which fell in 73). Jerusalem and its people paid an enormous price for having revolted against Rome, for an untold number died, the city was completely razed, and the Great Temple was leveled.

The reverse of Vespasian's sestertius celebrates the Jewish victory he and Titus had achieved. The inscription IVDAEA CAPTA echoes the design, which shows a mourning Jewess seated at the base of a palm tree (a symbol of Judaea), before which the victorious emperor stands in full

Coin 41: brass sesterius of Vespasian

Coin 41: brass sesterius of Vespasian
Late in the reign of the emperor Nero (54–68) a revolt broke out in Judaea which demanded much attention from the Romans. It cost the lives of more than a million people and caused the destruction of Jerusalem. On this coin the victorious general-turned-emperor Vespasian celebrates Rome's triumph.

military attire, placing his foot on a helmet and holding a sheathed sword and a scepter.

After a highly successful decade as emperor, Vespasian died in 79. The throne was passed to Titus, who ruled briefly until he died in 81, and then to his brother Domitian. For two decades Domitian had lived in the shadow of his dynamic older brother, and had missed out on military glory. But he was now 30 years old and was the undisputed ruler of the Roman Empire.

The ancient sources are hostile to Domitian, describing him as a tyrant who rode roughshod over the senate. However, he did enjoy the support of the army, and in that regard he was a wise emperor, for soldiers were the most likely source of rebellion. Further, Domitian thirsted for military glory on a scale even greater than his father and brother.

This collection contains a remarkable aureus of Domitian (**coin 42**) that honors his substantial conquests in Germany with a reverse type that shows a mourning figure representing the barbarian nations of Germany. She is seated upon a highly ornamented shield, beneath which there is a spear that is broken midway down its shaft.

Because the inscriptions indicate Domitian had held his twelfth consulship, had renewed his imperatorial acclamation for the twelfth time, and had renewed the tribunician power for the fifth time, we can precisely date this coin to the year 86, marking it as one of the earliest issues to feature the mature portrait style by which Domitian is best recognized.

Domitian ruled for 15 years before he was murdered in a palace coup in 96. Though his death was met with approval by many in Rome, it infuriated the soldiers who had respected him for his courage in battle and who had appreciated his financial generosity. Adding insult was the fact that the senate had appointed one of their own, a senator named Nerva, as Domitian's replacement without consulting the army.

Nerva was elderly and childless, and he ruled only two years before he died of natural causes. But before his death he adopted a military man, Trajan, as his son and successor because the army was on the brink of rebellion throughout his brief reign, and this gesture likely prevented a widespread revolt.

The army welcomed the death of Nerva and the accession of Trajan, who ruled for nearly two decades, from 98 to 117. During his reign Trajan waged numerous wars that enlarged the empire to its greatest extent.

Coin 42: gold aureus of Domitian

Coin 42: gold aureus of Domitian
Upon becoming emperor in 81, Domitian sought military glory with campaigns against the German tribes. This aureus celebrates those victories. Like many Roman coins, this one can be dated rather precisely based upon the honors and titles named in the inscriptions. It was struck in 86.

Rome had entered an era of prosperity that would last throughout the reigns of Trajan and his immediate successors Hadrian (117–138) and Antoninus Pius (138–161), and which is often described as a golden age of Rome.

This collection contains a superbly preserved aureus of Trajan (**coin 43**) struck in the middle of his reign. It shows on its reverse a standing female, representing the province of Arabia (Nabataea), who holds a parcel of trade goods and a branch over a camel (a symbol of Arabia). When Trajan added Nabataea to Rome's territories in 106 it must have been welcomed, as it contained important trade routes from the East.

Coin 43: gold aureus of Trajan

> *Hadrian's imperial travels inspired a series of commemorative coins.*

When Trajan died in 117 of natural causes the empire was inherited by a younger relative of his, named Hadrian. It was clear that Trajan had conquered more than could be effectively ruled, so Hadrian devised a plan to immediately set upon a course of withdrawal from the most troublesome and remote territories. He went further still by fortifying the empire's borders, including building Hadrian's Wall in northern England.

Instead of conducting aggressive military campaigns as Trajan had done, Hadrian's agenda involved visiting each of Rome's provinces personally—a task which, due to the largely ceremonial nature of his visits and the great distances involved, occupied much of his 21 years on the throne. To commemorate his travels, Hadrian issued a series of coins naming the provinces he visited, and celebrating his departures and safe returns.

Coin 44: gold aureus of Hadrian

The aureus of Hadrian in this collection (**coin 44**) is nearly perfect, and must have been buried soon after it was struck. Its high level of artistry should not surprise us, for this emperor was enamored with art and, after Augustus, was Rome's greatest patron of Greek culture.

The seated figure of Jupiter (Zeus) on the reverse, however, relates to an unfortunate aspect of Hadrian's personality—his obsession with Jupiter, and his megalomaniacal belief in his final years that he shared a special relationship with the supreme god of the Greeks and the Romans.

Coin 43: gold aureus of Trajan This forceful portrait of Trajan is a fair indication of his personality, for he was a tireless conqueror.

Coin 44: gold aureus of Hadrian This coin reflects an unhealthy obsession with the god Jupiter that Hadrian assumed later in his reign.

Coin 45: gold aureus of Marcus Aurelius

Coin 46: gold aureus of Lucius Verus

The Decline

After the reigns of Hadrian and his mild-mannered successor Antoninus Pius, the age of tranquility ended for Rome. Though nearly 320 years remained before the empire collapsed in the West, few of these years held cause for celebration. The era of Rome dominating its enemies had finally come to a close.

Signs of trouble came early in the 160s, when for the first time in Rome's history it was ruled by legitimate co-emperors, Marcus Aurelius and Lucius Verus. When these two young men jointly ascended the throne in 161 it was fortuitous, for military crises erupted simultaneously on Rome's eastern frontier and on the northern border in Europe.

We are fortunate that this collection contains gold aurei (**coins 45 and 46**) of both of these emperors, in virtually unimprovable condition. The coin of Marcus Aurelius (**coin 45**) was struck a dozen years before his accession, during the more than two decades he served as Caesar (a subordinate position) under his predecessor Antoninus Pius. Thus, we do not see the image of a war-weary emperor that appeared on his later coins, but a young nobleman at the peak of his youth. It is not surprising that the portrait is a perfect match for numerous marble busts of this emperor since the artists who cut the portrait dies based their work on busts in-the-round.

By the time the aureus of his co-emperor (**coin 46**) was struck in 163–164, Lucius Verus had already been in the East for more than two years defending Rome's borders and enforcing its policies. The reverse design is both a remarkable composition and a reflection of an historical event: Verus providing a new king, Sohaemus, to Armenia, a nation that had long served as a buffer-state between Rome and the enemy Parthians in the East.

Verus and his generals continued to score victories against the Parthians, sacking their capital in 165 and forcing them to sue for peace in 166. Then he returned victoriously to Europe to join Marcus Aurelius in his ongoing campaign against the Germans. Verus died early in 169, seemingly by a seizure, but not before he learned that the legions he had led back from the East had brought with them the plague, which swept through Europe and almost completely depopulated some regions.

Rome was thus experiencing the beginning of a new reality, which only continued through the reign of Marcus Aurelius and his son and

Coin 45: gold aureus of Marcus Aurelius The empire's fortunes began to slide under Marcus Aurelius, who, ironically, was one of Rome's best emperors.

Coin 46: gold aureus of Lucius Verus On the reverse of this aureus the emperor Lucius Verus is shown appointing a new king of Armenia.

successor Commodus (177–192), who ranks among the most dysfunctional of Rome's emperors. Much like Caligula and Domitian before him, Commodus had succumbed to an especially intense megalomania, and he had alienated those in a position to harm him most. After 15 years of behaving like a despot, Commodus was poisoned and strangled in a palace coup on New Year's Eve of 192.

The empire was now on the brink of a civil war much like the one it had experienced from 68 to 69, following the death of Nero. In place of Commodus the senate appointed as emperor a well-intentioned senator named Pertinax, whose constructive reforms—like Galba's of some 125 years before—were rewarded with resentment and bloodlust.

The praetorian guards seized the moment and murdered Pertinax only 86 days after he was hailed emperor, and found a novel way to select his replacement: they held a public auction at which they sold the throne to the highest bidder.

The wealthy senator Didius Julianus placed the highest bid, the equivalent of 250 gold aurei per guard. With so substantial a reward awaiting them, the guards rallied behind their candidate and supported him until, less than ten weeks later, a Roman army from the provinces invaded the capital, dragged Didius Julianus out of the palace, and murdered him.

Like most short-lived emperors Didius Julianus was able to produce coins, and we are fortunate to examine one of his gold aurei (**coin 47**). This particular coin bears an interesting reverse type, for on it Didius Julianus claims to be RECTOR ORBIS, "Master of the World." Though it was not unusual for Roman emperors to make false, hopeful, or delusional claims on their coins, this one is particularly absurd.

The army that dethroned Didius Julianus had marched at a breakneck pace from their station in Balkans. Their general Septimius Severus was determined to get to Rome before any other commander, and thus to claim the throne for himself. He knew that the commander who first arrived in the capital and overthrew the tyrant would be hailed emperor out of fear if not gratitude.

His instincts served him well, and the other two generals who had responded to the Romans' pleas for deliverance, Clodius Albinus in Gaul and Pescennius Niger in Syria, were marginalized. But Severus could not afford to ignore them, for they had entered the contest and had support-

Coin 47: gold aureus of Didius Julianus

Coin 47: gold aureus of Didius Julianus The empire was thrown into chaos late in the reign of Commodus, who was murdered on New Year's Eve of 192. Afterward there was a quick succession of five emperors. The second man to fall was Didius Julianus, who degraded Rome by purchasing the throne at a public auction held by the praetorian guards.

ers, even in the capital. So after he had consolidated his authority in Rome Severus set out to eliminate his rivals.

After he pacified Clodius Albinus with the subordinate title of Caesar, Severus marched eastward to defeat Pescennius Niger. He achieved that by late 194, after which he returned to the West and turned his attention to Clodius Albinus, whom he eventually defeated in February 197, leaving him Rome's only emperor.

When he had earlier campaigned against Pescennius Niger, Severus had followed up his victory with a quick campaign against the Parthians, some of whom had supported the rebel. Thus, soon after his defeat of Clodius Albinus, Severus returned to the East to lead a full-fledged invasion of Parthia in 198.

Coin 48: gold aureus of Septimius Severus

The superb aureus of Septimius Severus in this collection **(coin 48)** celebrates that event. The reverse is inscribed VICT PARTHICAE, and it shows a Victory, holding a wreath and a trophy, advancing with a captive Parthian at her feet. The victory was worthy of celebration: not only did the Romans gather a great amount of booty, but they also killed all of the men who had remained in the capital and took perhaps 100,000 women and children as slaves.

At the same time Severus restored a temporary stability to the empire, he also established a dynasty initially comprised of himself, his wife Julia Domna, and their two sons, Caracalla and Geta. The hope Severus and Domna invested in their family dynasty is expressed by one of the best-preserved coins in this collection, a virtually flawless aureus of Julia Domna **(coin 49)** depicting on its reverse the confronted heads of Caracalla and Geta accompanied by the inscription AETERNIT IMPERI, which calls for the continuance of the Severan dynasty.

Coin 49: gold aureus of Julia Domna

After nearly 18 years as emperor Septimius Severus died early in 211 and was jointly succeeded by his sons, with whom he had shared his authority before he died. However, they despised each other so much that their plan to divide the empire was averted only because Caracalla murdered Geta ten months later. But Caracalla's remaining six years were deeply troubled with declining health and, seemingly, a touch of insanity. He was murdered in an undignified manner by soldiers within his own bodyguard as he was traveling in Mesopotamia in 217.

The original component of the Severan Dynasty had thus expired, and the army hailed Macrinus, one of Caracalla's two senior-most offi-

Coin 48: gold aureus of Septimius Severus The defeat and devastation of Parthia, Rome's ever-present enemy in the East, is celebrated on this aureus.

Coin 49: gold aureus of Julia Domna The empress is shown with her sons, who became emperors before Caracalla murdered his brother Geta.

cers, the new emperor. His reign lasted only 14 months before he was unseated by an army supporting another member of the Severan dynasty.

The Severans were thus restored to power and would stay there for nearly the next 18 years. But it would not be a glorious finish to the dynasty that Septimius Severus had so energetically founded. The matriarch of the new dynasty was Julia Maesa, the sister of Septimius Severus' wife, Julia Domna. Maesa had two daughters, Julia Soaemias and Julia Mamaea, each of whom had one son. These were the boys who, in turn, were the next emperors of Rome.

The first to reign was the eldest, Elagabalus, who was all of 13 or 14 when he was hailed emperor by the Roman army in Syria that had defeated Macrinus. His suitability for the throne derived not only from his being a member of the dynasty, but also from the rumor that his true father was Caracalla, a cousin of his mother's. The soldiers had come to mourn Caracalla, and thus eagerly transferred their hopes to Elagabalus.

The brilliant aureus of Elagabalus in this collection (**coin 50**) portrays a well-kempt young man and bears a thoroughly Roman reverse type celebrating victory in battle. However, it was yet another case of false advertising, for Elagabalus turned out to be perhaps the most loathsome character ever to be hailed emperor. His religious and sexual excesses were beyond all reckoning, and he never did anything as constructive as leading an army to victory.

The matriarchs of the dynasty were not blind to the state of affairs, and they thus raised to the rank of Caesar the emperor's younger cousin Severus Alexander. As Elagabalus' behavior descended to an intolerable level he lashed out against his cousin on March 11, 222, demanding that the praetorian guards strip him of his subordinate rank of Caesar. Being forced into a choice, the guards murdered Elagabalus and supported his cousin as the new emperor.

Severus Alexander was a refreshing change, for he was a mild-mannered boy with a domineering mother who would keep him in line. He ruled in his mother's shadow for 13 years, during which time he brokered peace with Rome's enemies rather than waging long or perilous wars, and he allowed imperial policy to be determined by his mother. It was these very qualities that caused his downfall 13 years later, for the soldiers would tolerate no more.

Coin 50: gold aureus of Elagabalus

Coin 50: gold aureus of Elagabalus
Along with Caligula, Elagabalus ranks among
the most depraved of Rome's emperors. The
comparative innocence of this portrait hides an
unflattering truth of unimaginably foul deeds;
the empire was fortunate it enjoyed peace during
his reign, for this emperor was unsuitable to lead
an army.

Most of Severus Alexander's aurei bear generic reverse types, and we are fortunate that the example in this collection is his most prized issue, for it depicts the Roman Colosseum, a structure as famous today as it was in ancient times. The coin **(coin 51)** was struck in 223 to celebrate the re-opening of the Colosseum after the completion of extensive repairs to its interior, which had been badly damaged in 217 by a fire caused by a lightning strike.

This aureus is one of the great prizes of Roman numismatics, and it seemingly is the best of only two known examples. Aside from coins and medals of Severus Alexander, the only other Roman issues with an image of the Colosseum are rare sestertii of Titus (79–81) and medallions of Gordian III (238–244).

Beginning with the murder of Severus Alexander and his mother in 235, Rome's fortunes began to decline at an alarming rate for the next two generations, during which it must have seemed there was no hope for a Roman recovery. There was a rapid succession of emperors, with the average successful emperor achieving five years on the throne.

One notable exception was Gallienus, who ruled 15 years, from 253 to 268. His longevity is remarkable since he ruled during what in many ways was the low point of five centuries of Roman history. Thus, his long reign tells us a great deal of Gallienus' intelligence, resilience, and courage. He is often described as a tyrant and as being addicted to pleasure, but these certainly are unfair charges considering his unwavering devotion to duty.

The beautiful gold coin of Gallienus in this collection **(coin 52)** is a reflection of the hard times in which he ruled, for the terrible economic conditions meant that the weight of gold coinage varied from year to year. Gallienus struck aurei, heavy aurei, light aurei, as well as double-aurei and half-aurei. The probable explanation is that in many cases—especially when bonuses were due to the army—the weight of the coins was determined by dividing the amount of gold bullion available by the number of coins that needed to be struck.

In this case we have what is best described as a "heavy aureus," even though it weighs only 60 percent of an aureus of the early empire. Its reverse celebrates the loyalty of the army (FIDES MILITVM), and it was struck as part of a bonus paid to the soldiers at the start of Gallienus' celebration of his tenth year as emperor.

Coin 51: gold aureus of Severus Alexander

Coin 52: gold "heavy aureus" of Gallienus

Coin 51: gold aureus of Severus Alexander The most famous building of imperial Rome—the Colosseum—is shown on this exceedingly rare aureus.

Coin 52: gold "heavy aureus" of Gallienus The loyalty of the army was essential for any emperor, and Gallienus here requests it during dark times.

The chaos of the age is also illustrated by another rare and spectacular aureus in this collection. It was struck by a rebel named Postumus, who in 260 was hailed emperor and unlawfully assumed control of the empire's westernmost provinces. However, Rome's armies were stretched so thin that the West suffered from frequent barbarian invasions across the Rhine, and local commanders such as Postumus had to muster whatever armies they could to defend their homeland.

But even in times of extreme hardship emperors and rebels could show mercy. The reverse of this Postumus aureus (**coin 53**) is dedicated to the "dutiful generosity" of the emperor (INDVLG PIA POSTVMI AVG) for remitting tribute to his subjects and for releasing condemned criminals. The latter action is puzzling to the modern mind, but it was a traditional act of celebration.

After the death of Gallienus the empire began to make a slow recovery under several energetic emperors who built upon his recent successes, including Aurelian (270–275) and Probus (276–282). Though both of these emperors were extremely effective, like Gallienus they both paid for their dedication by being assassinated by those who either disapproved of their constructive reforms or were envious of their power.

Coin 53: gold aureus of Postumus

The Christian State

In 284 a brilliant man was hailed emperor near Nicomedia, in northwestern Asia Minor. He came to the throne like most every recent "military emperor": he was chosen by soldiers after their former emperor had been murdered. His name was Diocletian, and over the next two decades he worked tirelessly to reform the Roman world. He was an exceptional administrator who paid attention to every detail of life, with no aspect too obscure or too overwhelming to escape his attention.

Though many of Diocletian's reforms were successful, they only lasted as long as he was in power, for without his genius at the helm Rome and its subsequent rulers fell back into the familiar patterns of hereditary monarchy and civil war. Diocletian was remarkable in that he voluntarily shared his power with three colleagues and, in 305, he abdicated the throne so that others might rule in his place.

This collection contains an impressive gold aureus of Diocletian (**coin 54**) bearing on its reverse an image of the supreme pagan god

Coin 54: gold aureus of Diocletian

Coin 53: gold aureus of Postumus
When the empire began to dissolve in 260 a quasi-Roman empire was founded in the West by Postumus.

Coin 54: gold aureus of Diocletian
Coin portraits lost much of their individuality as a consequence of the "new age" ushered in by Diocletian.

Jupiter, who in the inscription, IOVI CONSERVATORI, is described as the protector of the emperor. Early in his reign Diocletian swore allegiance to Jupiter and had his first colleague, Maximian, do the same with Hercules.

So intense was Diocetian's devotion to the traditional Roman religion that in 303 he initiated a persecution of Christians throughout his empire. To what degree it was his idea or that of his ambitious and incompetent successor Galerius (305–311) is not known, but the persecution was brutal, and ultimately ineffective.

If anything, the Great Persecution gave momentum to Christianity, which by 312 had been adopted by another of Rome's most famous emperors, Constantine the Great (306–337). In many ways the rise of Christianity from a persecuted cult to the official state religion by the late fourth century is the most significant development of Late Antiquity.

Coin 55: gold solidus of Licinius

> *Licinius tolerated Christianity, but his coins showed where his true loyalty lay.*

But Rome was by no means ready to abandon paganism—or to embrace Christianity—when Diocletian abdicated in 305, let alone by the time Constantine died in 337. It would require many more decades of the Church benefiting from imperial patronage before paganism became the persecuted religion of the minority.

Diocletian's model of shared rule collapsed in the civil wars that raged from 305 to 313. From these great contests two men emerged victorious: Constantine and Licinius, who ruled separate halves of the empire until 324, when Constantine finally defeated Licinius.

Though Licinius (308–324) had been tolerant of Christianity, he was never its champion. A superb gold solidus of Licinius in this collection (**coin 55**), struck late in his reign, c. 321–322, helps illustrate that point, for Jupiter is shown on the reverse and is described as the protector of Licinius (IOVI CONS LICINI AVG).

His portrait is spectacular, and it is of great interest because it is shown fully facing, something that Roman die cutters seldom attempted prior to the late fourth century, when it became a standard portrait style.

Coin 55: gold solidus of Licinius
Licinius was only a lukewarm supporter of
Christians, who at the time constituted what
was little more than a modern cult, or a novelty
religion. His co-emperor and rival Constantine
the Great, however, recognized Christians as a
well-organized, vital force in Roman society
and openly sought their support.

Coin 56: gold solidus of Constantine

Coin 57: gold solidus of Romulus Augustus

While Licinius continued to support paganism, Constantine became the standard-bearer for Christianity, or, at least, his brand of Christianity. There is sufficient evidence to suggest his devotion to Christianity was sincere, but he viewed the Christian God from the perspective of a pagan soldier, for his devotion was based in his belief that the Christian God was the guarantor of his victories in war.

The gold solidus of Constantine in this collection **(coin 56)** is also virtually perfect, and it bears a portrait of Constantine from not long before he died. We see an image that is quite different from the soldier-emperors of old: he has long hair, is beardless, and he wears a jewel-encrusted diadem rather than a laurel wreath or a radiate crown, as was traditional for Roman emperors.

Even though Constantine had championed Christianity, he could not abandon an emperor's practicality, and so for about a decade after his conversion in 312, he openly honored the pagan gods in official art, which included his coins. Even on this coin, struck about 23 years after his conversion, Constantine still depicts the pagan personification of Victory, which by then had lost much of its religious significance.

Not long after Constantine died in 337 another important development occurred. In 364, the Roman world (which had been united since 31 B.C.) became divided between the East and the West, and with the exception of two brief interruptions due to military emergencies, it would remain divided until the West fell to barbarians in 476.

Though the East remained relatively prosperous, the West was on a path of steady decline. From about 455 onward the emperors were mere puppets for the barbarian soldiers who appointed and deposed them with impunity. It was a sign of the times, and a consequence of the unwillingness of Romans to serve in their own army.

This collection contains an exceptional gold solidus **(coin 57)** of the boy-emperor Romulus Augustus, who is generally described as the last Roman emperor. Perhaps more than any other Late Roman coin it illustrates the shameful decline of the Roman world during the final years of the Western Roman Empire.

Romulus Augustus was the son of Orestes, the highest-ranking soldier in the West. When in 475 Orestes overthrew Julius Nepos, the last legitimate emperor of the West, he soon appointed his son emperor. Father and son then fell victim to a counter-revolution less than one year

Coin 56: gold solidus of Constantine This solidus from Antioch expresses Constantine's vows in anticipation of reigning 30 years as emperor.

Coin 57: gold solidus of Romulus Augustus The portraits on the last Roman coins are mere caricatures, a reflection of the state of culture at the time.

later by resident Germans. This resulted in Orestes' death and the dethronement of Romulus Augustus.

But before he had lost his empty title of emperor, the Rome mint issued this gold solidus on the young man's behalf. It depicts an anonymous emperor identifiable as Romulus Augustus only by the inscription that contains his name. Such were the depths to which the art of coinage had sunk by the time the West collapsed.

The Roman world survived in the East for another thousand years, based in the walled capital of Constantinople. A long sequence of emperors reigned over what modern historians have identified as the Byzantine Empire, though that term was unknown in ancient times. Those emperors were quite unaware of the lesser status that would be accorded to them by modern historians, and throughout the centuries they never hesitated to describe themselves as Romans.

CHAPTER THREE

COINS *of the* MIDDLE AGES

Robert Wilson Hoge

A brief survey of the monies of the so-called Middle Ages reveals fascinating aspects that help delineate history in its complex and contradictory reality. Some modern historians have seen the "middle period" as merely a colorful interlude between the high-achieving ancient or classical civilizations and the more enlightened world of their own lifetimes. Yet a closer look reveals that the thousand-year period from the fifth century to the 15th was in many respects a true continuation or extension of patterns from the late Roman world, as well as a nurturing ground of transition leading to the more significant changes that we think of as being characteristic of recent history. Many medieval patterns, even some involving coinage, are still with us today.

In numismatics, it is possible to observe numerous signposts along the way, demonstrating both this continuity with late classical cultures, and the clear changes exemplifying the new occurrences in Western Europe. These coins—these specific objects which humanity created, used, and held dear—can serve as a window to provide a view to the prevailing political, socioeconomic, religious, literary, artistic, and technological tendencies of their times.

The End of the Ancient World

Just when "ancient times" came to an end can remain a matter of debate for historians. Certainly by the middle of the fifth century, the face of the Roman World had changed dramatically. While the imperial government still held sway (at least theoretically), Europe, North Africa, and the Middle East had witnessed significant changes during the previous century. Successful invasions and permanent settlement by Germanic and other tribes within the empire, plus the adoption and installation of Christianity as its state religion, eventually necessitated a permanent administrative division between the Western and the Eastern provinces. Along with these social and political changes, economic forces had been shifting as well. These were augmented or hastened by the capture and devastation of urban centers. Rome itself was sacked by the Visigoths in 410, and again by the Vandals in 455.

In modern popular imagination, Rome's Empire "fell" to the invading Germanic tribes, initiating an era called the Dark Ages. Certainly, recurring migrations and incursions of large foreign or outsider populations into civilized regions over a number of centuries characterized these times. In the late Roman Empire, a form of largely self-sufficient, hierarchical, agrarian life emerged as a primary resource for sustenance and status for both the Latins and the Germans. Accompanying this was a reduction in the importance of towns as cultural and administrative centers, yet these, nevertheless, continued to function as entities for the bureaucracies of the Christian faith, as well as remaining defensive strongholds in times of peril. And most notably, the warlike and largely uneducated Germanic "nobles" adopted Christianity and moved to the top of the social system, providing defenses for the natives of the provinces, who mostly devolved into the general work force.

Medieval coinages as a whole show much greater variety than can be found in the basic monetary systems of the ancient world. Yet paradoxically, at the same time, they perpetuate certain features over centuries, thus demonstrating an underlying continuity with antiquity. The Roman World of the fifth century presents a series of numismatic stereotypes, well removed from the normal earlier practice of utilizing coinage as a vehicle for topical propaganda. Changes in minting were at first subtle. As German "barbarians" gained control of mints in the West, they tended to retain imperial approaches to legends and imagery, no doubt regarding themselves as the legitimate continuators of the official Roman tradition. Gold was still minted on a relatively large scale by both imperial and "barbaric" mints, and was undoubted utilized not only for providing emoluments to high-level bureaucrats and military personnel, but also for mollifying both actual and would-be enemies. The gold solidus, a denomination introduced by Constantine the Great in A.D. 309, was still struck in quantity by the empire. For the barbarians, though, the smaller tremissis, one third of a solidus, became increasingly the preferred coin, and the characteristic one to be struck by the various Germanic groups in imitation of the imperial issues.

A fine example of a Roman coin of the mid-fifth century is a solidus **(coin 58)** of the Eastern Roman emperor Marcianus (Marcian), which might well have been used to bribe barbarian tribesmen to depart (or at least to make war on someone else), or to help pay for military defense.

This coin presents a standard example of the gold that served as a prototype for the wandering German tribal peoples of early-medieval Europe. Its obverse design employs a stylized effigy of the emperor as a military man, boldly facing forward with plumed helmet and cuirass. He

Coin 58: gold solidus of Marcianus (shown enlarged on page 79)

holds a spear over his shoulder and a shield with a horseman (spearing a fallen barbarian, incidentally) design on it.

The coin's reverse features a Roman Nike or "Victory" which, to the new Christian way of thinking, was a manifestation of an angel, shown holding the symbolic cross of the Crucifixion. To the angel's right is a symbolic star. The legend, appropriately enough, reads VICTORIA AVGGG, ("Victory of the Emperors"), followed by Z, the Greek numeral for 7, indicating the seventh atelier or *officina* of the Constantinople mint. The great mint of Constantinople, noted in the exergue with the mint signature CONOB (an abbreviation for *Constantinopolis Obryzum*—"Gold of Constantinople"), at times had up to 15 such factories in operation.

Ruled from Constantinople, the site of the former Greek city of Byzantium, the new capital of the Roman Empire was established by Constantine the Great a little more than a century earlier, and named for himself ("City of Constantine"). Constantinople and the Eastern Roman Empire were to survive invasions by Germanic tribes, Huns, Avars, Arabs, Normans, Frankish Crusaders, Italian mercantile interests, and many others, until falling before the Turkish onslaught in 1453. Its vast and intricate coinages reveal "Byzantine" institutionalized power, religious struggles, and iconography of the state, and the influence of dominant personalities.

Threats to Rome

Over the centuries, Roman rulers had become quite adept at playing one group of people off against another to their own advantage. When, for example, out of the Eurasian steppes in the fourth century charged a highly mobile and fiercely warlike people known as the Huns (relatives of the later Mongols), the Romans utilized these dangerous tribesmen as a tool against other, closer barbarians such as the Visigoths. However, in the 450s, under their formidable leader Attila, called the Scourge of God, the pagan Huns wrought havoc on the empire's frontiers and the people who lived in these regions—both the Christianized Germans and their increasingly demoralized Roman citizen neighbors. Alliances and tribute payments from the Eastern emperors bought off the Huns for some years, but Marcian discontinued this practice, infuriating Attila and providing him a pretext to attack!

In punitive confinement because of a scandalous sexual affair, Honoria, the sister of the Western emperor Valentinian III, sneaked a message

Coin 58: gold solidus of Marcianus
Struck in the imperial mints in Constantinople, the official capital of the Roman Empire, this gold piece clearly reveals how low representational coin portraiture had sunk. Also, indicative of the rise of faith-based kingdoms in this period, the Roman image of Victory on the reverse is evolving into that of an angel holding the cross of faith.

to the savage king of the Huns to come to her aid. Spurred by his ego and lust, and prompted by the absence of golden tribute, Attila decided to oblige. He turned his forces to the western provinces of Gaul, but at the great battle of Châlons-sur-Marne in 451, in what is now the Champagne region of France, a gigantic army of Huns and their allies was turned back by the empire and its Germanic soldiers—Visigoths, Alans, Burgundians, and Franks. Following his withdrawal from Gaul, Attila then marched into Italy, destroying Aquileia, and was descending on Rome when he was somehow persuaded to desist by the bishop of Rome, Pope Leo I, in 452. (A miracle was declared!)

To the relief of the Roman world, Attila died of a hemorrhage in 454, as the result of excessive conjugal festivities. The threat that he embodied disappeared. His Hunnish armies subsequently became stalwart soldiers of the Eastern emperors. While the Huns under Attila were settling in one way or another into life in the West, their eastern cousins, called the *Hephthalites* ("White Huns"), were invading territories of the Roman Empire's most dangerous traditional opponent.

The greatest threat to the Romans on the eastern borders of the empire at the start of the Middle Ages was the dynamic Sasanian kingdom of Persia, headquartered at Ctesiphon on the River Tigris, near where Baghdad lies today. The Sasanians had come to power with the overthrow of the Parthian kingdom by Ardeshir I in the 220s. Just as the Parthians had adopted the Greek coinage system model of the silver drachm and tetradrachm, the Sasanians took that drahm as their standard coin, accompanied by occasional small bronzes and rare gold issues.

Coin 59: gold dinar of Persia

An outstanding example of Sasanian Persian coinage is a rare gold piece **(coin 59)**, equivalent to a Roman solidus, issued by Khusru II (called Chosroes in Greek), whose rule marked the culmination of Persian power.

Among the most extravagant rulers in history, with thousands of concubines and many wives (one of whom was the daughter of the Byzantine emperor Maurice Tiberius), Khusru invaded Palestine during the reign of the Byzantine emperor Heraclius, and succeeded in carrying off the most sacred relic of the Christian faith, the "True Cross" upon which Jesus had been crucified—"discovered" some 300 years earlier by the mother of Constantine the Great. Khusru's coins were struck at a good number of mints throughout his long reign, with the mint names and regnal years generally written out in Pahlevi script on the reverse. In

Coin 59: gold dinar of Persia The Sasanian gold dinar was equivalent to Rome's golden solidus. This issue of Khusru II (590–627 A.D.), showing the goddess Anahita with a nimbus of flames about her head, is without a doubt the most visually striking issue in the entire Sasanian series.

the central area of the reverse on the dinar is an impressive facing bust of the fertility goddess Anahita, wearing a tiara within a nimbus of flames, to the right of which is the legend MAY HE CAUSE IRAN TO PROSPER and to the left, the regnal year 21 (although, in the deceptive Pahlavi script, it could be interpreted as 23). On the obverse appears a stylized portrait bust of the king wearing a turreted headdress plumed with two wings. The legend reads, on the left, MAY KINGSHIP INCREASE, and on the right, KHUSRU, KING OF KINGS. Each Sasanid king adopted a particular form of distinctive headdress, by which his numismatic effigy may be identified.

Consolidating their rule through identification with the Zoroastrian religion and the great land-owning families, the Sasanian kings controlled a vast region extending at times from Egypt eastward to the Indus and north to the central Asian steppe. They profited enormously from trade in the riches of the East over the famous silk route and the Indian Ocean. Their religion, Zoroastrianism, is based upon the duality of the struggle between the forces of good (Ahuramazda) and evil (Ahriman). Elements of this dualism entered early Christianity in the concept of God versus Satan. In addition to their impact on religion and numismatics, another important legacy of the Sasanians may be noted. In warfare, a great part of the success of the Persian armies against the Romans and others was due to their development of perhaps the first use of heavily armored cavalry. Their combatants made use of full-body armor for both man and horse—a custom that was adopted by the Byzantine Romans and spread to Western Europe in the form of the "knight in shining armor" of the High Middle Ages.

*T*he heavily armored cavalryman of the Persian army became the knight of medieval Europe.

With the death of Khusru, the Sasanian dynasty and the entire Persian state spiraled into rapid decline through internecine strife. Outside encroachments had already weakened their borders, but it was not these threats that felled the four-centuries-old kingdom of the Persians. From the heart of Arabia swept the Arab peoples under their new religion of Islam ("servitude" to the One God: Allah) proclaimed by the prophet

Muhammad. In just one century following Muhammad's death in 632, his adherents spread their domain and the teachings of their sacred book, the *Qu'ran* (or *Koran*) not only throughout the Middle East but also across North Africa, Spain, and southern France, reaching far into central Asia and to modern-day Pakistan. Islam was a religion of toleration and brotherhood, but it was at the same time a religion of forced conversion. Its conception of politics, of the religious State on earth, was something new, although built upon the Judaic tradition of the One God and the Christian Roman model of a catholic unity of peoples and spirituality. The Muslims' faith was likewise reflected in their coinages. Acceptance of the Mosaic commandment regarding "graven images" is apparent in the mature Islamic issues, which, for the most part, are devoid of figural devices. Because their extensive series regularly bear statements of place and date, the Islamic coins comprise an important resource as historical markers for numismatic and archeological research.

Meanwhile, one of the invaded areas where the natives were slowest to accept the new faith was a Roman ally and buffer state against the Sasanians. Christianity had spread through the Roman Empire, and from Egypt had reached up the Nile and into Ethiopia. There the Egyptian, or Coptic, mode took hold in the powerful kingdom of Aksum. Nestled beyond the great horn of Africa, and situated on the frontier that controlled trade into the heart of East Africa, Aksum served as a guard to the lucrative Red Sea trade. At about the time of Constantine, the Aksumite king Ezenas converted to the new religion then fostered by the emperor, and his territories became the world's first Christian state. The first bishop of Aksum was commissioned by the emperor Constantius II in 356.

For a period of nearly 400 years, Aksum produced a striking coinage, typically utilizing as its type images of the kings and the Christian cross. Legends on the coins appear in a combination of scripts derived from Coptic, expressing the rulers' names and titles in Greek, the official language of the entire Eastern Roman World, and the native language Geez. A rare and interesting example of the Byzantine satellite coinage of Aksum is an anonymous gold unit (coin 60), presumably struck during the early Christian period in the latter half of the fifth century.

This coin is reverse die-linked to the coins of two named kings of this era, Nezana and Nezool, whose coins are not dissimilar to those of

Coin 60: gold unit of the Aksumite Kingdom (shown enlarged on page 85)

still another, very slightly later, king, Kaleb, documented as being a contemporary and ally of the Byzantine Emperor Justinus (Justin) I (518–527 A.D.). Both obverse and reverse feature a right-facing bust of a king, the one crowned and the other wearing a head-cloth, within a wreath of two grain ears and accompanied by an unintelligible Greek-letter legend interspersed with crosses. On the obverse the Geez letter for M is to the right of the king's effigy.

Aksum became isolated from the rest of the Christian world, and then overwhelmed by Islam in the seventh and eighth centuries. No longer able to withstand Islamic political domination, let alone to mint coinage, its cities and economic influence withered. Christianity, however, survived in this region of Africa in spite of wars, slave-raiding, and attempted conversions by its Arab neighbors.

Aksum's stalwart adherence to its faith, almost alone within a sea of Islam, is but one thread of the weave of religiosity that will characterize the medieval period, also known as the *Age of Faith*. Yet, in this era, it was a faith of a harsh and confusing kind. The forms of early Christian worship and practice varied considerably, as had been the case with Judaism during the same period. Already by the time of Aksum's conversion, opposing Christian views had become entrenched and hostile to one another, leading to denunciations, proscriptions, and civic strife. By the reign of Justin, widespread fighting between Christian groups was breaking out. It must have been difficult for converting pagans to comprehend the dictates of their new faith (the Roman Church partially ameliorated this by incorporating popular old pagan customs into the new theological framework). Earlier pagan gods and various polytheistic manifestations, including allegorical personifications of virtues and ideals, were conveniently provided with a new host of patron saints and martyrs who could be represented and venerated in the same sort of way. God as well was multi-faceted, indeed tripartite. The exact nature of the Holy Trinity was a matter of hot debate, and frequently vicious conflict.

Indeed, reacting to the strong monotheism of the Muslims, many Christians saw doctrinal problems with their own faith's proliferation of holy icons. These Christian images seemed, in a way, to have become replacements for the old polytheism's artistic renderings. Others saw the icons of the sainted as their aids to atonement and salvation. These

Coin 60: gold unit of the Aksumite Kingdom The currency of Aksum was the first ethnic African coinage seen on the continent. Adopting Christianity early in the fourth century, the Aksumites remained defiantly so even as the lands around them became a sea of Islam.

opposing views, and others more materialistic, became a hallmark of the spiritual contradictions of life in medieval times. Similarly, much of the animosity felt toward some of the German barbarians was due to the fact that they had been converted by "heretical" Christian missionaries, and were therefore regarded as unacceptable by orthodox Catholics. Themes of this sort recurred throughout this period in Western Civilization, and at times strongly colored its history.

Characteristics of Medieval Coinage

A traditional date often used for the beginning of the medieval period is 476, when the barbarian general Odovacar, of the Herulian tribe, declared an end to the reign of the emperor Julius Nepos in the West. He deposed his own young puppet-ruler Romulus Augustus (who was the son of Attila the Hun's prime minister, Orestes), sending the imperial regalia to the Eastern emperor Zeno with the remark that there was no longer a need for them. But Odovacar and other Germanic rulers, heretics though they might be, continued their own version of Roman coinage, which was gradually transformed into the money of the European nations. During the thousand-year period that followed, money gradually became quite different from the familiar coinages of Antiquity.

Wars, victories, legislative acts, holidays, gods, goddesses, religious observances and attitudes, peoples, provinces, monuments, and ideas of many kinds had been commemorated on Roman imperial coins. And many Roman issues can be closely dated through the formulae of names and titles used by the rulers and, later, through sequences of mintmarks. Every year the Romans struck millions of coins for the empire's enormous financial needs. As they were put into circulation, these then served as a direct means of communication with the masses—an immense opportunity for state propaganda. The rulers of the Hellenistic kingdoms and early Roman empire took advantage of this possibility to foster personal power, and their numismatic portraiture reached an artistic level of realism that has never been surpassed. Until a more stylized, hieratic imagery appeared in the late third and fourth centuries, most of the rulers could be instantly recognized by means of the effigies on their coins. In contrast, however, most European coins of the Middle Ages made no attempt to project topical relevance other than to include the almost universal symbol of the cross, professing adherence to Christianity. Other than on some non-Christian coins, and apart from regnal-dated Byzantine issues until the eighth century, dates of issue were also essentially absent—perhaps implying a kind of timelessness, an other-worldliness in keeping with the ideals of the Church. For the State had become this religion, and this religion had become the State. It is called the Roman Catholic Church for good reason. The Roman Empire did not perish; it was merely transformed into an exaggerated manifestation of some of the most important of its later features.

The artwork and the craftsmanship with which coins of the medieval period were minted are also unlike those of their ancient models. With a few possible exceptions, of which we will make note, there was no real attempt at portraiture basically from the fourth to the 15th century throughout Europe; human images often appeared crude, stiff, linear, and poorly executed in comparison with their earlier counterparts. Instead of being struck on individually prepared blanks, as in previous centuries, typical coins of the post-Roman era were struck on thin blanks cut from hammered-out sheet-metal strips. The dies that were used to strike these planchets were simplified, with their designs and inscriptions primarily cut onto the surfaces by means of combinations of conveniently shaped punches rather than by fine engraving tools. The finished results normally showed low relief, uneven lettering, and conventional, stylized imagery. Nevertheless, these new kinds of coins show many interesting features, and help convey a sense of the peculiar wonder and attraction of this age of excesses and contradictions.

> *These coins convey the peculiar wonder of this age of contradictions. . . .*

It is worth remembering that always in the background of medieval Europe persisted the on-going Roman Empire based at Constantinople, the majestic "Byzantine" capital. Through most of the period, the imperial coinages greatly eclipsed their Western counterparts in quantity and quality. During most reigns, coin types remained relatively consistent in a number of ways although they too underwent clear transition and development. Before we proceed to survey Western issues, imperial Byzantine coins deserve further examination.

While gold such as the solidus of Marcian represented a continuation from late antiquity, economic factors and the coinages in the other metals changed substantially. In 498, Anastasius I reformed the minor coinage used in everyday transactions, introducing the copper follis (worth 40 nummi, as indicated by a large Greek numeral M—or 40—on the reverse) and its 1/2, 1/4, and 1/8 fractions (marked K, I, and E for the number of nummi each represented—20, 10, and 5). Along with the gold solidus (this denomination was called the *nomisma* in the Eastern, Greek-speaking, Roman Empire), the follis remained current into the 11th century, when new coinage systems were introduced, including so-called scyphates—cup-shaped coins of varying values, properly referred to as *trachea*. Silver coinage was sparsely minted, but was evidently significant for some purposes, often for limited ceremonial distributions. The late Roman siliqua and miliarense continued with modifications, and the emperor Heraclius introduced a new, heavier denomination, the hexagram. In the Late Empire, in its impoverished state under the Palaeologan dynasty, silver became the sole coinage medium from the mid-14th century until after the Turkish conquest of 1453.

Christianity, Islam, and Medieval Money

Traces of the Christian Church's conceptual struggle involving representations of holy icons can be discerned in many Byzantine issues. Characteristically, Eastern Roman coins show formal images of Jesus, Mary, and various saints along with members of the imperial family—as well as of the emperors themselves. But this had not always been the case. An important step was taken in the reign of a most unfortunate, and villainous ruler, Justinianus (Justinian) II, namesake of his illustrious predecessor, Justinian I (ruled A.D. 527–565). The second Justinian ruled from A.D. 685 to 695, and again from 705 to 711. What did he do? He placed a full-faced icon of Jesus prominently on one side of his coins!

During his first reign, in response to religious provocations on the part of the Arabs, who had recently succeeded in capturing the vastly important province of Egypt, Justinian decided to retaliate in a visual way with an image sure to annoy the infidels. They responded by introducing their own, an iconographic series of coins (which become the model for most Muslim issues for the next millennium). Many Christian Romans themselves disapproved of such imagery, and for the next 150 years, the Byzantine state was wracked by the struggles of those who favored the holy images, the *iconodules*, and those who, like the Muslims, regarded this practice as anathema, the *iconoclasts*, or "idol-breakers." Justinian's icon of Jesus, the first representation of Jesus in numismatic history, showed his effigy as *Pantocrator*, "ruler of all," wearing long hair and beard, in what has since become a traditional religious image. But on the solidi or nomismata of the second reign, Jesus was startlingly depicted as a facing, draped bust with a very short beard and short, very curly hair, with a cross behind his head, holding the Gospels with his left hand and raising his right in benediction (see **coin 61**). The effigy was probably derived from some unknown lost icon (much religious iconography was destroyed during the iconoclast struggles). Curiously, this second visage of Christ, to modern eyes, is almost as disturbing as the first was to Justinian's subjects. No longer the viral image of the Pantocrator, this Jesus, who was raised in the household of a carpenter, appears as elegantly manicured and coiffed as any fashionable Byzantine courtier or eunuch of the time would have.

This solidus' obverse legend reads D[ominus] N[oster] JHS[us] CH[ristu]S REX REGNANTIUM—"Jesus Christ, King of Kings." The reverse features half-length facing busts of the emperor, on the left, draped and wearing a cross-topped diadem, and on the right, his son and heir Tiberius, likewise arrayed, both holding the shaft of a cross in their right hands. The legend reads D N IUSTINIANUS ET TIBERIUS P[rincipes] P[erpetui]—"Our Lords Justinian and Tiberius, Perpetual Rulers." The main aspects of coins such as this one (a flat look, with somewhat clumsy lettering and a religious orientation, with prominence given to the cross)—so different from the solidus of Marcian—were to influence Byzantine and other European coins for centuries to come.

Justinian was deposed and purposefully maimed with his nose being cut off (historians call him *Rhinotmetus*, "slit-nose"), theoretically disqualifying him from holding again the sacred office of emperor because the imperial person was supposed to be protected by God. Still he succeeded in regaining the imperial throne and assiduously pursued vengeance against his enemies. For good reason, the Byzantine world has gone down in history with the reputation for political intrigue, subterfuge, backstabbing, violence, and massacre. Monks and hermits, priests, functionaries, and high ecclesiastics on the one hand met rioting

Coin 61: gold solidus of Justinian II (Eastern Roman Empire, Constantinople Mint)
(shown enlarged on page 91)

chariot factions, uncouth provincial soldiers, encroaching foreign enemies, and urban mobs on the other, with the imperial families, courts, and corps of eunuchs in the middle. It was a world characterized both by sophistication and savagery, debauchery and asceticism—constant tension between civilization and the abyss. Paler reflections of this tension also characterized Western Europe during the period. While the level and breadth of cultural attainment may have been more subdued, atrocities were every bit as convincing.

Christian fervor in the Middle Ages was real. In place of the faltering empire, the Church had become the center of education and jurisprudence. To expiate their transgressions, to achieve atonement, to become worthy of the kingdom of heaven, and to find solace in a world of chaos and carnage, legions of men and women dedicated their lives to the service of Jesus. Convents of rigorously observant believers—monasteries, cloisters, abbeys—were established throughout the former Roman territories and beyond, as Christianity spread into Central and Eastern Europe.

The emperor Basil I introduced a new iconographic design on his gold coinage (coin 62), one that would find a place in European numismatic typology for a good 500 years. This new design was an image of Jesus Christ enthroned on the coin's obverse, with the same legend as on Justinian's coin of nearly 200 years earlier. The reverse rendering was also not unlike that of the earlier coin, with half-length figures of the emperor and his son Constantine holding a cross between them and a similar arrangement of the imperial names and titles.

Basil was a good-looking and utterly unscrupulous and immoral Macedonian peasant who beguiled and murdered his way to the throne. The Arabs had continued to whittle away at the imperial provinces, but Basil was actually able to drive them back in Asia and establish his own strong and wicked dynasty. His successors maintained themselves for nearly 200 years while fighting incursions by new enemies, the Bulgars and the Turks, who had converted to Islam and become the vanguard of a new wave of Muslim expansion. In the 11th century, weakened by Norman invasions and defeat by the Turks at the Battle of Manzikert (1071), by which the Byzantines lost most of Anatolia, the empire was just beginning to reassert itself under the new dynasty founded by Alexius I Comnenus (1081–1118) when the first of a series of waves of Western Europeans arrived to unhinge the course of civilization. These were the Crusades.

Coin 62: gold solidus of Basil I (Eastern Roman Empire, Constantinople Mint)

Coin 61: gold solidus of Justinian II (Eastern Roman Empire, Constantinople Mint) Justinian II shocked his subjects, but made numismatic history, by introducing a facing portrait bust of Christ to his coinage. That seen here is the second version, dating to Justinian's second reign.

Coin 62: gold solidus of Basil I (Eastern Roman Empire, Constantinople Mint) Nearly 200 years later, the enthroned facing figure of Christ saw its first usage on the gold of Basil I. The iconography would be replicated on numerous other European currencies for another 500 years.

To return now to events in the former Roman Empire in the West, eventually many of the newly settled Germanic peoples took up minting. Coins were struck by Ostrogoths, Vandals, Visigoths, Suevians, Burgundians, Franks, Lombards, Angles, Saxons, Frisians, and others. Initial issues were based squarely upon the late Roman models, and at first gold and copper predominated. But from the 8th century to the 13th, Christian European coinage was minted almost exclusively in silver, and in only one denomination: named *denarius* in all Latin documents but called *denier* in French, *denaro* in Italian, *dinero* in Spanish, *pfennig* in German, and *penny* in English. The Herulian Odovacar (476–493) had his name and bust only on small silver and bronze coins, but other early Germanic rulers also minted gold—in some cases virtually to the exclusion of the baser metals. The extent to which their coins really played a role in commerce is not always clear, but the barbarian kingdoms did produce fairly extensive coinages. A fine example of a Germanic gold piece of the so-called Dark Ages is a tremissis of the Lombard king Liutprand (**coin 63**).

Coin 63: gold tremissis of Liutprand (Lombardic Kingdom)

On this coin appears a stylized, linear imperial-style draped and diademed bust of the king to right, with the legend D[ominus] N[oster] LIVTPRAN[dus] R[e]X—"Our Lord King Liutprand." The mark of the mint, M, appears to the right of the bust. The reverse features a stylized, linear, winged angel holding a labarum, with the legend S[an]C[tu]S MI[c]H[a]IL, identifying him as the archangel Michael. Thin, broad, royal tremisses were minted by the Lombards from the reign of Cunincpert (A.D. 688–700) until that of Desiderius (A.D. 757–774). The latter submitted to Charles the Great—Charlemagne—who was to form a new empire in the West.

Milan would have been the principal mint for the Lombards, but Byzantine minting continued in Italy while most of the land came under the control of the Germans. The Byzantines had used the Lombards (the *Longobardi*, or "long beards") to help crush the heretical Ostrogothic kingdom, which was among the most advanced of the Germans in cultural attainment. But in 568, under their king Alboin, the Lombards had returned and taken almost the entire Italian peninsula. Rome and the popes remained attached to the imperial idea, but sought a new protector. They found one among the Catholic Franks, north of the Alps, whose king Charles (Charlemagne) was crowned as the "Holy Roman Emperor" by Pope Leo III on Christmas Day in the year 800.

Coin 63: gold tremissis of Liutprand (Lombardic Kingdom)
The lightweight tremissis, a one-third fraction of a Roman solidus, became the gold coin of choice of the Germanic kingdoms occupying the former Roman lands.

Coin 64: silver denarius of Charlemagne

Under the previous Merovingian dynasty, the Franks had gradually consolidated a kingdom in the Low Countries and Gaul, now to be known by their tribal name as *Francia* (France). Under their chief administrator, Charles the Hammer, they had been able to turn back the tide of Muslim advance at the battle of Tours, in 732, paving the way for the eventual Christian re-conquest of the Iberian peninsula. Charles' son Pepin the Short overthrew the last Merovingian king, establishing the Carolingian dynasty, and his son Charlemagne greatly extended Frankish authority across the Pyrenees, into the German heartland and on into Northern Italy. The characteristic Merovingian coinage had been of gold tremisses, but a great economic change was taking place and under Pepin silver became dominant, with the denarius (the denier) assuming the role of the main European coin. Charlemagne continued this trend, although he did strike limited gold, some of it evidently in imitation of contemporary Islamic dinars of the Abbasid caliphs of Baghdad. The popes in Rome began minting the Frankish-style denarius, commencing with Adrian (A.D. 772–795). Charlemagne and his Carolingian successors provided the prototypes for much of Western Europe's coinage for the next 400 years.

One of Charlemagne's denarii **(coin 64)**, probably from the mint of Milan after it had been taken from the Lombards, is fairly typical. Simple in design, it bears the king's name on the obverse and his abbreviated title R[e]X F[rancorum]—"King of the Franks," on the reverse. Later Carolingian issues, from the establishment of Charlemagne's *denarius novus* ("new denarius"—a thinner, broader coin) about 794, typically employed monograms of the king's name and cross motifs, as well as occasional figural images and stylized chapels. These became the prevailing imagery not only of royal coins but also of the abundant feudal series that developed out of the socioeconomic and political changes that came about as part of the "Carolingian Renaissance."

Under feudalism, the system of land tenure based upon military support owed to an overlord, the right to mint coinage often passed from the central authority to his adherents. With its institutionalization, minting came to be considered in most regions as attached to the rights of a *comes*, a "count" or companion of the ruler, although noble lay magnates (petty kings, barons, etc.) of other degrees also struck coinage, as did ecclesiastics (abbots, bishops, archbishops, and popes). In practice,

Coin 64: silver denarius of Charlemagne Charlemagne was the first ruler of a united Western Europe since the fall of the Roman Empire. During his rule, the silver denarius, or denier, became the preeminent coin of the realm.

almost anyone rich and powerful enough to exert economic control over a populous area might arrogate the right of coinage, the *droit du seigneur*—the "right of a lord." These rights were an inescapable adjunct to one of the central themes of life in medieval Europe—namely the system of rewarding loyal followers, principally by gifts of land (*fiefs*), along with their appurtenances. At the top of the hierarchies, this right and ability to bestow titles and offices assumed profound importance. The popes contended with the emperors, and the kings with the archbishops, to appoint vassals of their choosing to the highest posts. Who had the right to appoint or anoint whom? This bureaucratic battleground is called the *investiture controversy*, primarily affecting the Holy Roman Emperors from the 10th century to the 13th. Religious leaders believed they had the right to anoint secular rulers, and the secular rulers felt they could appoint religious prelates. While the struggle reached everywhere, nowhere did it wreak more havoc than in Italy, where entire cities revolted on behalf of one side or the other. It led to long-term party politics, often affecting all levels of society.

Whether the minting authority was lay or ecclesiastical, a profit called *seigniorage* (from *seigneur*, "lord") accrued to every issuer. This was the differential in value between the official purchasing power of the coin and its production cost in labor and materials. Differing coin quality, fineness, and exchange rates meant that as merchants and travelers moved from one region to another, they would have needed to carry quantities of coin with them and exchange them, sometimes at unfavorable rates, wherever they might need to carry on transactions. Standards varied from one locale to another, and moneychanging became a common and lucrative business in towns and at regional trade fairs.

Across all borders in Europe, the motif of a cross in various forms was ubiquitous on medieval coins. In many areas of the continent, designs were "immobilized" for long periods, often imitating those of the Carolingian dynasty's monograms and chapels.

Medieval Coinage in England

In England, after the consolidation of the early Anglo-Saxon period, the kings were able to keep in check some of the tendencies of feudalism that dominated the political and economic life of most of Western Europe. The original seven kingdoms of the Anglo-Saxon heptarchy and the powerful earldoms came to be dominated by a supreme ruler, called the *bretwalda*. In the late 8th century, this was Offa, the Anglian king of Mercia. The first identifiable Anglo-Saxon coins cannot be readily attributed to specific individual rulers. They are pseudo-imperial gold tremisses, called *thrymsas* in Old English speech, similar to the contemporaneous Merovingian coinages. In time, the gold content disappeared from these issues, replaced by silver and, in Northumbria, later by copper. The latter two coinages are called *sceattas* and *styccas*. As elsewhere, cross types are most commonly encountered on coins of the Anglo-Saxons, although earlier, presumably pagan issues show a range of interesting mythological and figural representations. As was also the case on the continent, English coin legends characteristically began with a cross as an initial mark.

Bust types gradually became the norm on English coinage, and it is possible that an actual attempt at portraiture appeared during the reign of Offa, who adopted the new denarius denomination being promulgated by Charlemagne in France.

Coin 65: silver denarius (penny) of King Offa, Mercia (shown enlarged on page 99)

On this Mercian penny **(coin 65)**, found in North Yorkshire, the king's draped and diademed bust faces right, with the inscription OFFA REX—"King Offa"—displayed across the field in four lines. The plastic modeling of his face is remarkable for this era of stylized linear depictions. On the floriated reverse are the letters IBBA in four quarters, indicating the name of the king's moneyer. Offa's Mercian penny was minted in many varieties, all of which are today rare, but which in their time must have represented a fairly substantial output. From this time forward, gold became excessively rare in Western Europe, apart from Spain and southern Italy, until the 13th century.

It was during Offa's reign that raiders from the north first attacked the British Isles. These were the Vikings, also called the Danes, Norsemen, Normans, and Norwegians. Their first forays were the beginning of a phenomenon that caused panic, destruction, and dislocation through much of Europe. By the middle of the next century, they were coming not only to raid and pillage, but also to stay. No one knows fully why the Vikings suddenly spewed out of the Baltic regions; probably they were pressured by population growth, but the accumulating wealth of the Carolingian Empire must also have held great appeal. From their swift, practical, and highly maneuverable "dragon-ships," the Vikings raped and burned along the coasts and rivers of northern Europe and the Mediterranean alike, and even made their way to the Ukraine, some of them becoming imperial bodyguards in Constantinople. They imported vast amounts of Islamic silver coinage to their homelands, and sought more in France and the British Isles. By the latter part of the 9th century, they were attacking Paris, and seemed on the verge of conquering England, when they were confronted by a stalwart king of Wessex (the land of the West Saxons) who finally was able to curb their drive.

Alfred the Great holds a well-earned place in English history. As he thrust back the Danes, it is from his reign that London became the capital city and principal mint. Alfred's penny **(coin 66)** shares clear affinities with Offa's coin of 100 years earlier: a draped, diademed bust with rather disjointed lettering on the obverse, and a moneyer's name on the reverse—typical characteristics of the English coinage. The obverse reads [AE]LFRED REX—"King Alfred"—while the reverse inscription is TILEVINE and MONETA ("Tilewine, the Moneyer") above and below, and a stylized monogram of LONDON between two crosses. Winchester had been the capital of Wessex, but with the capture of London, circa 866, a shift occurred, and the great mercantile city was to grow and serve the kingdom ever after. The age of Alfred was to be looked back upon by Englishmen of centuries to come as a time of prosperity and success although the wars with the Danes continued for more than a century still. Alfred's coins were widely imitated, forming prototypes for coins of the Vikings themselves.

Although Western European monetary systems were basically dependent upon a single denomination of coin, surviving records make regular reference to other moneys of account. These were the libra, solidus, and marcus—the "pound," "shilling," and "mark"—used to reckon valuations for many purposes. The pound was originally the old Roman pound, which was re-determined in the 12th century due to the prevalence of trade centered in the great annual fairs held at Troyes, in the Champagne region, giving rise to the dual system of *troy* and *avoirdupois* ("by weight") measurements that have survived to the present day. Whereas the libra and solidus came to refer to an amount in terms of accounting norms, the *mark* normally meant an actual weight in precious metal.

Coin 66: silver denarius (penny) of Alfred the Great, Wessex

Coin 65: silver denarius (penny) of King Offa, Mercia This penny of Offa is one of the most remarkable portrait coins of its day. Offa's reign suffered through the first wave of the Viking raids.

Coin 66: silver denarius (penny) of Alfred the Great, Wessex Alfred the Great earned a special place in English history by preventing the Danes (Vikings) from wholly overrunning English lands. During his rule London, the name rendered as this distinctive monogram on his coins, became the designated capital of England.

In spite of the efforts of Alfred and his successors, the Viking Danes were able to maintain a strong presence in the North of England, establishing their own kingdom based upon the old Roman city of Eboracum ("York"), which they called Yarvik. They also invaded and captured most of Ireland, where they were the first to mint a native coinage, known as the Hiberno-Norse series. Their rare and interesting coins include some pagan design elements, such as the raven of Odin (the king of the gods) and the hammer of Thor, but they soon adopted Christianity as they settled down, and their coins not only resemble those of the Anglo-Saxon kings, but also include a series in the name of St. Peter. A fine example of Viking-Age coinage is a silver penny (coin 67) of the little-known king Anlaf Guthfrithsson, who is believed to have ruled out of York around A.D. 940.

Coin 67: silver penny of Anlaf Guthfrithsson, York

Around its raven obverse, within circles, is the legend ANLAF CVNVN-CIG—"King Anlaf." The reverse, clearly resembling many contemporary coins of the English, features a small central cross and the legend, within circles, A.D.ELFERD MINET RG—"Aethelferd, the King's Moneyer."

From this time forward, the naming of both the moneyer and the mint city became standard on English coins. Altogether, there were eventually 75 boroughs that housed mints, and major cities often employed multiple moneyers in their production. London had more than 50 at one point. Coinage production reached enormous levels during the reign of Aethelred II, "the Unready" (978–1016). He required great sums of silver to buy off the Danes, who imposed a "Danegeld" upon the country (today, great quantities of these coins have been found in Scandinavia, evidence of the cost of keeping the Vikings away). But this ransom was not enough. King Sweyn of Denmark, and after him his son Cnut, gained ever-greater control, and upon Aethelred's death Cnut was able to name himself King of the English and marry Aethelred's widow Emma, sister of the Viking descendant Duke Richard of Normandy. By Cnut, Emma had a son, Hardicnut (or Harthacnut), who was destined to become king of England and Denmark.

Coin 68: silver penny of Hardicnut, England

This coin of Hardicnut (coin 68), from the mint of Taunton, depicts the king's diademed and draped bust, holding a scepter, with the legend HARD[i]CNVT REX—"King Hardicnut." On the reverse is a common feature of many of the reverse coin types of the era, a "voided" or double-lined cross in the center which served to facilitate cutting the coin into segments for small change. (This was not unusual in England, where the

Coin 67: silver penny of Anlaf Guthfrithsson, York Despite the wars waged against them by Alfred and his successors, the Viking presence remained well entrenched in northern England, their lands centering around present-day York. Also, the Vikings for a time captured and controlled much of Ireland.

Coin 68: silver penny of Hardicnut, England Hardicnut occupied the thrones of both Denmark and, more briefly, England (1040–1042). His reign was quarrelsome and oppressive. His sudden death at a drunken wedding party was met with relief.

halfpenny was rarely minted and the quarter-penny, or *farthing*, was not struck until 1279.) The reverse legend names the moneyer and mint: BOGA ON TANTVNE—"Boga, at Taunton."

During the Late Anglo-Saxon Period, it became the common practice to make a major change in the national coinage type every few years. Hardicnut's short reign did not permit this, but that of his half-brother Edward the Confessor (1042–1066) did. London became the production center for all dies, which were then shipped to the respective mints out in the shires. Issuing coinage was a royal privilege and prerogative jealously guarded as a political and economic tool. The fees charged to moneyers for supplying them with their replacement dies at times of design changes were a source of regular revenue for the English kings.

All of the English penny obverses from the time of the church reforms of Edgar, father of Aethelred II, had included an effigy of the king. Harold Godwinson, who had himself proclaimed king by the English royal advising-council, the *Witan*, upon the death of Edward in 1066, was no exception. But his one reverse type implores what he was not to have—peace.

The obverse of Harold's penny **(coin 69)** is not unlike the image on the coin of Hardicnut from 25 years before, but for a much greater verism to the portrait, and an inscription now reading HALOLD REX ANG[lorum]—"Harold, King of the English." The reverse reads PAX— "peace"—across the middle, with the marginal legend, starting at 9 o'clock, naming the moneyer and mint.

Harold's "peace" was in death. Having ruled for only ten months, he died in battle on Senlac Hill, some ten miles from the Sussex port town of Hastings, opposing the invading Normans under Duke William.

William's first coinage issue **(coin 70)** closely resembled that of Harold, but with a floriated cross as the reverse type in place of PAX. On the pictured example from the historic town of Hastings, the obverse legend reads PILLEMVS REX ("King William"); the reverse, DVNNIC ON AESTI ("Dunnic, at Hastings").

Although in a way William was but one of a long list of Viking marauders, he is a pivotal figure in Western European history. By his conquest of England, he brought that country into the mainstream of the continent (which would precipitate his descendents' later attempts to expand their holdings in France). The invasion also returned to the

Coin 69: silver penny of Harold II, England

Coin 70: silver penny of William the Conqueror, England

Coin 69: silver penny of Harold II, England This coin bears an exceptional medieval portrait of the last Anglo-Saxon king of Britain, who was slain at the battle of Hastings while opposing William the Conqueror's invasion.

Coin 70: silver penny of William the Conqueror, England In the person of William the Conqueror, who was of Viking descent, the Vikings can be said to have finally won all of England. William was a pivotal figure in both English and European history.

island both the lay and ecclesiastical traditions of the Late Roman Western World. Before the coming of the Normans, English law had become more closely aligned with old Germanic customs.

Although a bastard, William was the son of Duke Robert the Devil, the brother of Queen Emma, and thereby first cousin to both Hardicnut and Edward the Confessor. His wife, Matilda, was also a descendent of Alfred the Great. Thus William's dynastic claim to the English throne was real, if perhaps stretched. In 1066 he obtained the blessing and sanction of Pope Alexander II to invade and conquer his "birthright." With some 700 ships and many allies, and under a sacred banner given by the pope, William felt justified in attacking. He claimed that Edward had named him as his heir, and that Harold, whom he had previously rescued and knighted, had sworn to support him in his goal.

William was crowned by the archbishop of Canterbury on Christmas Day, in 1066. He proceeded about the country, building fortresses and establishing his companions in extensive landholdings taken from the English followers of Harold, and making numerous other changes. However, in the English monetary system he found a stability that was lacking in the feudal economies of the continent. He made essentially no changes, and issued eight sequential basic coin types.

The English practice of issuing successive royal coin types continued into the reign of William's grandson, Stephen of Blois (1135–1154), but was then undermined by civil war. When order was restored by Stephen's nephew, Henry of Anjou, the Plantagenet (Henry II, ruled 1154–1189), the continental idea of a single coin type minted for long periods took hold. From 1158 to 1180, his *type immobilisé* ("immobilized type"— known as the *Tealby Type* from a major find of these coins in his name, made in 1807 near that Lincolnshire town) used as its reverse design four small crosses in the quarters of a central cross, combined with a crude, facing bust of the king holding a scepter on the obverse.

In 1180 Henry II introduced a new, better-executed coinage with a design not unlike that of the Tealby Type but having a voided cross in the center of the reverse. Known as the *Short Cross Type* coinage, its design and legends continued essentially unchanged on subsequent issues through the reigns of his sons Richard I ("Lionheart") and the infamous John, and that of his grandson Henry III until 1247, when the voided cross was extended to the edge of the coin to help combat the nefarious practice of clipping off portions of the coins' edges in order to steal some of its metal. The design then continued, again without a change in the king's name, until the seventh year of the reign of Henry III's son, Edward I, in 1279, when a major re-coinage came about.

Banking the Crusades

Upon the death of William the Conqueror, his eldest son (the rebellious Robert) had become Duke of Normandy, while his second son (William II, "Rufus") was crowned king of England. Robert pawned his duchy to his brother and set out as one of the principal leaders of the most striking enterprise of the age, the Crusades. This first of nine waves of Western Europeans to carry war to the Levant was a vast popular movement intended to free the Holy Land from control by the Muslim Saracens, and to secure the original holy places of Christianity for pilgrimages. But it was also a quest for territorial gain and military glory, all combined with religious zeal and intolerance. While the Westerners' grip on the Levant tended to remain tenuous, these evangelical wars nevertheless led to important changes in European ways of life, particularly in regard to emerging trade and reawakening knowledge about faraway parts of the world. Italian maritime cities prospered by providing supplies, money, and transport for the traveling avengers, whose largest number came from French-speaking territories.

The Crusading idea was not a new one. Christians had been fighting Muslims for 450 years, but recently the zealous Sunni Turks had made headway in conquering and consolidating territories in the East. Meanwhile, in the late 11th century, the rivalries between Islamic states were becoming increasingly bellicose. Also, the Christian Armenians had become surrounded by Muslim states, and sought help from their co-religionists, while the Shiite Fatimid dynasty in Egypt and North Africa was actually encouraging the Christians to disrupt their opponents. At the same time, Normans had captured southern Italy and Sicily and were invading Greece, diverting the attention and energy of the Eastern Roman / Byzantine Empire from handling the Muslims. An opportunity seemed to be there for regaining Palestine for the Cross of Jesus (and riches and blessings for the participants). Jerusalem and the Palestinian coastal plain were conquered, and a Christian kingdom of Jerusalem, with attendant feudal entities, was established.

In 1118, at the start of the reign of King Baldwin II, Hugues de Payens (a knight of Champagne) and eight companions bound themselves by a perpetual vow to defend Christian Jerusalem's domain. Baldwin accepted their services and assigned them a portion of his palace, adjoining the temple of the Holy Sepulcher; hence the title of this Crusading Order, the *pauvres chevaliers du temple* ("Poor Knights of the Temple"—or Knights Templars). Hugues journeyed west to the Council of Troyes (1128), at which he assisted and at which St. Bernard of Clairvaux, instigator of the Second Crusade, was the leading spirit. There, besides their crusader's vow, the Knights Templars formally adopted the Monastic Rule of St. Benedict, accepting a monk's three austere rules concerning the chapel, the refectory, and the dormitory. The Templar Order encompassed four ranks of brethren: heavily armored knights; *serjeants*, who formed light cavalry; chaplains, who were vested as priests to minister to the spiritual needs of the Order; and *farmers*, who were entrusted with the administration of temporal affairs. Recruits flocked to the new order and it grew rapidly. In it were combined those two great passions of the Middle Ages, religious fervor and martial prowess. Ecclesiastical and lay authorities heaped favors of every kind on the Templars, and made use of their services in several ways.

Banking practices (extending credit, lending, transferring balances, converting currencies, investing, making change) date back to antiquity, but they expanded and became increasingly formalized during the Middle Ages. Much of the development was certainly stimulated by the Crusades, as large numbers of feudal landlords mortgaged their estates to raise funds to support their extended travel and military commitments, and needed methods to obtain money far from home. With their great reputation for probity and disavowal of personal gain, the Knights Templar made this kind of activity part of their program of supporting the crusading movement and protecting travelers and pilgrims, thus greatly enhancing their own revenues. Payments from one region could be sent to another through a bill of exchange by paying for the order in a local currency, which would be paid out in another's coin upon receipt (with appropriate service charges, of course).

Gradually, networks of international banking houses, mostly North Italian, grew into great companies that had offices in all the leading commercial centers of Europe and the Levant. In London, the district where their business was conducted thus acquired the name *Lombard Street*.

English coinage was greatly in demand outside the country due to the high standards ("sterling" purity—calculated at 925 parts silver per 1,000) that had been retained by the dutiful regard of the kings. With his reforms of 1279, the English crusader King Edward I (1272–1307) instituted new silver coinage types and denominations that were to survive, with only slight value reductions, for more than 250 years. In the Low Countries and northern Germany, in particular, the *esterlins* or *easterlings*, as the sterling pennies were called, were highly favored and widely imitated. But the German states were not without their own resources; in fact, the silver in English coins had to be imported in the first place, since England was without sources of its own. Finds of silver ore occurred in the mountains of Germany in the mid-12th century, quickly leading to a proliferation of minting. Broad, thin, embossed bracteate ("leaf-like") pfennigs—still called *denarii* in Latin documents—became popular around 1160. Although, like foil, they were so thin that they could not carry a different design on both sides, these bracteate denars offered a wider field for artistic scope, and their types provide the most appealing suite of fanciful medieval numismatic designs. A charming representative example is a bracteate minted in the bishopric of Erfurt. It seems probable that the fragility of the coins was intentional; by breaking easily, they often needed to be replaced, to the profit of the mint!

The large bracteate of Erfurt **(coin 71)** features a tonsured facing bust of the city's patron, St. Martin of Tours, holding a bishop's crozier in his right hand and the Gospels in his left, above an arch of the city's walls between two towers. Below and within the city enclosure is the archbishop, facing upward and outward, supplicating, with traces of his name (Heinrich = [H]ENR[icus]) above his hands; the city name ERPES-FORD ("Erfurt") appears to left and right of the saint's head. Erfurt was one of several bishoprics under the authority of the archbishop of Mainz. It was a major commercial center of the era, controlling the trade in woad (a blue dye made from a weed-like herb) and other commodities at the Gera River crossing of the *Via Regia*, the medieval highway that extended from Paris to Novgorod. Under Erfurt's authority were 82 villages and five castles. It was a technological center of the time, and the capital of the region of Thuringia.

Coin 71: silver denar of Henry I, Erfurt, Germany (shown enlarged on page 109)

St. Martin was the patron saint of Erfurt, but his name in numismatics is much more closely associated with another coinage entirely: that of Tours. There, the Abbey of St. Martin enjoyed an extensive minting. In fact, it was at times the most important under the control of the kings of France, and its deniers tournois became some of the most popular and widely recognized issues in Christendom. When, in the Fourth Crusade, the Ferengi crusaders were sidetracked by the wily Venetians and overthrew the Byzantine emperors, establishing their own Latin Empire and setting up their own feudal states in Greece, they chose the coinage designs of the Abbey of St. Martin of Tours as their own, and issued extensive billon imitations of the French deniers. These are known as *torneselli*—the "little tournois." The Venetians minted their own versions of torneselli as a colonial coinage for their growing holdings in this region as well.

Around the year 1200, larger, heavier silver coins, multiples of the ubiquitous denarius, had appeared in the more commercially advanced Italian city-states—Genoa, Venice, and Milan—and by the end of the 13th century were also widely minted elsewhere. These coins were generally referred to as "big ones." Thus, "big" in Italian provided the denominational name *grosso*; in German, it was the *groschen*; in French, the *gros*; and in Middle English, the *groat*. This last substantial silver coin was introduced by the Plantagenet king, Edward I (1272–1307), in 1279. It was a four-penny piece, while the French gros, first struck in 1266 by Louis IX (St. Louis, 1226–1270) was worth 12 deniers tournois—thus clearly illustrating the differential in purchasing power between the corresponding smaller coins of the two kingdoms at this time. The French coin, the gros tournois, carrying the design of the old deniers of the Abbey of St. Martin of Tours, the *châtel tournois*, was widely admired and imitated, sometimes with similar designs and sometimes with new ones. A gros tournois was among the last issues of the Crusaders in the Holy Land, before Acre, the main city and mint of the Crusaders, fell to the Turkish Mamluk sultan of Egypt and Syria in 1291.

Although the Knights Templar are not known to have minted coins, when their order was abolished by the pope and destroyed by King Philip IV of France (called Philippe *le faux monnoyeur*—Philip the Counterfeiter) in the early 14th century, all their great lands, assets, and practices were turned over to their rival order, the Knights of the Hospital of St. John of

Coin 71: silver denar of Henry I, Erfurt, Germany The thin, foil-like "bracteates" were peculiar to the German states and parts of central Europe, and one of the most distinctive money types seen in the Middle Ages. Some, of impressive size, were true masterpieces of early medieval art.

Jerusalem (also called the Knights Hospitallers or Knights of St. John), which also received the remaining Templars as members. It is small wonder that the Hospitallers began their own grosso coinage at this time. From their headquarters on the Greek Island of Rhodes, they emitted a coinage on the gros tournois model with their own designs, derived from those of Naples and Provence.

Gigliati (or gillats) of the Knights of St. John were issued in the names of their grand masters. This typical example (**coin 72**) from the rule of Grand Master Helion de Villeneuve shows him on its obverse, kneeling on the right, facing outward, toward a patriarchal cross on the left. Its legend reads FR[ater] HELION' D[e]' VILINOVE D[e]I GRA[tia] M[agister]R—"Brother Helion de Villeneuve, by the Grace of God, Master." The coin's reverse displays a floriated cross consisting of a crusader's shield and two wings at each end of a cross potent (known as a "lilied" cross, hence the nickname *gigliato*). The reverse legend reads [H]OSP[i]TA[l]I' S[ancti] IOH[ann]IS I[e]R[usa]L[emita]NI Q[ui es]T R[h]ODI—"Hospital of Saint John of Jerusalem Which is of Rhodes."

With larger denominations becoming increasingly popular, and these new coins fostering expanded trade, a series of monetary conventions and alliances arose among issuers. Certain types were widely adopted and imitated as international banking and mining activity grew in the 13th century. Surreptitiously introduced into commerce in England, foreign imitations became an annoyance to the government on many occasions. Significant early grossi were minted by the kings of Bohemia at Prague or Kutna Hora, near where extensive silver and gold deposits started to be found in the late-13th and early-14th centuries. The Low Countries began to have a strong impact on international banking, related to woolen trade with England and a growing weaving industry as well as the establishment of a major shipping transport system.

Gold Coins of the Middle Ages

The use of gold coinage had never quite disappeared from southern Italy and the island of Sicily during the Middle Ages, thanks to proximity to the cultures of the Eastern Roman / Byzantine empire and the Islamic World. Gold coinage was initiated at Brindisi, also in Italy, by the "Wonder of the World," the Holy Roman Emperor Frederick II Hohenstaufen (1216–1250). His gold augustalis was a remarkable coin (and fairly

Coin 72: silver grosso gigliato, Order of Knights Hospitallers

Coin 72: silver grosso gigliato, Order of Knights Hospitallers
The gigliato was a larger and heavier silver issue first struck in Naples in 1303. Within Europe it circulated mainly in Italy and Avignon, France. However, its greatest employ was in the Levant, where it was widely imitated by both Moslem and Crusader states.

heavy at about 5.24 grams), harking back to Roman imperial prototypes, but was relatively unsuccessful in gaining acceptance. This was one of the problems with high-denomination money. Gold coinage was truly relaunched shortly after by the great mercantile commune of Florence (in 1252), and later by the seagoing republic of Venice (about 1280). Both of these lighter-weight coins gained wide acceptance due to the commercial and banking strength of their communes. The Florentine fiorino d'oro ("gold florin") was widely imitated, and survived as a denomination for centuries under the name *gulden*. The Venetian ducat became the most long-lived coin in history, struck continuously without major design change until 1797, and even sporadically thereafter; imitations can sometimes be seen even today.

The Italian maritime communes—Venice, Genoa, Naples, Salerno, Amalfi, Bari, Brindisi, Pisa (until its domination by Florence)—enjoyed prosperity during much of the Middle Ages. There, the old Roman worldly orientation seems not to have disappeared although it was surely changed. The Venetian economy, like its navy and its artistic output, became the admiration of much of the rest of the world. Its coinage became so prominent in Eastern Mediterranean trade that the very word *sikkah*—"coinage," in Arabic—came to be applied to it, and the mint of Venice was thus referred to as the *zecca*. The abundant Venetian gold coins were called *zecchini d'oro*—the "little gold mintings." Fortunately, many official records have survived in the archives of Venice, so we know a considerable amount about the medieval minting of *la Serenissima*, the "Most Serene," as the city was called. Part of the popularity of the Venetian zecchino is well illustrated by one of its emulators, a coin probably struck by one of the Gattilusi lords of Mytilene, on the Aegean island of Lesbos (or by the Genoese rulers of Chios, or possibly by Robert of Anjou, the Duke of Achaea, one of the Ferengi states created by the crusaders in Greece).

On the obverse of a representative piece **(coin 73)**, which purports to be an issue of the Venetian duke (or *doge* in the local dialect) Andrea Dandolo (1343–1354), St. Mark, the patron saint of Venice, on the left, hands the Venetians' sacred banner, the gonfalone, to the doge, who kneels on the right. Downward along the staff of the gonfalone is the word DVX ("duke"), while the legend reads S(acra) M[oneta] VENETTI ("Sacred Money of Venice") from top to bottom on the left and ANDI

Coin 73: imitation of gold ducat of Venetian duke Andrea Dandolo

Coin 73: imitation of gold ducat of Venetian duke Andrea Dandolo
The preeminent gold coin of commerce in this era, especially for the eastern Mediterranean and Levant, was the gold ducat of Venice. It was often copied by numerous minting authorities, as seen in this example (which was probably struck in Chios, Greece).

DANDNV (for "Andrea Dandolo") on the right. The inscriptions show a barbarous haphazardness that would not be found on a genuine piece. The reverse is emblazoned with Christ standing within a mandorla, with stars to either side; the legend is a very corrupted version of the standard Venetian form *Sit tibi, Christe, datus, quem tu regis, iste ducatus*—"May this ducat (duchy) which you rule, Christ, be given (dedicated) to you." This was the wording whence came the coin's usual name, *ducat*, the abbreviation for "duchy." The coin's Oriental colloquial name *zecchino* became *sequin* in English, a term still used to describe little round glittering ornaments! *Zecca*, the term used to refer to the Venetian mint, replaced the Latin Italian word *moneta* as the standard word for "mint" in the Italian language.

Not surprisingly, the initiation of gold coinage lagged somewhat in England. It was not until the reign of Edward III that an attempted gold coin was introduced in 1344 and quickly withdrawn due to an inadequate correlation with the silver currency. It is sometimes called the *florin*, after the name of the Florentine fiorino d'oro, but is also known as the *double leopard piece*—its half being the actual leopard. Shortly after, a second attempt was more successful, with a gold noble valued at eight shillings and six pence (102 sterling pennies). At the time of the introduction of the noble, Edward was engaged in a prospective war of conquest in France; it is thought that the legends and types may allude to this.

The representation of the English king in a ship on the noble may refer to the naval battle of Sluys, the harbor town of Bruges. Edward's mother was Isabella, the sister of King Charles IV of France, who died without male heir. Edward's claim to France had no standing under French (Salic) law, by which descendents on the female line were barred from royal inheritance. Under English law, however, which he naturally preferred, he was the legitimate king of France. He maneuvered for a time, then the hostile fleets met at Sluys in June of 1340. Edward led his fleet in person against a much larger force of some 400 French, Spanish, and Genoese vessels. The English broke to catch the wind and get the sun behind them, leading the French to believe they were retreating in fear. The French fleet let loose their linking chains, permitting English ships in units of three (two of archers and one full of men-at-arms) to come among them one at a time, sinking, capturing, or severely disabling almost all of the French fleet. The clever Genoese sailors got away, but French and Castilians who struggled to make it ashore were killed in the shallows by the Flemish allies of the English.

After Sluys, the English attained a number of other famous victories, such as that at the village of Crécy-en-Ponthieu in August of 1346. It was this victory that allowed Edward to besiege and take Calais. Chased northward by superior French forces following a failed attack on Paris, Edward's army of some 10,000 (including 2,000 men-at-arms, 5,000 archers, and 3,000 infantry) had to battle across a ford on the River Somme before turning to fight. King Philip VI of France led a much larger force of 12,000 mounted men-at-arms, along with 6,000 Genoese crossbowmen, and perhaps 10,000 other infantry. However, he was unable to make effective use of his larger army. This battle was the first great encounter of the English employing the longbow, and is believed to be one of the first where cannonfire was also utilized. The French were strung out in a long line of march and their crossbowmen were outshot by the English archers; then a series of uncoordinated cavalry charges was flung against the defenders. Edward had disposed his archers and men-at-arms in mutually supportive ranks that hurled back these attacks. Some 1,500 French knights were killed and Philip withdrew.

The elaborate gothic designs of the English gold noble (**coin 74**) are among the most appealing of the Middle Ages. On the obverse a half-length facing figure of the king, in armor, is shown standing in a cog, a medieval warship with castles fore and aft, a rigged mast, and a pennant of St. George (England's patron—the "Red Cross Knight") mounted on its stern. The ship's rudder and tiller can be seen, as well as the ocean waves below. Within beaded circles, the legend runs EDWARD[us] D[e]I GRA[tia] REX ANGL[iae] & FRANC[iae] D[omi]N[u]S HIB[erniae] + AQVITT[aniae]—"Edward by the Grace of God King of England and France, Lord of Ireland and Aquitaine." The reverse bears the scriptural legend IHC (Jesus) AVTEM TRANSIENS PER MEDIUM ILLORVM IBAT (Luke iv.30, "But Jesus, passing through the midst of them, went his way"). The reverse design is a floriated cross with two scrolls and a fleur-de-lis at each end, a crown above a leopard in each quarter, and an E within an ornamented quatrefoil in the center, the whole within a tressure of eight arches with a *lis* at each point.

Much of Edward III's success in France was attributed to his son, the Black Prince, Edward Prince of Wales, who won a major victory over the

Coin 74: gold noble of Edward III, England (shown enlarged on page 117)

French at the battle of Poitiers in 1356. There, commanding some 7,000 English, he defeated around 18,000 men under French king John II. The English took up strong positions behind lanes and vineyards with their longbowmen and flanked and routed the French, who lost some 8,000 men while the English losses were slight. King John was taken prisoner and held for a gold ransom of 500,000 pounds sterling. He was kept in honorable captivity while his government minted a vast gold coinage intended to recover their king. He was released, but upon France's inability to pay the entirety of the huge indemnity, he voluntarily returned to England, where he died, his chivalry intact.

When peace was declared by the treaty of Brétigny in 1360, Edward agreed to remove the offensive title "King of France" from his protocol and his coinage inscriptions. The gold noble described above is attributable to the French coastal city of Calais, whose mint had been turned into a thoroughly English facility in 1363. It dates to Edward's fourth period of issue, 1369 to 1377, following the expiration of the treaty of Brétigny, one of the few interludes of peace during this so-called Hundred Years' War. In 1361, a complete new monetary system was introduced by the English for the coinage of now wide holdings in France. Edward and the Black Prince, who was named ruler of Aquitaine in 1362, issued multiple types and denominations for their extensive French domains, known as the *Anglo-Gallic* series. While Calais struck exclusively English-style coins, Agen, Bordeaux, Dax, Figeac, Limoges, Poitiers, La Rochelle, and Tarbes all served as Anglo-Gallic mints. They generally (all but Dax, which used an AS monogram) incorporated in their designs the first letter of the town's name as a mintmark—a practice which became increasingly standard and has survived into the coinages of the present day. Previously, issues of the same coins from different mints in France had been marked in more cryptic ways. Small changes were taken seriously. This was the age of chivalry, of heraldry, and of curious privy marks on coinage—*points secrets*—which were utilized as production controls and indicators in the Late Medieval mints. By means of slight variations, it becomes possible for numismatists to attribute coins to specific times and places in the absence of dates and mint names.

Edward and the Black Prince took a great interest in coinage for their French possessions, and great volumes must have been struck. However, due to the exigencies of the wartime economy, and continuous revalua-

Coin 74: gold noble of Edward III, England The elegant noble was England's first successful effort at a large-scale gold coinage.

Coin 75: gold leopard of Edward III, for England's French possessions The territorial ambitions in France of England's Edward III resulted in a vast gold coinage that melded both French and English traits.

Coin 75: gold leopard of Edward III, for England's French possessions (shown enlarged on page 117)

Coin 76: gold pavilion d'or of the Black Prince, England (shown enlarged on page 121)

tions, all but a small amount has disappeared. A gold écu had been minted by 1348, and in 1355 the handsome leopard d'or was introduced.

Coin 75 features the blazon of the English *pard* (leopard) passant, crowned and bearded, its head facing outward (guardant), as its obverse type. This contrasts considerably with a sheep (the "lamb of God") introduced shortly before as a new French gold coin type, the mouton d'or. This choice of type would have been not only an heraldic gesture, but also a ploy of political propaganda to contrast the fierce emblem of the English king with the pacific one of King John of France. The coin's obverse legend reads EDWARDVS DEI GRA[tia] ANGLI[a]E FRANCI[a]E REX—"Edward, by the Grace of God, King of England (and) of France." The reverse legend reads XPC (Christus) VINCIT XPC REGNAT XPC IMPERAT—"Christ Conquers, Christ Reigns, Christ Commands." The reverse type includes a floriated cross within an ornamental quadrilobe, with a pard passant in each angle.

Edward's leopards are classified into four issues, of which this is the second, dated to July, 1356, when the initial value of 20 solidi (French *sols*, or *sous*) was reduced to 18 sols 4 deniers bordelais ("of Bordeaux"). French and Anglo-Gallic issues of the period are extraordinarily complex. Understanding of these coins is complicated by the fact that they involve successive and simultaneous series of gold, silver, and "black" money. The silver alone is broken into 27 types. Added to this, some 60 issue-marks are known. Black money consisted of the small, base-metal coins of everyday commerce, generally despised by almost everyone and not hoarded, so that today they are extremely rare. They nevertheless have provided us with the origin of the term *blackmail*, from *maille noire*, the maille being a fraction of the silver gros.

Turmoil in Europe

In 1367, the Black Prince (seen in Gothic splendor on **coin 76**) set out to Spain to help King Pedro the Cruel of Castile and Leon regain the throne, from which that harsh monarch had been deposed. English arms helped reinstate Pedro, but he did not fulfill the financial obligations undertaken on his behalf, and the Anglo-Gallic economy faced a crisis in 1368. A variety of expedients were adopted. In 1372, Edward III re-assumed dominion over his Aquitaine possessions. It was during his long reign that heraldry and chivalry truly came to the fore, with the establishment of the order of the Knights of the Garter as the highest emblem of nobility in England. But it was also during this reign that the bubonic plague, the "Black Death," struck down an enormous proportion of the population of Europe, in some places killing nearly everyone and averaging a quarter to a third of the populace overall. A resulting labor shortage led to economic changes, as people began to make greater use of money to get out of feudal obligations, and to demand payment in money for services rendered, leading to pressure on landed aristocracies to maintain their affluence.

From the reign of Edward III onward, English coinage remained very constant until the Renaissance, even through the various national crises: the great plague of 1348 to 1350, the Peasants' Revolt in 1383, the factional Wars of the Roses between the houses of Lancaster and York, and the establishment of the Tudor dynasty under Henry VII in 1483. But a variety of changes were occurring elsewhere. While France and England were going through their Hundred Years' War, their neighbors Spain and the Low Countries were facing their own wars and gradually increasing their strength and prosperity through consolidation. The plague struck Gibraltar in 1350, killing Alphonso XI of Castile and bringing to the throne the 16-year-old Pedro, who by the time he was 20 had had three wives! He fathered at least nine children, all of whom could be considered illegitimate, two of whom married younger brothers of the Black Prince. His sexual "connections" contributed to ten years of rebellions on the part of jealous nobles fearing the growing power and wealth of the Castilian kingdom, fostered and supported by the Aragonese and later the French. It was during this time that Pedro perpetrated a series of murders that gave him his nickname. After being restored to his throne, Pedro was again attacked by the refractory nobility and their foreign allies, and was murdered and succeeded by his bastard half-brother Enrique, the great-great-grandfather of Queen Isabella, "the Catholic," who united Spain by marrying King Ferdinand II of Aragon in 1469.

Although crusading ferment from the 11th century onward led to the eventual *reconquista* of the Iberian peninsula from the Muslims, the Spanish kingdoms reflected an unusual degree of religious toleration, a trait that had been characteristic of Iberian Muslims in their heyday. Arts and commerce prospered; not only were Muslims and Jews *not* persecuted (as they elsewhere), but they were even allowed opportunities for advancement. Pedro was in fact partly disliked by the nobles because of his favors to Jewish financiers and his protection of the merchant class. On account of its contacts with the rest of the Muslim world, unlike the rest of Western Europe, Spain never went without a gold currency: the Visigothic tremissis; the mancus, dating from Carolingian times; dinars of the Umaiyad Muslims and their successors; and the Christian maravedí (a name for gold taken from that of the dynasty of the Morabides), at first imitating Muslim coins but then becoming an integral part of the Castilian monetary system. After Alfonso VIII introduced a lighter-weight gold piece, also called a maravedí, the standard-weight coin became known as the *dobla*, or "double." The value of the maravedí rapidly degenerated, to the extent that by the beginning of the 16th century it was no more than a nearly worthless small billon (copper/silver alloy) coin, 34 of which would make one silver real ("royal", a standard silver coin more or less a counterpart of the grosso).

Coin 77: gold dobla of 35 maravedis, Spain

This dobla of Pedro *el Cruel* (**coin 77**) depicts the emblematic types of the joint kingdom of Castile ("castle") and Leon ("lion"), with the namesake heraldic castle and lion disported respectively on the coin's obverse and reverse, each within a gothic tressure of ten arches and angles within a dotted circle. The mintmark S, for Sevilla, is beneath the castle on the Castilian side of the coin. Heraldically, old Leon's blazon is a lion rampant. On this side of the coin (for convenience called the reverse), the gothic legend reads PETRVS DEI GRACIA REX LEGIONIS ("Peter, by the Grace of God, King of Leon") while that on the other side replaces the last word with CASTELL[ia]E ("of Castile"). Although Spain did not witness the feudal fragmentation of coinage rights that permeated France and Germany, it was still a land of separate monarchies and privileged nobles. With the conquest of Granada and the expulsion (or forced conversion) of Muslims and Jews in 1492, united Castile/Leon and Aragon, now called the *Kingdom of the Spains*, was ready to take its place on the world's political and economic stage. Following many vicissitudes, the dobla was replaced in 1497 by the excelente denomination, based upon the value of the Venetian ducat, that great international trade coinage.

With the re-establishment of gold currency in Western Europe in the late-13th and 14th centuries, the territories in modern Belgium, Luxemburg, and the Netherlands saw the introduction of many new coinage issues. As feudal vassals of both France and the Holy Roman Empire, and as the prin-

Coin 76: gold pavilion d'or of the Black Prince, England Edward, the Black Prince, was one of the notable figures of the 14th century. His pavilion d'or, wholly French in inspiration, remains as the most handsome of the Anglo-Gallic issues.

Coin 77: gold dobla of 35 maravedís, Spain Spain never truly suffered a shortage of gold coin, unlike much of Europe in the early Middle Ages. This elegant dobla, struck in Seville, exemplifies Spanish coin design at its best.

cipal trading partner of England, the Flemish were in a position to capitalize on the dangerous game of international politics, as reflected by their coins. The richest series of gold was produced under Count Louis *de Maele* (called *Lodewijk van Male*, in Flemish), who minted 11 different types.

The last and most beautiful of Louis' issues (**coin 78**) was modeled on the French kingdom's chaise d'or ("golden chair"), portraying as its obverse type the diademed count enthroned in gothic splendor, wearing plate armor and holding an upright broadsword in his right hand while placing his left atop a shield emblazoned with a lion rampant, which gave the coin its alternate Flemish name, the "new golden shield with a lion." The legend reads LVDOVICVS DEI GRA[tia] COM[es] & D[omi]N[u]S FLAND'[riae]—"Louis, by the Grace of God, Count and Lord of Flanders." On the reverse was a pleasing ornamental cross and quadrilobe motif, not too dissimilar to that already seen on the golden leopard of Edward III (surprisingly, the reverse inscription on de Maele's coin is identical to that on Edward's gold leopard). Louis de Maele managed one of the longest and most stable rules of his time, helping to pave the way for an explosion of prosperity and creativity in the Low Countries for the next 300 years. With the marriage in 1384 of his daughter Margaret to the Duke of Burgundy, Philip the Hardy (the youngest son of King John of France), and with the union of his descendents with Holland and Brabant, a new European power arose—one that would be joined to the Austrian imperial house of Habsburg at the close of the Middle Ages and come to dominate the world.

From Dark Ages Into the Light

We call the 15th century's flowering of artistry and appreciation of the classics the *Renaissance*. In numismatics, certainly, it marked an important rebirth. Wealthy and scholarly people began collecting and studying coins of the Greeks and Romans, while ambitious leaders sought to enhance their images by producing issues of comparable artistic merit. For the first time since antiquity, artists of the highest caliber employed their talents as die engravers. Their accurate, representational portrait effigies became the chief characteristic of the handsome, new, and larger silver pieces typically known as *testoni* (from *testa*, Italian for "head"). Beyond coinage production itself, Renaissance artists created the medium of medallic sculpture as we know it today.

Coin 78: gold chaise of Louis of Maele

Coin 78: gold chaise of Louis of Maele Generally the finest coin art of the period can be seen in the counties comprising the northern Lowlands, due to their ascendant prosperity in the 13th and 14th centuries. The nearly 40-year reign of Louis de Maele provided the richest series of gold issues made at this time—striking 11 different gold types, based upon both local and French models.

Innovations leading to the Renaissance included the use of gears, swivels, screws, springs, and new kinds of "mills" (wind-, water-, and animal-powered). Much engineering activity was stimulated by medieval increases in commerce, mining, and minting, not to mention thoughtful inventions by monks, such as improvements in the fermentation of liquors and experiments in alchemy. German and North Italian commerce centers were early leaders in the field. Inquisitive minds such as that of Leonardo da Vinci invented apparatus for minting mechanically rather than performing all such labor by hand. Dating coins by their years of issue A.D. became prevalent for the first time towards the end of the 15th century. Major discoveries of silver in Bohemia, in Germany, and later in the Spanish New World, encouraged production of large, high-value silver coins, while banking and commerce rapidly expanded.

So the trends of the past continued in the late Middle Ages. Many economic changes had occurred, and more were to follow. Banking followed trading networks, which followed the Crusaders throughout the Mediterranean. Re-exposure to gold coinage came to Europeans through the Byzantine and Islamic worlds, and as commerce and urbanity increased, a greater need for higher-valued coinage was felt. Prices rose and workers demanded pay in the wake of the Black Death's decimation. Individuals used money to buy their way out of feudal service obligations. Increasing royal power and emerging nation-states placed a greater prestige on minting authority, while larger minting establishments required more sophisticated administration and improved accounting systems. Bigger economies saw more inflation, which governments sought to control by manipulating coin contents and values. New sources of ore were tapped, and mining methods progressed.

These centuries of the "Middle Ages" somehow seem today to be both appealing and repellent, noble and servile, ideal and idiotic. It was a time of supreme contrasts and contradictions, full of woe and wonder. If it was scholarly and sublime, it was also at least equally cruel and crude. People erected soaring architectural monuments, yet lived in squalid mud-and-straw hovels. Enough documentary source material has survived to tell a story rich in detail, yet tantalizingly silent about many day-to-day activities. The coins produced then can somehow help to fill out these gaps.

CHAPTER FOUR

COINS *of the* EUROPEAN RENAISSANCE

Bruce Lorich

The human spirit at the beginning of the 21st century glows with freedom and a boundless sense of inquiry. But it was not always so. The world was once dark. The only light was the sunshine, roughly half of each day. The human spirit did not shine. Most of the time it was like the half of the day that lacked sunshine.

The era of the medieval world stretched for nearly a thousand years, from the 5th century into the 14th. What was left of a once-great and shining culture in Italy fell into ruin as invading barbarians, whose culture was the horse and the weapon, chased away an educated world, killed men of learning, murdered not only their bodies but also their spirit. Ancient Rome had been a glowing light in an otherwise dark and fearful world. Once Rome was decimated, all the Western world fell into darkness.

For centuries superstition and mystery replaced knowledge. All the learning and recorded history that had been centered in Rome was forgotten in dusty versions of early books. What was once known was now forgotten, lost to the Dark Ages. Invaders came from distant shores, striking fear in the hearts of huddling villagers. Heads rolled, genes mixed, and gradually kingdoms emerged from isolated villages.

Throughout what we now call Europe, the future loomed. Mankind began to rally around "champions" and local warlords, working all their lives for the keeper of the castle. In the Middle Ages the knight was a man of power and dignity in shining body armor. He lived by a code of honor called *chivalry*. For his lord, he roamed the land and undid injustice, protected vulnerable servants of the lords, and roused many a poor soul. People no longer huddled in dark fear. The human mind began to be aroused once again. But the focus of interest was God. God was the light in the midst of eternal suspicion of the unknown. Religion was the center of life. Latin was the language of the Church, and monks were the carriers of the spirit of God, and its recorders on parchment that could be read to the people.

The Rebirth of Rome

The center of this new learning, focused on a Heavenly afterlife, a relief from the drudgeries of a usually brief existence here on Earth, was the same place where the ancient civilization had once shone so brightly: Rome. It was believed that one of Jesus' own disciples, a man who knew the Son of God himself in life—a man named Peter—had been buried not far from where the Caesars had once ruled the known world. On this spot grew a new shining light, called the Vatican. It was the very center of the focus of all the rest of Europe, the place where God was worshipped in a stylized, orderly way that commanded the attention of mankind throughout the Western world. The Middle Ages had a light of its own, focused on God's promise of a future eternity of goodness.

The nature and manifestations of God were studied endlessly, written about until there seemed to be nothing left to explicate. But all movements have an end, and slowly the Middle Ages wound down. Slowly yet another new light emerged, and this one would change the world for good.

This change in human history has come to be called the Renaissance. Everyone remembers from school that the word itself means "rebirth." This new light shone on mankind's mind, opened a new world.

The Renaissance was more than the emergence of all that we know today. It was a hinge—between the almost forgotten past and the yet-to-be-invented future. It was arguably the most important development in the entire history of the human race.

The darkness, the mystery, the superstition, the fear that pervaded the Middle Ages slowly drained away. The change began in Italy at the very end of the 13th century. Those church people, the monks and priests, had scattered strokes of genius. They came upon some ancient writings that were not just about God. Among the dusty manuscripts that had lain unread for hundreds of years, those church scholars found that the Greeks and Romans—a thousand and more years before—had observed Nature, had formulated ideas or "laws" about how things worked, had written revealing and sometimes humorous stories about their fellow men and their relationships not with God but with each other, and had even expressed their observations in stone and in words. Art and literature in the ancient world had been realistic, true to Nature.

In the Middle Ages, art had grown static. It had become highly stylized, cold, emotional only in its passion for God, and imitative. It was unrevealing. In the beginning of what we call the Renaissance, the churchly scholars began to see that there was another kind of art that had gone before, but was forgotten until the time of its rediscovery. Over time, these men of learning stopped focusing on God and began to focus on humanity, on what Man was, on what he looked like, what he felt inside himself, what he thought and how he wished to express his thoughts and feelings. Art began to be reborn.

The knight errant of the Middle Ages was replaced by the wandering student of humanity, who came to be called a *humanist*. He wrote, he painted, he sculpted, he studied, he lectured and spread knowledge. He changed everything. It was as if a new, brighter sun had risen over the edge of the world. That sun was the creativity of the human spirit.

Dante of Florence (1265–1321), the "glimmer of the dawn" of his age, took aim at the obsessions of the church in his *Divine Comedy*, and he did it not in Latin but *in Italian*. His fellow townsman, Francesco Petrarch (1304–1374), composed poetry also in Italian and became the great poet-scholar of the early Renaissance, collecting and relishing Greek texts that he never learned to read! But he was driven to discover, and his influence was monumental. Another of his countrymen, Giovanni Boccaccio (1313–1375), is thought to be the first Italian in centuries who learned to read classical Greek, and from inspirations gained there he wrote his book of witty stories called *The Decameron*, revealing people in their often embarrassing humanity. The veils of mystery so prevalent in the earlier Middle Ages began to disappear as literature was reinvented.

Art and Money of the Renaissance

As we gather an idea of what the Renaissance really was, how it formed the modern world, take note of the dates of these men who changed the world each in his own way. We will see these times on the faces of the money created in this age. Their images came from the inspirations of Renaissance writers, scholars, artists, craftsmen, inventors, and explorers. We cannot speak to those humanists, but we can "listen" to what they said by seeing how they said it, on metal.

Italy's first awakening to the glories and knowledge of the ancient or classical world spread in due course throughout Europe. The fine arts were revived using nature as the living model, instead of images of God copied and endlessly refined by imitators. The inspiration was the remains of what the Greeks and Romans had sculpted in marble and painted on clay and even on the walls of their homes, and assembled in tiny colored stones on their floors. This inspiration took many forms during the four centuries that mark the period we call the Renaissance.

Poetry, dramatic plays, novels (or *romances*) revealed the human psyche. Greek oratory became the modern arguments called conversation and debate. Music and new musical instruments, the "science" of the old laws of Nature so minutely observed by the Greeks, the study of politics, the nature of government and the structure of towns, and inventions (gunpowder, the compass for navigation, and most of all the printing press)—these bursts of genius of the human spirit, set free from the chains of the dark past, ushered in the world as we know it today. They led to the revival of city life, therefore of new industry, out of which grew merchant and craft guilds or unions of workers, who revived the marketplace, which demanded money, which led to the invention of banks and bankers, who dreamed up the concept of buying on credit, which was sometimes so uncertain that it needed to be insured, while the former autocratic lords became town officials who established centers for trade, which sought new markets. Exploration was conceived by this collective human energy, colonies were established in foreign lands outside Europe, and as we all know a New World was "discovered" by an Italian sailor looking for a trade route to India, financed by a Spanish king and queen. The modern age was born.

To modern eyes, coins made during the Renaissance look crude, at first. Compared to coins made by the machinery used in the 19th and 20th centuries, they are indeed crude—but they possess a charm nowhere to be seen on today's coinages. Take a look at the images of coins shown elsewhere in this book. Later coins have squared, sharp rims. Their surfaces are smooth and often reflective of light, sometimes mirrorlike. There is an evenness of design, pleasing and more or less uniform from one coin to the next. The real breakthrough for this kind of coin came in the late-18th century, from the workshop and mint of Matthew Boulton, of Birmingham, England. He invented the modern coin, largely as an anti-counterfeiting feat.

Now compare the images of coins you see in this chapter with those of ancient Greek and Roman coins. Even here, Renaissance coins are relatively crude in fashion, lacking the high relief seen on the Greek and Roman to a great extent. Numismatic art reached a zenith in the fourth century B.C. in Syracuse, Sicily, by Greek engravers working by hand. We still don't know how such style was achieved oh so long ago—for style it surely was, and deeply detailed. Some of the finest ancient art extant is that seen on coins.

Coin 79: 7 ducats of Maximilian and Mary, Holy Roman Empire
(shown enlarged on page 133)

Renaissance coinage, however, is also known for its artistic details. To be understood in its true light, it must be compared to the stick-like, stiff images seen for hundreds of years on coins of the Middle Ages. Those coins too had style, but it was charming only in its crudeness, intended to instruct an illiterate public.

The traditional purposes of coins made through all the ages up to the 14th century continued in the hard money of the Renaissance issued throughout Europe. Now, however, a new sophistication was lent to the purpose. It was no longer enough to proclaim the image of the ruler shown on the coins as *sovereign*, and for the fineness of the metal to be accepted for local use. No, much more was now communicated, and its origins, its inspiration, lay in the artists and scholars and inventors whose activities gave a brilliant rebirth to ancient ideas.

Renaissance coinage, in gold and silver, as well as remarkably sculpted bronze medals (mostly showing portraits of rulers and family members), burst onto the European scene much as the sun itself still lights up the continent—with varying shades, in stages, rising here and there across the broad land—until light shone in constant brightness. It is time to consider some of the great coins of this age, and where better to begin than with one of the most valuable (in its day and presently) golden issues of the late 15th to early 16th century. The impressive 7 ducats **(coin 79)** of the Holy Roman Emperor Maximilian I (1459–1519), struck at Hall, underscores the newfound celebration of marriage and romantic inclinations which came out of the Middle Ages metaphorically stillborn, but flourished again beneath the sunshine of the artistic and political spirituality of this new age.

Courtly chivalry of the previous centuries, in its ritual stiffness, gave way in this era to idealistic but sensitive romance, often compromised by politics. But such was not the case in the marriage celebrated here. There was no compromise in the romantic expression broadcast by this coin! Dated 1479 beneath the queen's bust, it was probably struck in remembrance of Maximilian's beloved first wife, Mary ("Maria" on the coin), whom he married in 1477 while still archduke of Austria. It is believed that this memorial coin was created shortly after 1511, following the death of Maximilian's second wife, another Mary—Maria Bianca Sforza (an important aristocratic name which will appear again later in our discussion of this age). Take notice of the very unusual numbers which appear: the 19 after the initials ETATIS split to right and left of Maximilian's portrait, and the 20 similarly placed on the other side. These stand for the respective ages of the newly married couple in 1479.

This young woman was eagerly desired by other princes, as she was the only child of Charles the Bold of Burgundy, a rich and influential part of the Low Countries with which the king of France and others sought alliance. The French connection was especially appealing but Mary wisely distrusted the Dauphin. She chose Duke Maximilian of Austria instead, and the very selection would have been impossible in the Middle Ages. This, however, was not an arranged marriage. We do not know all the personal reasons for her choice, but it became a signal event because it placed the Hapsburgs in the Low Countries and set off what would be a very long rivalry between France and Austria. The archduke became an elector of the Holy Roman Empire in 1508 and his influence and his portion of the empire flourished along with the age in which he lived.

Maximilian lost his wife in 1482 to an untimely death just a few years after they married, and took other wives partly to consummate political goals, but he seems to have carried a gentle love for his young first wife, testament to which is this marvelous coin. It shows him as a youth with a laurel tie around his lengthy hair and an apropos sunburst initial or mint mark at 12 o'clock in the obverse legend. Mary is also sensitively portrayed, and their long titles appear in Latin abbreviation. The style here is remarkable after the stilted artistry of the centuries that preceded it, and is so fitting for a coin which, itself, broke tradition. There is much to be admired in the die engraving of this piece. Consider the coins that come next, then admire this coin once again—for it will shine ever brighter once the other coins are explained.

In the golden 4 excelentes (coin 80) of the Catholic king and queen Ferdinand V and Isabella I of Spain (a type struck during the period of 1469 to 1504; this one minted at Segovia about 1497), we have another excellent example of Renaissance coinage art as it emerged from the Middle Ages. In their day Ferdinand and Isabella were known as *los Reyes Católicos*, two monarchs unified in their insistence on one religion and politically tied to the pope in Rome. They had married each other in October 1469, eventually uniting the two kingdoms of Aragon and Castille and Leon, which led to the unification of other parts of the nation later known as Spain. (Ferdinand was also king of Sicily, thanks to the ambitions of his father.)

Coin 80: 4 excelentes of Ferdinand and Isabella, Spain (shown enlarged on page 133)

Look at this coin. Husband and wife, king and queen, face each other, a symbolic stance of union. They wear crowns reminiscent of headgear shown on some medieval coins, but more finely rendered. Their hairdos are representative of the time. Isabella wears jewelry around her neck. They have faces perhaps flatly engraved, but not just the crude outline drawings that represented monarchy in the Middle Ages. Their titles in Latin surround—and two symbols of the place of manufacture appear by—their heads. The smooth, fine gold shows the pair inside a kind of cartouche, an idea taken from the Middle Ages' coins. Unlike medieval coins, though, this is gold—high-grade gold meant to be taken at its intrinsic value not just in Castile and Aragon, but beyond. That was a distinctive, breakthrough feature of Renaissance money. It could be spent "abroad"!

The coin's reverse is where the real departure from earlier coins may be seen. Here are humanistic images, not the symbols of God of earlier centuries (one or another form of the Cross appeared on the backs of most medieval coins), but more a political message recalled from the coins of the Roman emperors of a thousand years past. Abbreviations of Latin titles surround on the outside of the coin, but behind a complexly drawn shield of the kingdoms of Ferdinand and Isabella appears their nimbate eagle, literally holding their heraldic arms for the world to view.

And the world indeed had much to see. Ferdinand and Isabella were the financiers of the "captain from Castile," Christopher Columbus, who doubtless carried coins exactly like this one on his voyages of discovery. This was money created by the inventions of humanists, by a concept not dissimilar from that of the single most influential new machine of the Renaissance, the printing press. Duplication of a technical quality not previously known was suddenly possible. Printed engraving was a new art form. The products of the printing press spread the revival of learning throughout the continent of Europe. Money more finely engraved, and uniformly coined, spread an influence every bit as important as the word and the artistic picture. It had been done before, but not for a thousand years.

And what of Ferdinand and Isabella? They initiated the dreadful Spanish Inquisition, which in another three-quarters of a century spread all the way to England, strengthening the power-grip of the church at Rome on the peoples of solidly Catholic lands, but wrenching apart oth-

Coin 79: 7 ducats of Maximilian and Mary, Holy Roman Empire
Only two examples are known of this romantic memorial coin, which honors the emperor's first wife.

Coin 80: 4 excelentes of Ferdinand and Isabella, Spain These symmetrical portraits were remarkable for their time, with equal size and position stressing equality in power. This imagery was stipulated in Isabella's marriage contract.

ers and leading to yet another version of this faith called Christianity. Isabella died in 1504. Her two eldest children died young. Surviving daughter Joan "the Mad" never knew her mother's power or influence in Aragon. Widower Ferdinand remarried into the French royal lineage but his new son also died young. (Life was not easy before modern medicine.) Ferdinand ruled Castile alone until his passing in 1516, never understanding the importance of the voyages made by his Captain Columbus. All the Spanish kingdoms passed to his grandson, Charles of the Netherlands, who became Charles V of the Holy Roman Empire. Even the name recalled the glories of an empire of Caesars, long gone but no longer forgotten.

Let's turn our attention next to a coin, also of Spain, that was made just prior to the 4 excelentes above. The golden enrique (**coin 81**) has a classic Renaissance design, but its image of the king owes much to its medieval predecessors. Enrique IV ("the Weak") (1454–1474) is depicted on a throne, but he is not at all lifelike in appearance. His static facing picture resembles all those "outline images" of kings of the Middle Ages. His face could have been lifted unchanged from any English silver groat. However, this is not a silver coin. *It is gold!* Gold might almost be said to be the metal of the Renaissance. It could be traded for its content abroad. It fostered foreign exchange, and therefore broadened its "market." And, unlike medieval coins, it said and showed very clearly where it came from. The sovereign's titles in Latin surround him once again, he appears on a throne, and wields an image of might (even though he himself was not mighty). On the other side, more Latin abbreviations of titles, all around the arms of Castile and Leon, the two kingdoms of his royal house—standard elements of design for a reverse side, yet more elegant in conception than may be seen on all but the latest medieval coins.

Importantly, each side bears a cross at the top of the images. This is a very religious piece of money, intended to tell a story abroad and at home. Similar to it is another large, thin coin of fine (very pure) gold, struck almost a hundred years later but obviously owing much in its design to the Spanish coin. Curiously this ruler was also Catholic, and even married for a short time to a Spanish prince. Mary Tudor was the eldest child of the English king Henry VIII, child of his union with Catherine of Aragon. It was Henry's father who first caused this gold coin

Coin 81: gold enrique of Castile

Coin 81: gold enrique of Castile
King Enrique IV of Castile was nicknamed
"the Impotent." It was rumored that his
sole child, a daughter, was illegitimate. In
spite of the innuendos, the king is shown
on this coin as powerful and authoritative.

to be minted in England, and it was named after him, a *sovereign* (**coin 82**). This kind of coin first appeared in the 1580s and clearly shows the influence of foreign Renaissance artists in its conception.

On the sovereign of fine gold of Bloody Mary Tudor (1553–1554), who brought the Inquisition to England in her zeal as a Catholic and in her marriage to the man later to be crowned as Philip II of Spain (who believed that his mission in life was to make Spain a world power), the stiff image of the earlier Spanish coin gives way to a portrait only possible as a creation of the Renaissance. Like Enrique, Mary is seated on a throne and holds a symbol of power. Here, though, the Catholic image of the Cross is much subdued, appearing atop Mary's crown in miniature. Her titles still appear in Latin abbreviated form, and the verse of holy Scripture (in Latin abbreviation, it translates to "This is the Lord's doing and it is marvelous in our eyes" (Psalm 118:23) around the reverse design pays homage to her religion, but the "drawing" here of the monarch is more realistic than ever could have emerged during the Middle Ages. The queen is in relief against a diapered background, including symbols borrowed from ancient Rome; it is an image not of godly splendor but of human power. On the reverse side, the entire picture is dominated by the Tudor rose, opening around the regal shield. It is florate, owing its inspiration to the art of Florence and of Venice, as will many other coins over the next few centuries.

Another classic gold creation of this era is the doppia (**coin 83**) minted for Philip II of Spain (born 1527, ruled 1556 to 1598) at Milan. After Mary Tudor died, Philip was ejected from the court of England. He sought to spread Spanish influence, and the Catholic faith, throughout Europe and even into the New World. This coin, dated 1578 below his portrait, shows him at the height of his powers. The classical influence may be seen in Philip's profiled portrait, wherein he looks much like a crowned Roman emperor with perhaps the top of a toga showing. Such a portrait could never have appeared on a medieval coin, and it demonstrates the influence of the new artistic standards of the Renaissance,

> *King Philip looks much like a crowned Roman emperor. . . .*

Coin 82: gold sovereign of Mary Tudor, England

Coin 83: Italian gold doppia of Philip II, Spain

Coin 82: gold sovereign of Mary Tudor, England The violence with which England was returned to Catholicism earned its queen the nickname Bloody Mary.

Coin 83: Italian gold doppia of Philip II, Spain Mary Tudor's husband was maneuvered out of England after she died. He consolidated Spain's empire, increased the flow of bullion from the New World, and promoted Catholicism throughout Europe—but was unable to conquer Protestant England.

which attempted to capture human dignity lifelike, rather than static and stylized as in previous centuries. It was a realism not seen since the portrait coins of the Roman Empire. The tidy crowned shield on the other side is again ornamented by a floral style, simple but balanced. The coin is literally an advertisement for acceptance in international trade. Just ten years after it was minted, however, Spain's armada met and was defeated by the new ships and naval strategies of the English navy, ending Spanish ambitions for dominance of the old world and the new.

Renaissance Painting and a New Realism

Renaissance paintings—much like the king's picture on the Spanish doppia—attempted to capture human dignity, as lifelike as was possible using the techniques of the time. This new realism could communicate, and in the case of gold coinage it could communicate both majesty and distinct value. This art first flourished in the 16th century. The sovereign of Queen Mary owes its existence to a succession of artists who took inspiration from an Italian who lived at the very beginning of the Renaissance, Giotto of Florence (1266–1337). His bell tower, which still stands in the *Piazza del Duomo* (Plaza of the Dome), is covered in images later transformed by an English engraver into symbols seen on Mary's golden coin. It is one of the supreme examples of the employment of the newly understood laws of perspective.

Looking again at Mary Tudor's coin, notice the improved structure of the image of the seated monarch, using perspective, compared to the gold piece of Enrique; the latter, of the 1450s, suffers from the lack of this perspective as it was made before understanding of these artistic laws had reached Spain. The English coin is all the better, and more modern, for using finer perspective in the image. So too is there influence in the design of this coin taken from the adornments of the painter Botticelli (1444–1510). Italy practically invented the new style and laws. All of Europe adapted them to diverse uses over time.

And what of Enrique the Weak? We are left with only his image. He bore no heir. His kingdoms passed to his sister Isabella and her husband Ferdinand. They would become Spain's most remembered rulers. Their Renaissance yearnings would lead to the discovery of America. And what of poor Queen Mary? We are left with rare images of her, as on this coin. She would die childless and her husband would return to

Spain. Her kingdom would pass to her brother (only son of Henry VIII), who would die a teenager and also without heir. After his death the kingdom would pass to the young Elizabeth, Henry's second daughter by Anne Boleyn, whose brilliance was perhaps among the greatest of all reflections of the Renaissance Age. Her navy would crush forever the ambitions of Spain to dominate the new world; she would do it using inventions inspired by the new learning begun in Italy, and she would practice statecraft as clever as any Roman emperor ever imagined and dared to attempt.

A Study in Old and New

Among the most elegantly conceived and engraved coins of this era is the splendid gold half pound (coin 84) of Elizabeth I (born 1533, reigned 1558 to 1605). Minted on new machinery, rather than by hand as was customary at the time, this is the product of Frenchman Eloye Mestrelle, who brought the new screw-press as well as improved coin dies with him on commission to the Royal Mint at London, inside the Tower of London. In marked contrast to the late-medieval gold angel of Henry VII (coin 85), which depicts the Biblical Saint Michael slaying Satan in the form of a dragon on one side and a ship of state on the other, Elizabeth's coin dramatically demonstrates the advances of art coming from France, and to France from Italy. The angel was made by the ancient hammer method, and shows the technology of that method in the wavy gold of its flan. This is a particularly well-struck specimen, while most of its kind are more uneven and far from round, often with deep splits into their sides. Not so, ever, the half pound of Elizabeth. The gold planchet was cut out to be exactly round with raised beading for its outer borders (also an anti-counterfeiting design). The queen's portrait is among the finest and most lifelike of all the Renaissance busts of monarchy, elegantly crowned and showing the fancy neck-ruff and jeweled dress that she so favored. A French initial mark of the moneyer, a fleur-de-lis, appears above her head, and the capital letters of her legend are more boldly styled, with a baroque panache, than had ever appeared on any English coin before it.

Now compare the reverse designs of the half pound and the angel. The latter is one-dimensional, even very shallow in its engraving. In contrast, the half pound features the royal shield topped by a crown featur-

Coin 84: gold half pound of Elizabeth I, England (shown enlarged on page 141)

Coin 85: gold angel of Henry VII, England (shown enlarged on page 141)

ing true perspective as well as "shading" to suggest the ermine and shadows within. Unfortunately, though a technical success, the coin was ahead of its time, and anti-Frankish prejudice at the mint caused Mestrelle to be ejected from his commission. Vengeful, he sank to counterfeiting and was hanged for his crimes, thus ending a glorious experiment founded upon the new technology and artistry.

While the discovery of the New World may have been the most important single event of the Renaissance, this was a period of time marked by discovery or invention in many fields outside of geography. New scientific laws were written as man observed Nature. New religious and political theories abounded—the Catholic Church espoused only one of various forms of Christianity, and statesmen came again to practice strategies so long tested by ancient Romans and summarized by new writers, among them Machiavelli (1469–1527) of Florence, famous for his volume *The Prince*. Science influenced how money was made, physically. Politics and faith may be seen in images of rulers on money. But it was in art that the new laws of perspective (how the images were seen) had the greatest influence on the circulating money. Coins changed from one-dimensional to multi-dimensional symbols of authority.

The Shift in Perspective

Coin 86: gouden leeuw of Philip the Good, of the Belgian Low Countries (shown enlarged on page 143)

Numerous Renaissance coins reflect this artistic change, but let us concentrate on just three. The gouden leeuw (or lion d'or, **coin 86**) of the Belgian Low Countries is very much a transitional piece, combining artistic conceptions of both the Middle Ages and the new times. This gold coin was struck from 1454 to 1460 for Philip the Good (born 1396, ruled 1419 to 1467), founder of the Burgundian state. Again, importantly, it was made of gold, the metal of international trade (within Europe), and it served a man of considerable political talent who balanced his alliance with both France and England, pitting each against the other, for his own purposes of expanding his influence, much as Elizabeth I of England would do a century later—both of them taking their cues from the new writing about the old rulers of ancient Rome. Philip is remembered for his use of art to serve his political ambitions: a flamboyant man, he even commissioned the artist Jan van Eyck to paint a portrait of his intended wife so that he might judge her before meeting her, and he employed talented artisans to create banners and tapestries

Coin 84: gold half pound of Elizabeth I, England This coin of the Virgin Queen, machine-minted rather than hand-struck, displays an elegant Renaissance portrait.

Coin 85: gold angel of Henry VII, England This late-medieval coin, struck by the ancient hammer method in the time of her grandfather, predates the gold half pound of Elizabeth I by more than 50 years.

and gold jewelry, and even the decorations on his carriages, to promote himself. And of course his coins.

Artistically, the floriated shield on this coin's reverse side (the quartered arms of Flanders and Bourgogne) is essentially medieval, but the embellishments at the four sides of the royal crest are nothing such. They are Renaissance in flavor. The little X's which serve as stops between the words of the legend in Latin, a sort of punctuation, come out of the Middle Ages—but the letters themselves are more ornate, and the cross pattée at the top of this side, in the legend, is an elegance not earlier seen on coins.

The obverse side of the coin, however, bearing the lion within a canopy, is entirely of the newer age. The structure is technically called a *gothic dias* and was surely inspired by the paintings of Flemish, Dutch, and German artists in oil. Gothic was a style that flourished during the Renaissance, with gothic cathedrals arising all over the landscape of Europe. The coin was minted in the middle of the 15th century, so its sense of perspective is simple, but decidedly new on a coin.

Coin 87: 10 ducats of Salzburg

Far more elegant and sophisticated a work of art, also in gold, is the wonderful and very rare large 10 ducats (**coin 87**) of Salzburg in Austria. Not only is this a marvelous study in the use of perspective, but it also captures two other images that could only have come from the Renaissance—the pope-like bishop on one side, and the tower of a city on the other. In the previous age, religious leaders urged believers to avoid the wickedness of cities because their pleasures and opportunities took away from the medieval focus of saving the soul. The traditional town, or *tun* in Anglo-Saxon, was a fortified place usually located at a crossroads or near a harbor or at a strategic spot along a river. In the Renaissance, towns were renewed as places having large markets offering numerous goods and services. Business thrived. Craft guilds of merchants were born. The city was a commercial trading center but religion remained a mainstay of the populace, the cement that held it all together.

These things are captured on this beautiful 10-ducats coin of the Austrian archbishopric. We see a tower assailed by the elements, the four winds, the rough sea at its base, but protected by an angelic force from above. The tempest was a topic of concern during this age, for man was

Coin 86: gouden leeuw of Philip the Good, of the Belgian Low Countries This coin's design mixes medieval and Renaissance features.

Coin 87: 10 ducats of Salzburg
The reverse design is likely an allegory of the disturbed times, where the tower is "Catholic Europe" assailed by destructive elements—but standing protected from these adversities by the blessings of Heaven.

still battling with nature theologically. The symbolism here, of the church and the town both threatened by outsiders, reflects the political scene of the day, that of the Holy Roman Empire's hostilities against the Ottoman Turks. The design is baroque—highly embellished by curling ornaments, adorned on both sides. Struck in 1593 (dated on the reverse in Roman numerals), it shows the arms of the city and the religious implements of the overriding faith combined on the obverse side in a message that anyone of the day could understand. Here was power, focused in a town filled with artisans and leaders of all sorts. The coin itself is a treasure of the use of perspective; its parts are balanced and inspiring and beautifully clear.

The Influence of Erasmus

It has been said that two influences, more than all the others, combined to spread the Renaissance northward from Italy, beyond the Alps. One was the invention of the printing press (about 1450), without which the intellectual energy of the age could not have spread. Almost immediately it made the medieval copying of manuscripts by scribal monks obsolete. Its invention may be likened to the advent of the Internet in our time.

The other huge influence of the early modern age was not a thing nor an invention but a person, the scholar Erasmus of Rotterdam (1466(?)–1536). A man of looming talents, he lectured and wrote about the revival of classical learning throughout central Europe and as far west as England, where he was befriended by no less a luminary than Sir Thomas More. Erasmus was an essayist of renown on social issues whose learned words spread to Switzerland and led to the founding of universities in Germany.

Erasmus' dual secular and religious influence might well be seen in the 1512-dated guldiner (or taler) of Zurich **(coin 88)**. Typical of Germanic silver coins of the time, its design is a complexity of symbols and images, though presented with great balance. The obverse features the three martyred patron saints of the city, each holding his own head! Haloes nonetheless adorn their shoulders. Their clerical robes are surrounded by a baroque curlicue, outside of which is the legend in elegant capital letters punctuated by classic medieval annulets (tiny circles), with a five-pointed florate star at top center—all holdovers from the earlier age.

Coin 88: silver guldiner of Zurich

Coin 88: silver guldiner of Zurich

Felix and Regula were siblings and soldiers of the Theban Legion, a Roman force that converted en masse to Christianity. The legion's officers were ordered to punish its men by *decimation*—that is, the summary execution of every tenth soldier—for refusing to sacrifice for the Roman emperor and take an oath against Christianity. The soldiers pledged their military loyalty to the emperor but refused to denounce their faith, accepting decimation after decimation until all were killed. Felix and Regula and their servant Exuperantius were all decapitated, after which they stood, carrying their heads in their hands, and walked 40 paces up a hill. There they knelt down and finally expired. Centuries later, a cathedral was built at the site of their martyrdom, which is in Zurich; hence their appearance on this coin.

Coin 89: silver taler of Schlick

**Coin 90: silver taler of Sigis-
mund, Austria**

The reverse, however, could only appear in the Renaissance. Noble shields surround the central crest, itself a study in stylized curves with its supporting lions. No medieval coin ever had such adornment. Although meant as a testament to the saints Felix, Regula, and Exuperantius, this riveting image also illustrates and possibly alludes to Erasmus' great and highly popular, witty treatise on the church, called *In Praise of Folly* (or *Encomium Moriae*, in the Latin in which it was published), which took to task the long-held practices of theological argument, superstition, luxuriant living by the "devout," and the stark monkish life. But, while he revealed these follies, he also published new editions of the works of early church fathers, which led to sounder Biblical theology. Erasmus was a man of many parts.

Very similar to the Dutch silver piece is the Austrian taler (**coin 89**) of the counts of Schlick, also struck at the beginning of the 16th century. Here too we see the dual influence of faith and politics. Saint Joachim stands by a crested secular shield, holding perhaps a shepherd's crook. Saintly and wizened, he is opposed by a rampant lion. While the entire design is rather flat in execution, it is highly balanced and busy with symbolism and legends (in bold and modern capital letters all well impressed), with a firm outer border. There is a sense of humanism in the depiction of the saint as a scholar among men, found on no coin of the Middle Ages.

We come now to the earliest dated silver taler (**coin 90**), that of the archduke Sigismund, also called a *guldiner*. It is dated in Arabic numerals 1486 and was minted at Hall in Austria, using silver from the rich mines of that area. It bears more than a slight resemblance to the second coin we examined (coin 80), the Spanish gold enrique. Gold was the metal of Spain, while central Europe mined primarily silver in the late 15th century. But it is the style of the two coins that is similar. Although animated, the Austrian knight on horseback is not lifelike, nor is the standing portrayal on the other side, a sort of stick figure much like the seated figure on the Spanish gold piece. However, the layout of the two coins is very balanced, pleasing, and full of detail. Much like the Zurich coin, the knight finds himself surrounded by a circle of shields, while a crude perspective marks the insignia around the standing portrayal of the prince and a crude cartouche appears inside the inner circle. The legend is made of bold capital letters. What we are looking at in the 1486

Coin 89: silver taler of Schlick The counts of Schlick held a very productive silver mine. To exploit its output they struck large coins, which became known by their location name of *Joachimsthalers*, later shortened to talers.

Coin 90: silver taler of Sigismund, Austria This 15th-century piece was the first taler-size coin to bear an Arabic-numeral date (1486).

Coin 91: silver double taler of Philip II, Spanish Netherlands

Coin 92: silver guldengroschen of Frederick III, "the Wise," Saxony

coin is one of the earliest of all Renaissance pieces. It is a mixture of the medieval and new styles of art. Crude but delightful.

We cannot seem to escape the influence, or the portrait, of Spain's King Philip II, and again we see his visage in the large silver double taler **(coin 91)** minted at Brabant in the Spanish Netherlands at the end of the 16th century. Here he looks more English than Spanish, with his neck-ruff (similar to that worn by Elizabeth I) and a tidy small crown very much of the English style. His dress is armor. The conception of the design layout is more Dutch or German than Spanish, owing more than a little influence to the English crown coins of the time, which themselves were often engraved by Dutch artisans. Both sides feature large capital lettering in the legends, and beaded edge bordering. While it was struck only a decade or so after the Milanese gold doppia of the same king, the double taler is far more modern looking. In fact, it bears the appearance of a fine engraving rather than a struck coin—printed engravings being inventions of the talented Dutch and Flemish artists of the Renaissance.

As we near the end of our journey, we must not fail to mention the contributions made to this age by the businessman. During the 16th century in particular, with towns flourishing and commerce growing via trade outside the close region of each town, marketplaces grew at a pace not seen before. Local merchants found it prudent, and profitable, to band together into guilds, each specializing in some sort of product or service. Butchers, green-grocers, shippers, accountants, lawyers—every sort of merchant, in fact—now found strength in numbers. This only promoted further expansion of town and trade, and enriched those who joined a guild. It was a centralizing of power, one of the hallmarks of the times.

This age saw new diversity as well, even within an individual. Previously, a man concentrated on one trade or skill. Now the world felt open, as it never had before, to those with foresight and talent. A superb example of a multi-talented artist who also had keen business acumen is the man responsible for fashioning the portrait of the Saxon elector Frederick II, the Wise (1463–1525), on his large guldengroschen **(coin 92)**. He was Lucas Cranich the Elder, whose sculpture of Frederick was transformed into a metallic portrait by die-engraver Ulrich Ursenthaler of Hall, in Tyrol. It is evidently a fine likeness of the ruler, and a splendid example of Renaissance portraiture.

Coin 91: silver double taler of Philip II, Spanish Netherlands In this coin of the late 1500s, King Philip of Spain appears more English than Spanish.

Coin 92: silver guldengroschen of Frederick III, "the Wise," Saxony Despite the fact that Frederick protected the rebellious Martin Luther, Pope Leo X sought his election as Holy Roman Emperor. Frederick himself supported Charles V, who was elected in 1519.

Frederick was a champion of local nobles as well as a protector of Martin Luther, rebel against the Church at Rome. In this he was forward-looking, "democratic" in an early sense of the word, in wishing to promote independent thought. In particular he forged reforms that would augment electors' powers at the expense of the emperor. Outside of politics, Frederick befriended humanists, founded the University of Wittenberg in 1502, collected art, and was patron to both Albrecht Dürer and Cranich. But the artist Cranich was even more of a Renaissance man: he attended university in Vienna, painted portraits of great quality and sensitivity (becoming court painter to Frederick in 1504), set up a studio to sell his works in quantity, became mayor of Wittenberg, and owned a variety of businesses, including a printing company. He embraced the discoveries and freedoms of his age.

Coin 93: silver testone of Antoine I, of Lorraine, France

> *No portrait of the Middle Ages ever had such style. . . .*

Frederick III's big silver coin shows the capped elector looking very much indeed like a guildmaster, in bold detail and sharp relief. He wears armored shoulderware and seems to stare ahead (at the future?) with great concentration. It might be said that no portrait of the Middle Ages ever had such style, but only those of the Roman emperors. There is sensitivity in his face, and elegant attention to detail in his thick beard. His nimbate eagle reminds us very much of that on the very first coin we examined in this chapter, the golden 4 excelentes of Ferdinand and Isabella. On Frederick's coin, though, the shield becomes tiny on the eagle's breast, the bird though scrawny more lifelike, even if still heraldic. While the obverse is spare and focuses on the persona of the ruler, the reverse is full of detail, balanced and clear and highly emblematic.

Coin 94: gold doppia ducato of Giovanni Sforza, Milan, Italy

This European movement we call the Renaissance began with the monks and scholars, so it is perhaps fitting that we end our look at the age they created by seeing resemblances of their images on a couple of coins. Two classics are the silver testone **(coin 93)** dated 1544 of Antoine I (1508–1544) of Lorraine in France, and the golden doppia ducato **(coin 94)** struck about 1481 in Milan, Italy, for Giovanni Galeazzo Maria Sforza (born 1469, coins issued 1476 to 1694). The reverses of these two

Coin 93: silver testone of Antoine I, of Lorraine, France Antoine I, duke of Lorraine, was stronger than this portrait might suggest; remove the coronet and he appears youthful and almost timid.

Coin 94: gold doppia ducato of Giovanni Sforza, Milan, Italy Giovanni succeeded to the duchy aged seven, on his father's assassination. He died in his twenties—probably in the typical courtly fashion, by being poisoned by his regent uncle, who became the next duke of Milan.

pieces share a similar conception, the crest or shield of arms of the royal family: one crowned, the other plumed by gorgons sliding through crowns. The ducat is balanced and refined in conception. The silver piece may be a simple shield surrounded by legend, but the layout is classic style of the mid-16th century. It could have been fashioned in any number of countries, and it again contains two annulets as stops or grammatical pauses.

It is the obverse side of each coin that most captures our attention and fully symbolizes the age that formed them. The French coin portrays the ruler almost as a monk would have looked, his hair styled as a tonsure, though crowned. He does not appear kingly; he seems almost scared, or excited, staring off into the unknown. Lombardic, curled, baroque lettering is marked by a cross right at the top center. The picture is nothing that ever appeared on the lifelessly styled coins of the Middle Ages. It bears a simple but rational beauty.

The gold piece of a member of the powerful Sforza family of Milan, however, is even more peculiar, suggestive of a scholar more so than a political ruler. The boy, Giovanni, was the son of a despotic genius who was also a patron of the arts and of musicians. When his father was assassinated, Giovanni inherited a brief, troubled reign. On this coin he has armored shoulders but a plain cap, not a crown, and above it in a small cartouche an icon. Giovanni's placid face has features only possible in metallic art of this era. Is it the visage of a moral philosopher or of a ruler? It has great dignity, much as do portrait paintings done in oil at this same time. It is a vast departure from the outline faces of just a hundred years before. It bears the principal hallmark of art of the Renaissance—realism. Serene and beautiful, it simply exemplifies its age.

And so we come to the end of our glimpse at this historical period.

CHAPTER FIVE

1600–1750
THE AGE
OF REASON?

Michael J. Shubin

Before the end of the 16th century the artistic light of the Renaissance had begun to sputter, its vitality drifting toward mannerism and affectation. Equivalent behavior could be seen in the world of European politics, where in the new century it ripened into incessant posturing, power plays, and political bluster.

The emergent trend of nations being controlled by centralized royal powers accelerated beyond that seen in the 15th century and sharpened in definition. This trend was stimulated, without a doubt, by the significant infusion of metal wealth, which suddenly began to pour in from the New World. The repercussions of this newfound wealth were not solely limited to economic and commercial spheres. It would influence all levels of society, and the reverberations would be felt well into the 17th and 18th centuries.

One factor, always present during the previous two centuries, continued merrily along during this period—war. While it cannot be said that the age was one of continuous conflict, it may sometimes have seemed that way. At the beginning of 1600, wars of religion still dominated the scene. By the end of the century, however, the reasons to wage war moved to causes perhaps more profane, maybe even mundane, as well. Kings and princes, ministers and investors, bankers and profiteers all began to view war in terms of profit, loss, or just "breaking even." Soon, many European wars and skirmishes became directly linked to controlling the incoming wealth of the Americas, or the trade with Asia.

The effect of these power struggles can be seen in the currencies of the 17th and 18th centuries. Financial disruptions resulting from those adversities are most clearly evidenced in the small change and everyday monies of the common man. But it is in the larger denominations of silver and gold, the coins that lubricated international commerce and paid for standing armies, that the history of this chapter is perhaps most vividly written.

Coin 95: 50 reales or cinquentin of Philip IV, Spain

Spain

When discussing coins of this period it is necessary to first look to Spain, the unwitting midwife to much of the nationalistic fervor and political activity of the era. The coin illustrated (**coin 95**) truly epitomizes the complexities and quandaries of Spain. It was struck under Philip IV

Coin 95: 50 reales or cinquentin of Philip IV, Spain Spain's vast holdings of American precious metals allowed it to experiment with larger silver coins of high value, in 50- and 100-reales denominations. Struck intermittently for nearly three decades, they never seemed to become a truly viable coinage. Very few examples of these have survived to the present day.

(1621–1665). The piece is huge for a coin, three inches in diameter, and weighs about five and one half ounces. The cinquentin, with its finely balanced and carefully executed designs, bespeaks imperial majesty, power, and tradition: the perfect currency for a world state, and a world power. Sadly for Spain, it was a role she never quite realized.

The massive infusion of New World gold and silver into Spanish coffers exacerbated and furthered huge price increases, already begun in the previous century, and which eventually spread throughout Europe. Sometimes termed the "European price revolution," this long-lasting inflationary cycle exerted economic stresses that eventually fueled much of the political, religious, and social unrest throughout Europe. During this period, Spain produced some of its most interesting coins. Of particular note are the large silver reales (minted in denominations of 100 or 50), issued during the reigns of Philip III and Philip IV.

Initially, these large multiples of reales were likely considered a convenient means of creating coins in a direct silver-to-gold ratio to Spain's gold escudos—50 reales then being equivalent to three escudos. But the production of cinquentins obviously taxed the limits of the technology of the time. Few were struck, and even fewer have survived to this day. Laminations, as seen on the obverse of this coin, were endemic to the series. These imperfections were due to refining and smelting irregularities. They became more noticeable when the metal was worked and rolled by means of a roller press into thick sheets from which the coins were struck and punched. It is also likely that the production of these coins was simply not cost effective. Still, numerous contracts continued to be signed for their striking. It is possible that these huge silver pieces evolved into quasi-medallic issues. This particular issue of cinquentin resulted from silver mined by the merchants Ulloque and Aramburu, who had a license to extract ore from the Ingenio region of Chile from 1633 to 1637.

Of the major European powers, Spain might be regarded as the "poor little rich girl." During its heyday, it possessed unbelievable material wealth, yet Spain's access to American precious metals seemingly afforded it little benefit. Spain suffered equally from Europe's "price revolution," the antecedents for which go back at least a half a century prior to Columbus' famous voyage. By the 1550s, the torrent of silver flooding in from the New World pushed inflation to new extremes. Even while this new wealth was also accelerating regional depression cycles, it created other economic disturbances as well. Europe wouldn't "normalize" until the 1630s, just in time for the devastating Thirty Years' War. Spain became embroiled in that conflict, while at the same time attempting to deal with insurrection in the Netherlands. This, in simplest terms, is the crux of Spain's failure as a dominant power: as a Hapsburg-ruled kingdom, or as a surrogate of the Holy Roman Empire (again, through its Hapsburg connection), Spain spent a vast portion of its American wealth on numerous ruinously expensive wars. Money that did not go towards directly supporting armies was spent servicing attendant loans, bankers, material suppliers, and transportation costs. Later, when New World bullion shipments began declining, Spain faced the fact that it was spending more to run its empire than it was receiving in bullion assets to maintain it. As a result, it frequently defaulted on loans. Historians have estimated that from the discovery of Spain's American possessions to about 1800, well over 158,000 tons of silver and gold were extracted from the New World.

The British defeat of its armada in 1588 marked the beginning of the end for Spain. A replay of this disaster occurred in 1639 against the Dutch at the Battle of the Downs, effectively marking the demise of Spain's maritime ascendancy, as well as its postion as a dominant power. Still, even with its decline and senescence clearly marked for the future, Spain's political influence remained significant until the end of the 18th century.

Coin 96: gold 5 ducats of Leopold I, Austria (shown enlarged on page 159)

The Holy Roman Empire

Another political entity whose day was passing, especially in the 18th century, was the Holy Roman Empire, embodied at this time by Leopold I of Austria, 1657–1705. Austria's golden 5-ducat piece **(coin 96)** shows Leopold's laureate and cuirassed bust on the face, while the reverse displays the double-headed imperial eagle, with Hapsburg arms at its breast. This early minted portrait of Leopold only hints at the facial peculiarities that increased as he aged, earning him the un-royal nickname "Hog Mouth." In the 15th century, the Hapsburg line picked up a genetic trait that, due to inbreeding, afflicted many family members (both Spanish and Austrian) in varying degrees of severity. The physical characteristics of the famed "Hapsburg profile" included mandibular prognathism, which caused the lower jaw to jut forward. This was unfortunately combined with a thickened lower lip and an oftentimes prominent, misshapen nose.

Leopold, the successor to Ferdinand III, ascended to the imperial throne during one of the most tumultuous periods in the empire's history. During his lengthy reign, he experienced incessant warring with a resurgent Ottoman Turkey and constant threats from an aggressive France. In the tradition of other Catholic Hapsburgs, he spent considerable energy attempting to eradicate Protestantism in his territories, especially Hungary. His efforts there often aroused hostility and rebelliousness, giving the neighboring Ottomans opportunities to exploit in order to press their territorial agendas in the area. In any event, the need for capital expenditures ensured that Leopold's silver coinages were among the most prolific of the Hapsburg emperors. Today, however, the larger-denomination gold issues remain rare to excessively so.

Leopold expelled the Jews from Vienna, asserting that their loyalty to the Crown was suspect. Ironically, it was the Jewish businessmen who helped to finance Leopold's (and his son's) imperial warfare. This same business community served as a convenient scapegoat whenever government economic policies ended in failure or bankruptcy. Leopold's reign also witnessed the rise of a movement anxious for the state's adoption of a mercantile economic policy. The Austrian Ostende Trade Company was the progeny of this enthusiasm.

Leopold's Holy Roman Empire was born of the eastern division of Charlemagne's conquered lands. In 800, Charlemagne received the title of *emperor* (much in the manner of the term employed by the ancient Romans) from the pope. Eventually the name "Roman Empire" came to be applied to the Germanic lands of Charlemagne's eastern holdings, the western part evolving into France.

The empire differed from other kingdoms in one significant way— since the 10th century it existed as an *elective* monarchy. As time passed, though, increasing limitations on the emperor's sovereignty began to accrue. The rulers of numerous Germanic states voted (as electors) one of their own to the imperial seat, hoping to gain privileges, status, and political potency via close proximity to their overlord. Further limitations on the sovereign were brought about by the existence of many principalities. These varied politically, existing as imperial holdings, clerical states, or free city states—many with shifting loyalties and differing

Coin 96: gold 5 ducats of Leopold I, Austria Leopold I's unusually long reign (1658–1705) covers one of the most important and tumultuous periods of European history. The result of his involvement in numerous wars against the Turks, and especially France, has allowed the coins of his rule to survive in great numbers, making them easily available to collectors of this day.

agendas. Because of this, the national and political unification enjoyed by France proved impossible in the German lands. Imperial sovereignty was further weakend in 1700 when Leopold, greatly in need of help for an impending war with France, granted additional concessions to some of the German electors. Subsequently, Hapsburg sovereignty became increasingly marginalized, wielding less and less power outside the Austrian border.

France

Without doubt, France was one of the greatest political players of this period. Producing handsome portrait pieces of taler size, as illustrated here **(coin 97)**, was a new venture for France. The 60-sols portrait coin was now the largest silver issue of the land, and it was born of a need to put the country's disordered currency on a more rational footing. This became necessary not only domestically, but also to facilitate France's participation in the international markets. Louis XIII initiated a major re-coining in 1640. The new minting not only replaced defective, out-of-date currency, but also provided a for-profit enterprise that benefited the State. Worn, defective, or antiquated coin was devalued by proclamation and returned to the mint by royal decree. There, replacement coin was offered at a taxed or otherwise inflated price. Often this process was designated as needed "coinage reform." Between 1689 and 1715, France saw five so-called reformations, all profiting the Crown. One such reformation in the early years of Louis XV's reign taxed the public in this manner at 20 percent. To save expenses, coins were not always melted down but simply re-struck with a new design stamped over the old. Today, it is still possible to come across coins whose older undertype shows through a later design.

An ambitious France contributed greatly to the war-torn environment of 17th-century Europe. Both Louis XIII (1610–1643) and Louis XIV (1643–1715) ruled under the influence of dominant and persuasive ministers—such as Cardinal Richelieu and his successor, Cardinal Mazarin. The two clerics served as sequential ministers throughout the century, strengthening royal power and that of the State. Likewise, they encouraged and facilitated each king's desire of empire building. This was deemed vital for security, due to France's anxiety at the prospect of unification of Hapsburg Spanish and Austrian territories.

Coin 97: 60 sols of Louis XIII, France

Coin 97: 60 sols of Louis XIII, France The louis d'argent of 60 sols, or silver ecu, is the first taler-sized coin struck by France. The masterful portrait was engraved by the gifted Jean Varin of the Paris mint.

Coin 98: gold 5 ducats of Leopold I, Holy Roman Empire

Both Richelieu and Mazarin encouraged mercantilism as a means of fortifying their country militarily and financially, establishing colonies in North America, Africa, and the West Indies. Richelieu, in particular, shrewdly kept France out of actual military confrontations with the Hapsburgs by subsidizing other nations to serve as military proxies. Under the advisement of these and other ministers, Louis XIV eventually boasted a well-trained professional army of some 400,000 men—the first large-standing army seen in Europe in more than a thousand years. In addition, Louis now had the financial means to fund his territorial aggressions. So, while the French were careful to make political arguments for embarking upon war campaigns, most appear to be nothing but blatant land grabs. France soon posed a definite threat to the balance of European power.

In response to the French threat, an alliance, headed by the Netherlands, was formed between the Holy Roman Empire, Sweden, Venice, and the pope. During the long and exhausting war that followed, Louis sought to manipulate aid from fellow Catholic James II, king of England, Ireland, and Scotland. This, in part, led to James overthrow and replacement by his son-in-law, William of Orange. As king of England *and* stadtholder of the Netherlands (the original orchestrator of the alliance against France), William now posed a considerable threat to France.

Louis eventually realized he had overextended himself. A truce, resulting in the Peace of Rijswijk, was signed in 1697. It was a victory for the Alliance, and France was forced to give up many of the territories it had forcibly annexed. Celebration of the well-earned peace finds exceptional display on this large 5-ducat gold coin (**coin 98**), struck in the Imperial city of Nuremburg, by the Holy Roman Emperor, an older Leopold I. The obverse shows a delightful aerial view of the city. The reverse presents an allegory of Peace standing on a raised base, holding an olive branch and serpent-entwined staff. Below her, two cherubim support shields of arms.

Europe's nationalistic wars, it must be remembered, were not limited to the Continent. In North America hostilities erupted as part of "King William's War," the first of the French and Indian Wars (1689–1763). During the 17th and 18th centuries, colonial wars between Britain and France could usually be linked to the wars in Europe. Europeans considered colonial "skirmishes" to be a minor aspect of the greater struggle,

Coin 98: gold 5 ducats of Leopold I, Holy Roman Empire This large and elaborate gold piece celebrates the victory of the European alliance in 1697 against a very territorially aggressive France. The coin is an excellent example of the pictorial intricacy displayed on many coins of this era.

but to the settlers in America the rivalry of the two powers was the cause of great concern. The fighting inevitably led not only to French or British raids, but also the horrors of Indian warfare. As the British later learned, the wars created important political changes, particularly in the attitudes of the colonists toward their home country. The conflicts eventually fostered a resiliency of spirit, an attitude of self-reliance, and a healthy resentment of "foreign wars." This new colonial viewpoint would contribute greatly to the unrest that sparked the American Revolution.

Meanwhile, Europe had only a brief respite in which to catch its breath. By the start of the next century the War of Spanish Succession would begin, giving Louis renewed opportunities for French expansionism.

The German States

Coin 99: Reichstaler of Charles VI, Holy Roman Empire

In terms of coins, one can hardly think of a more vivid and explicit sign of the times than this Nuremberg German Reichstaler, following the Rijswijk gold coin by little more than a generation. This piece **(coin 99)** was struck by Holy Roman Emperor Charles VI (1711–1740). The obverse displays a popular heraldic type with a wreath bearing six shields of arms, the larger seventh hanging from a ribbon at center. More extraordinary is the reverse, dated June 8, 1733. It finely details a battery of four field cannons firing at a large round target. This fascinating scene highlights the artillery contests conducted in the city that year. The momentum for the War of Polish Succession (1733–1738) was moving forward and the various contestants were gearing up for the conflict. In 1733 Emperor Charles VI raised the Nuremburg 14th Infantry Regiment for service in the war, and perhaps this Reichstaler served as a patriotic booster for that campaign.

The volatile elements igniting this war were religion (once again), multiple claimants to the vacant Polish throne, and political meddling on an international scale from Austria, Russia, France, and the various German states. One of the royal claimants, former Polish king Stanislaw I, was supported by his son-in-law, Louis XV of France. Louis hoped to renew France's traditional alliance with Poland as a way to offset rising Russian and Austrian powers in Northern and Eastern Europe.

The war was relatively brief and a preliminary peace was agreed upon in 1735, ratified as the Treaty of Vienna three years later. As an appeasement to improve relations with Austria, the French (and her allies) now

Coin 99: Reichstaler of Charles VI, Holy Roman Empire The large taler coins that flourished in the 17th and 18th centuries were adaptable formats, suitable for several purposes. Some served at their most basic as mere conveyors of value and issuing authority. Others (as seen here) are windows to historical events of the time. Equally often, they were a canvas for artistic whimsies and allegorical flights of fancy more at home on medallic works.

**Coin 100: gold 8 ducats of
Joseph II, Regensburg**

agreed to recognize the Pragmatic Sanction (imperial decree) allowing Charles' daughter, Maria Theresa, to succeed him to the throne.

On a lighter note, despite suffering through decades of war the population and cities of Europe continued to grow, rebounding nicely after the devastation of the Black Death. While industry and commerce grew alongside the population, the gap between rich and poor grew steadily as well. Eventually, an alarmingly high percentage of people in many of the largest cities appeared to subsist on charity and alms begging. Perhaps as a consequence of decades of religious strife, the attitude towards these unfortunates began to harden. This can partially be traced to the divergent Protestant sects spreading across Europe that equated inherent goodness with thrift, labor, and industry. Before, it was one's Christian duty to assist the poor. Now they were looked upon with suspicion. One French official flatly stated, "Beggary is the apprenticeship of crime. . . ." All this would lead to social unrest, exploding later into revolution. Meanwhile, however, optimism and civic pride ruled the day as evidenced by the numerous "city view" coins that became highly popular during this era.

The gold 8-ducat piece **(coin 100)** of German Emperor Joseph II (1765–1790), originating in the imperial city of Regensburg, is a stunning example of its type. The obverse bears the well-known imperial crowned double-eagle, holding a sword and cross-topped orb with a crowned shield and order at its breast. The reverse shows a magnificently rendered scene of Regensburg, viewed from the north. The ample flan of the coin provided the perfect backdrop for the wonderful detail shown. Prosperous cities and courts boasted of the cultural figures they housed, and this same sort of hometown boosterism is evidenced on many German coins. City views became popular in the 16th century and were displayed on gold and silver coins of various sizes. By the 18th century, improvements in engraving and striking rendered them impressive vistas in miniature. The coins displayed a wealth of detail and information, extolling the prosperity, strength, and importance of the city depicted. Many cities made liberal use of the motif on trade-oriented gold ducats. No doubt these "little views" were an inducement, before the advent of high-tech marketing and customer manipulation, to think of the displayed city in terms of its wealth, power, and "golden" opportunities.

Pictorially related to these coins are some of the largest and most interesting issues struck in Germany, originating around the Duchy of

Coin 100: gold 8 ducats of Joseph II, Regensburg This impressive gold coin regales the viewer with an extraordinary view of the Imperial City of Regensburg, Germany. The popular "city view" coins were a reflection of both a civic and a growing "national" pride. The types achieved their greatest sophistication in the 17th and 18th centuries.

Brunswick. The coins are quite fascinating, and truly illustrate the times in which they were struck. Especially noteworthy is this Löser 3 talers **(coin 101)** of 1685, struck under Rudolf August (1666–1704) of Brunswick-Wolfenbuttel-Luneburg. The obverse depicts the hereditary family crest in the elaborate manner German engravers genuinely excelled at. The reverse shows a fanciful Lady Luck playing the lute upon a huge snail. A radiant sun illuminates one side, and the blessings of Heaven the other. The rather busy background depicts the silver-mining fields of the Hartz Mountains.

Detailed landscapes, such as noted on the 3-talers piece, often provided delightful contemporary "slices of life" peculiar to German coins. With so many minor German kingdoms striking taler-sized coins, coin designers occasionally resorted to intriguing imagery to make their issues stand out. Coins such as the popular class of "Mining Talers" were ideal canvases for such use. The details they provide have proven to be exceptionally valuable to students of both history and technology. This multiple-taler of Rudolf August happens to be one of the more charming examples of that series.

Generally known as "Löser Talers," once they exceeded two talers in size, these coins were the ingenious conception of Julius, Duke of Brunswick-Wolfenbuttel, who struck the first multiples in 1574. While silver output from his mines in the Hartz Mountains was on the upswing, times were becoming less certain. The Protestant Reformation initiated by Martin Luther was in full swing, the properties of the Catholic Church were being seized and sold off, violent pogroms levied against the Jews were increasing, and the Inquisition had already started burning Protestants at the stake. Allegiances were shifting, and soon nationalistic "saber rattling" could be heard across the Continent.

Julius devised a plan. As a means to store quantities of the duchy's excess silver as a hedge against the exigencies of war, he began striking a series of coins in denominations ranging from 1-1/4 up to 16 talers. Next, he ordered property owners to purchase at least one of these new coins, the size of the denomination depending upon the owner's wealth and rank. The owners of these larger coins had to be able to produce them on demand and redeem them, but only in exchange for the local debased coinage. While the coins could be pawned, they could not be

Coin 101: 3 talers, Brunswick-Wolfenbuttel-Luneburg

Coin 101: 3 talers, Brunswick-Wolfenbuttel-Luneburg The often visually intriguing German Löser talers rank among the largest coins minted in Europe, with some issues containing up to a pound of silver. Although wholly coin-like in appearance, their intended function perhaps should place them in the category of an elaborate ingot instead.

sold or traded. This resulted in a substantial amount of money remaining in "storage." In case of war or other calamity, the ducal wealth would be diffused throughout the country, thus minimizing the risk of losing quantities of treasure to invaders. For this reason, the coins' inscription reads, "Julius Löser" (redeemers) on the reverse of the 1574 issues—the appellation "Redemption Talers" attaching to these coins. The duke's scheme worked well. It would be needed for the time of tribulations ahead—the Thirty Years' War (1618–1648).

While the gargantuan coins (the 16 talers held more than a pound of silver) produced by the princes and grand dukes of Brunswick-Wolfenbuttel are reminiscent of the equally large 50 and 100 reales of Spain, there was also a significant difference. Those of Spain might be termed "active," initially coined with the intent to be used. The German löser coins instead should be considered "reactive," primarily produced as a unit of stored value, rather than circulating money.

Great Britain

During the 17th century, the German religious wars had a counterpart in Great Britain. The religious tensions existing in England since the time of Henry VIII were further complicated by the growth of Protestant sects. Some of these sects could be highly intolerant of other faiths—especially Catholicism. This was largely due to the population's fear of recurrent papal meddling in English affairs. The most remarkable salvo in this conflict centered on King Charles I (1625–1649).

Charles inherited the incessant financial problems of his father, James I, including a parliamentary refusal to grant royal funds unless he agreed to address the grievances of the nobility. At a time when Parliament and the nobility were determined to flex their legislative muscles, Charles determinedly clung to the idea that kings ruled by divine right. When he forced a showdown with Parliament, civil war resulted. The largely Puritan nobility was further upset by Charles' marriage to a devoutly Catholic French princess. His supporters were eventually routed by Parliamentary forces, and in 1646 the king was captured and imprisoned. Late in 1648 he was put on trial for high treason; he was executed the following year.

Owing to the remarkably diverse variety of denominations and issuing mints, the numismatic legacy of Charles' reign has proven to be particularly fascinating for scholars and collectors. Add to this the odd (but always interesting) siege money, which originated during the English Civil War. Note the largest English gold coin up to that time—the gold triple unite, struck at Oxford in 1644, at nearly an ounce of 22-karat gold **(coin 102)**. This is the extremely rare small "élan" variety. The obverse bears a crowned bust left of the king, holding a sword and branch, the reverse: a scrolled "Declaration."

When Charles declared war against the rebel Parliamentarian forces, he promised to "Preserve the Protestant religion, the known laws of the land, and the just privileges and freedom of Parliament." This declaration, with abbreviated Latin legend, is seen on the coin. The three plumes above it are the mark of mintmaster Thomas Bushell, of the Aberystwyth mint (Wales), which provided the equipment for the Oxford coinage.

Charles established his wartime headquarters in Oxford late in 1642, and began striking coins from plate donated by the university. Surprisingly, between 1643 and 1649, the Parliament-controlled Tower Mint of London continued to strike gold coins bearing Charles' portrait and titles. All undated, these pieces bear the royal coat of arms on the reverse.

Parliament ruled London and the prosperous southeast and much of the bullion it struck into coin came into the country via the usual trade and commerce sources. Charles had access to silver mined in Wales, which was still under his control. Additionally, private contributions from royalist supporters also proved very helpful. Charles rarely struck coins in gold, and his troops were paid almost exclusively in silver.

One aspect of English conservatism is readily seen in its coinage. Compared to other European monarchies, machine-struck coins came to England fairly late. Mechanized coin production was attempted during the reign of Elizabeth I, but ended in failure. This was primarily a result of conservative guildsmen (employed by London's mint), who feared that their professions might be jeopardized. These same men also harbored resentment towards the foreign French Huguenot, Eloi Mestrel, who was in charge of the project. Headway was made under Charles I, who made good use of another talented Frenchman, Nicholas Briot. Briot also faced considerable resistance in London, but managed to exert far better control over the York and Edinburgh mints. In fact, much of

Coin 102: gold triple unite, Great Britain (shown enlarged on page 173)

the Scottish product is unquestionably superior to the issues struck in England. After Charles, machine striking resumed once more, late in Cromwell's tenure. The resultant portrait pieces of the aged "Lord Protector," by the masterful Thomas Simon, are among the most compelling and dignified numismatic works in Europe during this time.

Upon Cromwell's death, the exiled Charles II was invited back to England and proclaimed king. His early coins were likewise of hammered manufacture, but the clipping and counterfeiting of these became so common that he was compelled to advocate machine striking. The addition of grained or lettered edges also served to foil clipping. In 1662, hammered coinage in England ceased altogether. Soon, gold denominations were reduced in number and simplified, while silver denominations, from crown to penny, remained unchanged.

Coin 103: gold guinea of Charles II, Great Britain

A number of Charles' issues include an elephant in profile.

An interesting and rare example of his early machine-struck coin is exemplified by the gold guinea, dated 1664 (**coin 103**). It was Charles' second bust-type coin, and bore the usual reverse of crowned cruciform arms, alternating scepters at angles, and central interlocking C's. It is remarkable, both as a work of art and as a historical piece—it is the tiny image of an elephant beneath Charles' bust that sets this piece apart.

The English guinea received its name from being struck from gold mined and imported from Guinea (now Ghana), in Africa. This gold was acquired and imported by the Company of Royal Adventurers of England Trading in Africa. The company traded in gold, slaves, and other African goods (in 1665, it was estimated that the company earned £100,000 from its slaving activities alone). A royal charter granted the company the privilege of affixing its badge to coins struck from their imported metal. Due to this, a number of Charles' issues include an elephant in profile (sometimes with a turret on its back) placed below his bust. The denomination was originally valued at one pound, or 20 shillings. But subsequent increases in the price of gold during his reign led to its being traded at 22 shillings, and this after a slight weight reduction in 1670.

Coin 102: gold triple unite, Great Britain The triple unite was England's largest gold coin up to that time. The numismatic legacy of the civil war brought on by Charles I make his coinages among the most varied and fascinating of British monies.

Coin 103: gold guinea of Charles II, Great Britain The first of Britain's gold guineas was struck under Charles II. The term *guinea* was derived from coins struck with gold mined and imported from Africa (modern-day Ghana), which was specially noted by the symbol of an elephant placed beneath the king's portrait.

Coin 104: gold 2 guineas of William III, Great Britain

Unusual for Charles' reign was the extraordinary abundance of large-sized silver crowns, which eventually became more plentiful than smaller silver pieces. The main source of this wealth derived from a payment received from Louis XIV when he purchased back for France the coastal port of Dunkirk. The ownership of the town, near the border of the Spanish Netherlands, had been contested by France and Spain throughout the 15th, 16th, and 17th centuries. It finally passed into French hands in 1658, as a result of French victories against Spain. France then ceded Dunkirk to England as a reward for her co-alliance against Spain. Afterwards, Charles II sold it back to Louis to ease the financial difficulties he faced upon re-establishing the monarchy. The sale from this, plus other confidential subsidies received from France, swelled the coffers of the London mint, and England soon experienced the largest silver surplus it had seen in decades. With good reason Charles' rule was regarded by many of his subjects as a return to the golden age of Elizabeth I. It was marred only by a few heaven-sent disasters: the bubonic plague that appeared in London around Christmas of 1664 (decimating the city the following year), followed by the great fire of London in 1666.

After the reign of Charles II, English coinage was basically "set" for the next two centuries, although the multiples of guineas expanded to five. However, incessant Catholic/Protestant skirmishes continued to trouble the kingdom. The partial resolution of these conflicting faiths contributed to one of the most artistic English coins seen at the end of the century—the "Fine Work" gold coinages of William III (1694–1702). The obverse of **coin 104** depicts an extraordinary portrait of the aged William, his luxuriant hair (or wig) supporting a classical wreath of laurel leaves. The reverse shows crowned cruciform arms with angled scepters, a lion in cartouche at center, and a divided date.

William was an outsider to English politics. He was stadholder of several Dutch provinces, and he and his wife Mary (sister to both Charles II and James II) were devout Protestants. William was soon invited by members of the British Parliament to take the throne from the despised James II, a Catholic. To further secure that British rulers would remain forever Protestant, Parliament passed the Act of Settlement in 1701. Subsequently, after William and Mary, and then Queen Anne, all died without heirs, the English throne passed to the German House of Hanover through Sophia, electoress of Hanover and granddaughter of James I.

Coin 104: gold 2 guineas of William III, Great Britain British coins seldom enjoyed the artistry achieved by many European currencies. The "fine work" issues of William III rank among the best of British numismatic art, and easily equal the best contemporary work seen in France, Italy, or Germany.

Coin 105: 5 guineas of Queen Anne, Great Britain (shown enlarged on page 179)

Between the 16th and 18th centuries, Europe suffered incessant religious, territorial, and commercial warfare. The costs of constant rebuilding and restoration while maintaining (or at least renting) standing armies (not to mention the costs of civil government) became enormous. One means of producing needed revenues was the development of an economic policy known as mercantilism. The nations that favored this practice (primarily Holland, France, and England—all leading maritime nations) capitalized upon the fact that precious metals were universally accepted and desired instruments for acquiring commodities. Likewise, it was soon accepted that encouraging foreign trade was the best way to accumulate this precious bullion. Similarly, industries involved in manufacturing and processing were favored over traditional economic bases, such as agriculture. The essential tenet of the mercantile system required nations to sell more than they bought, thereby accumulating bullion. To accomplish this required vastly increased government involvement not only in shipping and manufacturing, but also by employing revenue-raising practices such as duties, levies, tariffs, and taxes. Governmental involvement in commerce often resulted in the formation of corporations and trading companies. These organizations carefully regulated production of goods at home while securing quality goods and resources from abroad at the lowest possible prices. Soon, government treaties were signed which granted trading rights; next, trading posts and colonies and trading companies were established. A "low-cost" workforce was needed in these new colonies, and the promotion of slavery soon spread like wildfire. The so-called discovery of the New World, with all the opportunities that it presented, contributed greatly to promoting the growth of mercantilism across the globe.

Two outstanding mementos of Britain's mercantilist period, and its rise to pre-eminence as a maritime world power, involved her commercial clashes with Spain. The earliest was the creation of the largest multiple of guineas struck by the English, a 5-guinea gold coin **(coin 105)** of Queen Anne (1702–1714). The coin displayed shows an attractively draped bust of the queen to the left, with VIGO in bold letters below. The reverse depicts the usual crowned cruciform arms with angled scepters, this time with a rose at center.

Throughout the 17th century, rivalries between the English and Dutch resulted in both tenuous friendships and bitter war-making, often with Spain pulled into the fray. By 1701 Britain and Holland were once again "friends," unified now against Spain during the War of Spanish Succession (1702–1713), fought simultaneously in Europe and in the North American colonies. This proved to be the last European war resulting from Louis XIV's efforts to expand French power and territory.

Political and commercial harassment of Spain involved various joint Anglo-Dutch expeditions against Spanish targets. One such expedition was led by Sir George Rooke in 1702. Rooke sacked the Spanish seaports of Cadiz and Vigo, seizing a number of Spanish treasure ships in Vigo Bay. The booty brought back to England exceeded 11 million silver "pieces of eight," along with a small quantity of gold. To commemorate the event, silver coins struck from their haul (between 1702 and 1703) bore the word VIGO. Gold was likewise struck in this fashion and only a handful of five-guinea coins were made. The guinea and half guinea were the primary gold issues.

Later, but in the same vein, is the "Lima" crown (coin 106) of George II (1727–1760). This coin is of the Old Head type, with a laureate and cuirassed bust to left and LIMA spelled out below. The reverse is similar as before, but with a haloed cross at center.

During the reign of George II, gold and silver coins marked LIMA were struck from Spanish bullion seized by Captain George Anson during his trans-global ocean voyage of 1740 to 1744. In 1740, under royal orders, Anson circumnavigated the globe. He penetrated the Straits of Magellan and attempted to stir Spain's South American colonies into revolt while interfering with Spanish shipping. Outfitted with a six-ship squadron, Anson's trip lasted nearly four years. Scurvy and loss of life notwithstanding, Anson still managed to capture numerous prizes, sack and plunder enemy towns, and sink or damage many Spanish ships. Most importantly, he captured the rich Spanish trading galleon *Nuestra Senora de Covadonga*, which plied the Spanish shipping lanes between Acapulco and Manila. Her cargo totaled nearly 1.5 million dollars in value, adding 36,000 ounces of silver and other goods to Anson's earlier hauls. On December 1743 he turned towards home, arriving in England on June 15, 1744.

All this brigandage was part and parcel of England's supremely arrogant policy towards Spain (and France) to achieve maritime supremacy. Anson's voyage itself, as economic warfare and a commercial venture, was basically a failure—being extremely costly, while contributing little

Coin 106: crown of George II, Great Britain (shown enlarged on page 181)

to the war effort. But in terms of prestige and perception, the view of British naval superiority was hugely reinforced.

When it came to implementing colonial settlements in the Western hemisphere, Britain could be considered a Johnny-come-lately. Despite previous attempts by Elizabeth I, it was under her successor that England's earliest permanent settlement, Jamestown, was established in 1607. By that time Spain, Portugal, France, and the Netherlands had already established claims to much of the territory. Despite this, Britain was assertive in protecting her smaller holdings. Massachusetts evolved out of the Plymouth Colony, eventually merging into the holdings of the Massachusetts Bay Company. The area became dominated by Pilgrim colonists—among them, those who landed at Plymouth Rock (by accident) in 1620.

The so-called Pine Tree shilling was among the early coins struck during Britain's early colony-building period. The example illustrated **(coin 107)** is the large-planchet variety, the obverse depicting a pine tree on a base flanked by two pellets, with MASATHVSETS.IN around the perimeter. At the reverse's center, the date 1652 / XII, and around the perimeter, NEWENGLAND:AN:DOM. This coin was struck between 1667 and 1682.

The Pine Tree shilling is a classic of early American coinage. It is surprising that the law-abiding Pilgrim founders of the Massachusetts Colony dared coin money at all; at the time this was a jealously guarded prerogative of kings. In 1629, the founders of the colony were granted a royal charter allowing them certain rights and powers to govern the colony's affairs. There was nothing in the charter (explicit or implied) to suggest that coining was permitted. By contrast, coining was specifically allowed in the charter granted to Lord Cecil Calvert, the founder of Maryland.

The colonists were more than likely motivated to produce coins by the myriad problems created by the glut of foreign, English, token, and other local currencies then serving as New England's "coin of the realm." Widespread use of non-standard currency made it susceptible to the problems of "bad money." The New England colony's earliest coin consisted of a plain round blank of silver with NE stamped in one corner. It was highly prone to clipping and forgery. Records suggest that the problems inherent with non-standardized coin were seriously affecting

Coin 107: Pine Tree shilling, Massachusetts Colony (shown enlarged on page 181)

Coin 105: 5 guineas of Queen Anne, Great Britain This is a rare and impressive memento from Britain's commercial wars against Spain and its possessions. The 5-guineas piece, now the largest of Britain's gold coins, was struck from treasure seized in 1702 in Vigo Bay, Spain, during the War of Spanish Succession.

Boston's growing trade economy. The Pine Tree (and its predecessors, the Oak Tree and Willow Tree issues) proved a successful currency. So many of these coins were struck that huge quantities were exported back to London. Despite the fact that their manufacture spanned 30 years, these coins are all dated 1652. This may have been a wise precautionary measure on the part of the colony governors. Should King Charles II eventually learn of the unauthorized minting, he might be lulled into believing that it was only produced as a brief emergency issue, since the coins bore the date of a single year only.

The Netherlands

The Dutch nation was born during this troubled era, and symbolized both the best and worst of the times. The northern lowlands, comprising modern-day Belgium and the Netherlands, bore witness to a long, bloody, and turbulent history. In the early 16th century, Holy Roman Emperor Charles V (Hapsburg) gained possession of the lands. In 1555 he divided his estates among his sons, granting Spain and the Netherlands to his eldest, Philip II. Protestantism had already made significant inroads in the area and Philip felt dutybound to repress this heresy. Earlier grievances and political friction, combined now with vigorous religious suppression, made for 80 years of open revolt and rebellion (1568–1648).

In 1609, weakened by constant warring with England, France, and the Netherlands, with its area shipping overwhelmed by the aggressive maritime skills of the Dutch, Spain called for a truce. Although an actual treaty was not formalized until 1648, Spain was forced to tacitly acknowledge the independence of the Netherlands. This tentative acceptance of independence ushered in the Dutch *Gouden Eeuw* (Golden Age). After years of turmoil, destruction, and death, with this respite the Dutch experienced an almost explosive release of long pent-up energy. The nation all at once threw itself into exploration, art, science, and especially trade. The sudden and aggressive success of Dutch commercial endeavors soon instilled envy, and then fear, into the heart of the major supporter of its earlier rebellion—Britain. The 17th and 18th centuries would see four Anglo-Dutch wars fought over shipping and commercial rights.

As to be expected, the fuel propelling this "Golden Age" was money: money and goods that poured in from newfound overseas possessions,

Coin 106: crown of George II, Great Britain Struck in silver from booty garnered by Captain George Anson in South America, this coin is believed to be from the presentation set of Lima coins given by Anson to the captain of his treasure ship from the anti-Spanish expedition.

Coin 107: Pine Tree shilling, Mass-achusetts Colony Here is a particularly fine example of a Pine Tree shilling. This and its earlier brethren issues, the Willow and Oak Tree series, were coins of necessity (and probably illegal) that were struck by the colony over a 30-year period. Curiously all issues bear the date of 1652.

Coin 108: 3 gulden, Holland

Coin 109: Lionthaler, Netherlands

along with coin and bullion coming into the area because of Spain's continued aggressions in the southern Netherlands. The region was awash with ducats and doubloons, talers and reales—the Dutch made good use of them. By the mid-17th century the independent Netherlands was the foremost commercial and maritime power of Europe, and Amsterdam was the financial center of the Continent. Meanwhile, the southern Netherlands was still afflicted by Spanish repression. The resulting exodus of many of its intellectual, cultural, and financial elite to the northern free Netherlands contributed greatly to the Dutch Golden Age.

Dutch coin at this time was a sturdy, no-nonsense currency. Not especially beautiful, it was eminently adaptable for commerce. An exception is this finely styled provincial 3-gulden piece from Holland (**coin 108**). A Dutch maiden, represented as the Greek goddess Pallas Athena (warlike, but also noted for wisdom and prudence), is shown on the obverse. On the reverse, a heraldic rampant lion within a beaded circle appears. The coin is a rare, one-year type, with superbly engraved dies by Drappentier, and is truly suggestive of Dutch affluence.

By contrast, one of the true workhorses of Dutch currency was the famed Lionthaler, or Leeuwendaalder (**coin 109**). The constant demand for it is evident in the sloppy workmanship the coin often displayed, indicating mass production focused not on quality but on quantity. On the obverse, a knight in period armor stands behind a shield bearing a lion. The reverse bears the same lion, rampant, and the date of 1648 above. The coin illustrated here is an unusually fine example of the type.

The Lionthaler represented the archetypal Dutch trade coin. The first specimens appeared in Holland in 1575 during the war of independence. The seven free provinces struck various similar versions. While the type was devised as uniform coinage, it displayed obvious nationalistic intent. The coin was created to serve as a local currency, but through the travels of Dutch maritime traders it became one of the most widely used trade currencies in the Mediterranean, especially the Levant. Where trade was concerned, Dutch merchants played second or third fiddle to Venice, then foremost in Near Eastern trading (followed by Britain or France), often acting as trans-shippers for the Venetians. In 1590 there were more than 20 Flemish (southern Netherlander) merchant firms located in Venice. These firms managed to thrive by strong business rela-

Coin 108: 3 gulden, Holland The Dutch had an efficient coinage, eminently suitable for commerce and not especially noted for its beauty. An exception is this 3 gulden of Holland, struck from fine dies by Drappentier.

Coin 109: Lionthaler, Netherlands The numismatic workhorse of Dutch commerce was the Lion daalder, this one struck at Utrecht. It became the preferred trading coin in the Levant and eastern Mediterranean, but also saw service in the New World possessions of the Dutch. Like the earlier Venetian ducat, and the later Maria Theresa talers, it too was copied and imitated.

tionships with the Italians and the useful association with Dutch shipping firms. Prior to 1599, there appears to be little or no direct contact between Dutch merchants and the Levantine trade centers of the Ottoman Empire. After the truce of 1609, however, Spain removed many of the economic and political obstacles that had hindered the Dutch Republic. Armed with silver and spices (wrested from the Portuguese), Dutch merchants forcefully entered the eastern Mediterranean trade. Later events only increased their opportunities there—the Turko-Venetian war and the English civil war decreased the presence of both maritime competitors for some time.

Some of the luxury goods accessed by the Dutch proved extremely profitable—coffee and tulips, for example. Their large silver daalders quickly became the coin of choice of Muslim merchants, alongside the venerable gold ducat/zecchins of Venice. As with the later Maria Theresa talers, success bred imitation and a number of countries struck their own replicas of the coin, notably the Italian and German states. The Lion-thaler also saw service in North America, mixing with the Dutch currency used in New Netherlands, whose capital, New Amsterdam, would later become New York.

Coin 110: kroon, Netherlands

The excessively rare kroon, or reaal, of 48 stuivers (coin 110) of the Netherlands East India Company is another important coin of Dutch trade. This coin was one of the earliest locally produced currencies used for the Netherlands' Southeast Asia trade. The obverse bears an upright sword with a filleted laurel wreath behind, with BATAVIAE ANNO 1645 around the perimeter. The reverse has the Verenigde Oostindische Compagnie (VOC) monogram with the value above, and four arabesques around the perimeter.

The kroon was the first silver dollar-sized coin minted in the Orient. To combat a local shortage of silver in the Dutch Indies, pieces having a value of 12, 24, and 48 stuivers were cast locally to the somewhat lighter standard of the Spanish real. The real was equal in weight to seven-eighths of a Lionthaler. The coins were eventually withdrawn from circulation in 1647 due to problems with counterfeiting.

In 1602, the Dutch government had encouraged merchants trading in the East Indies to form the VOC (Dutch East India Company), and extended them a virtual monopoly of all trade and shipping outside the Atlantic Ocean. During its nearly 200-year history, the VOC became the

Coin 110: kroon, Netherlands
The VOC kroon was the first silver dollar-sized coin minted in the Orient, and also the first round silver coin made anywhere in the Orient. Issued to combat a local shortage of silver in the Dutch Indies, the cast coins were eventually withdrawn from circulation in 1647 due to problems with forgery.

Coin 111: ducatone, Austrian Netherlands

largest company of its kind and one of the most profitable, trading in spices such as nutmeg, cloves, cinnamon, and pepper, and other high-value/low-weight goods such as tea, silk, porcelains, and coffee. The VOC soon dominated the Eastern spice trade, eventually eliminating English and Portuguese competition altogether. From 1641 onward, the VOC established a trade monopoly with Japan, forcing out not only English and Portuguese competition, but that of the Spanish as well. By the 17th century, the VOC was the most important European company in the Asia trade, boasting more than 150 merchant ships, numerous warships, upwards of 50,000 employees, and a private army of 10,000 soldiers. The success of the company cannot solely be attributed to its extraordinary business acumen. Violence, or the threat of violence, aimed against local populations was often employed. In 1619 the VOC captured the Javanese city of Jakarta, burned it to the ground, and set up a new trading center it called Batavia.

The ducatone, originating in the non-Dutch Low Countries of the Austrian Netherlands, a commonly used coin during this time, was a holdover from the time of Spanish rule. This piece (**coin 111**) was struck by Maria Theresa (1740–1780), and dated 1747. The obverse shows a pleasant portrait of the youthful Austrian empress, and the reverse a crowned shield of arms. Its inclusion here is because it can be thought of as a younger, more petite "prototype" for the most famous silver trade coin in world history—the Maria Theresa taler.

With the Spanish finally removed from the picture, the lowlands of the southern Netherlands transferred in 1714 to the Austrian branch of the House of Hapsburg by means of the Peace of Utrecht. The "Peace" was actually a series of treaties that put an end to the French expansionism that had plagued Europe since the Thirty Years' War. As part of its arrangements, Spain allowed Britain sole rights to the slave trade in Spanish America, clearing the way for the rise of the British Empire. Austria didn't get to keep her territories for long, however. In 1795 Napoleon Bonaparte warred with Austria repeatedly—always to the latter's detriment. Out of this the Low Countries were seized and then merged to the Netherlands, with Napoleon installing his younger brother, Louis, as king over the greater Netherlands. Following the demise of Napoleon's empire, the whole of the Netherlands was incorporated into the United Kingdom of the Netherlands. In 1830, however,

Coin 111: ducatone, Austrian Netherlands This is an earlier version of the most successful trade coin in history. Maria Theresa's silver coins bearing her aged and veiled portrait were highly esteemed and desired throughout the Near East, Arabia, and portions of Africa. Her Austrian taler, dated 1780, has been in continuous production for more than 225 years!

the unhappy Belgians seceded from the union, with Luxembourg following suit not long after.

Meanwhile, returning to Maria Theresa, as the beneficiary of the Pragmatic Sanction brought about by her father, Charles IV, she finally succeeded to her disputed Austrian throne in 1740. As archduchess of Austria, queen of Hungary and Bohemia, and later (through her marriage to Emperor Francis I) Holy Roman Empress, she became the only female ruler in the 650-year history of the Hapsburg dynasty, and one of its most successful rulers, male or female. Despite this, the Holy Roman Empire continued to weaken and the Hapsburg influence was felt less and less outside of Austria's borders. Regardless, Maria Theresa appeared to be involved in every European war, treaty, and other major event occurring during her reign—with her only serious nemesis being the land-grabbing Frederick the Great of Prussia.

> *More than 50 million pounds of silver have been struck with the empress' likeness.*

Even as a reduced "empire," Austrian territories were not wholly land-locked. Austria still ruled Trieste, which provided access to the Adriatic, eastern Mediterranean, and ports further east. Austrian merchants did a lucrative trade in coffee, and the talers utilized during Maria Theresa's 40-year reign became well received, even preferred to the exclusion of other currencies in Arabia, the Ottoman Near East, and parts of Africa, especially the north. The empress' death in 1780 required the inevitable change of design and portrait, even though her aged, benign face on the silver coins was equated in the Muslim world with reliability and trustworthiness. Concerned, the silver and coin merchants of Augsburg petitioned her son, Emperor Joseph II, to allow his mother's 1780 talers to continue in production. Joseph gave his consent, allowing that they might be struck for the trade within the Levant, "as long as there is a need."

The coins have been in continuous production for more than two centuries from mints across the globe. Chester Krause and Clifford Mishler, in their catalog of world coins, estimated a total mintage of around 800 million pieces. If correct, this would mean that more than 50 million pounds of silver have been struck bearing the likeness of Maria Theresa of Austria!

Southern Europe

In southern Europe, Italy remained an important and influential commercial center. Even though the Americas were discovered by an Italian, the shift in European economies towards the New World eventually reduced the wealth and political significance of Italian mercantile centers.

Italy of old was home to several maritime republics, including Venice, Pisa, and Amalfi. Venice was the most powerful of these oligarchic states and the gold ducat, later termed *zecchin*, was the city-state's supreme coin of the international commercial world. Second only to Venice was Genoa, another maritime republic. Situated high on the northwest coast of Italy, its origins preceded those of Venice by many centuries. As economic rivals, the Genovese proved equally fierce and combative, engaging in numerous commercial wars with the Venetians. Genoa's respected banking houses played an important economic role in the history of that state, and one of the first incorporated banks in the world was found within the city.

The financial heyday of Genoa occurred during the late-16th and early-17th centuries, and was intimately connected to the imperial and fiscal business of Spain. During this troubled time, Spain suffered several bankruptcies and the Crown found itself unable to repay the loans of its German bankers. Afterwards, Spain found potential lenders increasingly reluctant to do business with it. The expenses of the Netherlands war needed to be met, however, and payment in specie and transfers of funds had to be easily managed. Since the English were supportive of the Dutch rebels, the waters of the north became off limits to Spain. The best alternative route was by way of Italy. The relationship resulted in a new source of loans for Spain and a boost for the Italian economy, which had been showing signs of stagnation. The taler-like scudo, coined sporadically in Italy, soon became plentiful. Italy's busy mints generally produced efficient, workaday products, often lacking in grace. Not so with the quaint issues of Genoa. The handsome scudo largo seen here **(coin 112)**, is nearly twice as heavy as a single scudo. The obverse shows a nimbus-crowned Virgin among the clouds, the infant Jesus at her side flanked by two cherubim. The reverse is engraved with a voided cross and delightful cherub heads in the angles.

Another port republic, that of Livorno, rose to power later than its sister cities. One of its large silver coins, a tollero (tallero) is illustrated

Coin 112: scudo largo, Genoa
(shown enlarged on page 189)

here (**coin 113**). The obverse is resplendent with an almost humorous portrait of the portly and portentous Cosimo III de Medici (1670–1723), one of the last direct scions of the famed Florentine merchant-banking family. He is depicted in the manner of an ancient Roman emperor—with radiate crown and armored bust right. The coin's large size provides the perfect format to depict the enlarged and renovated harbor of Livorno on the reverse. The scene not only shows the city's fortress and watchtowers, but the multi-oared galley ships, the notorious slave-driven workhorses of Venice's shipping industry, as well. The coin's commercial status is implied by its "tollero" designation. Thus its equivalency to the German taler, or Dutch daalder.

Coin 113: tollero, Livorno

Looking for a coastal outlet with maritime access, the republic of Florence purchased Livorno in 1421. The rise and the fortunes of the city soon became inextricably intertwined with those of the Medici family, long one of the most important in Tuscany. The Medicis eventually transformed the republic of Florence into a ducal state, ruled by hereditary succession until the 18th century. Developing the commercial potential of Livorno became a pet project of the Medicis, and in 1571 Cosimo I de Medici started the construction of the Porto Mediceo.

Livorno soon became known for its multi-ethnic, cosmopolitan character—quite unique for its time. In an effort to increase population and to recruit entrepreneurs, shippers, merchants, shipwrights, carpenters, sailors, and bankers, the dukes of Florence repeatedly granted protection, tax exemptions, and asylum to the persecuted and to those who may have had brushes with justice in their own countries.

Foreign émigrés invited by the Medici dukes included the Spanish, Portugese, and Germans. Remarkably, Jews from the Levant along with the Marranos (Jews evicted from Portugal and Spain) were also welcomed into Livorno. Perhaps more surprising was the wide range of privileges they were granted. Ferdinand I de Medici's charter offered Jewish immigrants religious freedom, amnesty from previous crimes, full Tuscan citizenship, and special courts with civil and criminal jurisdictions. Cosimo I, himself a merchant, recognized the vast potential of Jewish capital and entrepreneurs to benefit his port city. Not all was bliss, however. Cosimo's liberalism was limited in scope and pragmatic in principle. In practice, Medici rule was characterized by a shifting balance of privileges and concessions—a cyclical mix of status and repression.

Coin 112: scudo largo, Genoa
A number of Italian maritime republics dominated Mediterranean commerce for centuries. The greatest of all was Venice, with Genoa running a close second. During their heyday the two often tangled with each other in vicious commercial wars.

Coin 113: tollero, Livorno Livorno was a latecomer to Italy's important maritime centers. Due to the vision of the Medici family, who developed and enlarged the port, the city became remarkable in its time for its highly cosmopolitan and multi-ethnic character.

This unusual aspect of Livorno illustrates a recurring theme during the period of this chapter: the status of Jewry in Europe—especially as the social and political stature of some elements were increasing considerably throughout the era. Jews and Christians were uneasy bedfellows at the beginning of the Christian era—both groups being generally detested and misunderstood in the Roman world. Later, with the spread of Christianity and the rise of Islam, Jewish businessmen moved into areas of commerce such as banking and moneylending—professions discouraged by both Bible and Koran. This occurred in part because Jews were often forbidden to hold land or practice the more "acceptable" types of economic enterprise. Even though their financial services were widely used, Jews were still condemned for providing these very services. Their commercial and metallurgic skills did attract some degree of acceptance and status. In numismatic history, Jewish coiners and mint-masters can be traced back as early as the reign of the Frankish king Chilperic I (561–584). Jewish names are found on a number of medieval Islamic issues and the early coins of both Silesia and Poland. Some of the gold issues of Spain's Pedro the Cruel bear the initial of his chief treasurer and financial wizard, the Jewish Samuel Halevi Abulafia of Toledo.

The romance between the Jews and Spain ended in 1492, when Ferdinand and Isabella cast them out of the country during the *Reconquista* (re-conquest) of Spain from the Moors. What incipient damage this might have done to Spain's economy with the loss of this important middle class was masked by the influx of gold and silver starting to pour in from the New World. Spain again shot itself in the foot, economically speaking, a century later when Philip III expelled another industrious middle-class group, the Moriscos—Moors who had converted to Christianity after the Christian re-conquest.

The resulting flood of Jewish immigrants was not kindly received by the rest of Europe. Martin Luther's vitriolic anti-Semitic writings did nothing to engender the welcome of Jews among the adherents of his heretical "Protestant" religion. However, conditions were changing. With the rise of nationalism and the growth of absolutist monarchies, princes and rulers came to consider the Jews as a valuable resource, eventually welcoming them into the territories of Prussia, Hamburg, Frankfurt, Brandenburg, Pomerania, and Venice. Of course this welcome had numerous strings attached. Still viewed as socially and religiously suspect, the daily life of the Jews was highly regulated. The practice of confining Jews in walled quarters (ghettos), where they remained locked up at night, was common in Central and Eastern Europe. The Dutch, who had endured nearly a century of religious persecution from Spain, were more tolerant and provided a safe haven. Amsterdam in particular profited from their presence. Even Cosimo III, the most bigoted of the Medici grand dukes, realized the importance of Jews to Livorno's commercial life, and refrained from tampering with that asset too severely. Europe would still be wrestling with a satisfactory solution to the Jewish "problem" at the close of the 18th century. It would be a few more generations before a final solution was devised.

Back to Cosimo III briefly: as a ruler, he can be considered a blight on his duchy and his subjects. As a good Catholic in the Hapsburg manner, he sought to enforce purity of thought (and religion) in his territories. Preceding grand dukes had protected the likes of a Galileo from the Church, but under Cosimo scholars and philosophers were tortured by the Inquisition. His restrictions and taxes interfered with the productivity of his domains, and hastened the decline of Tuscany. Shortly after Cosimo's death Tuscany was eventually given to Francis of Lorraine, an Austrian duke, as part of the settlement resulting from the War of Polish Succession.

The Papal States

In Rome, the papacy, the spiritual force that for centuries had directed, influenced, or manipulated European politics, entered a period of slow decline. Two hundred years earlier, the territorial ambitions of Pope Julius II (the patron of Michelangelo) bordered on naked aggression, yet his fervent concern for the welfare of the Church elicited both fear and admiration. By the late 17th century, however, the Church's passion for Reformation had begun to slow, and its worldly influence was starting to dim. Despite this, the papacy continued relevant to important issues during this period.

Over the centuries papal coinage was serviceable, fairly attractive, and, on occasion, masterful. Its first taler or crown-sized coin appeared in 1579. The adoption of machine striking greatly enhanced papal minting. When the Holy See combined this with the regular employment of gifted die engravers such as Giuseppe Ortolani and the Hamerani family

Coin 114: piastra, Papal States

Coin 115: novodel ruble, Russia
(shown enlarged on page 197)

(medallists and coin engravers employed for nearly two centuries at the Papal Zecca of Rome), papal coinage experienced a metamorphosis. The much improved craftsmanship lent the papal issues an elegance truly worthy of the prestige and dignity of the Holy Church. This large silver piastra (**coin 114**) of Pope Innocent XII is a handsome example of what papal coinage had become.

In his coin portrait, Innocent XII is finely rendered, his benevolence and piety almost palpable. The coin is dated Year III on the obverse and stamped 1693 on the reverse. Also depicted on the reverse is the sedate image of Charity as a mature woman with children about her. Her presence is enlivened by the almost fevered rendering of the folds of her garment, a clear indicator of the Baroque art trends then ascendant. The inscription, Latin for "The just man understands the cause of the poor," is truly applicable to the views of this most admirable pope.

Immediately after his election, Innocent XII issued a papal bull forthrightly declaring against the practice of nepotism in the papacy, one of the Church's greatest scandals. In addition to other public benevolences, he proved instrumental in raising monies for Leopold I of Austria. This papal assistance helped to bring about the decisive victory against the Turks by Prince Eugene of Savoy in 1697. Just like the propagandistic coins of the ancient Roman emperors, these later military successes played across the coins and medals of papal Rome.

Russia and Sweden

Further to the north, Russia, led by Peter the Great (1682–1725), was gaining as an important regional power. This gold strike (**coin 115**) of Peter's new ruble denomination is perhaps most evocative of the country's latent strength. The obverse shows the youthful bust of Peter facing right, wearing an ornately embellished leather breastplate. The reverse displays the Russian imperial double-headed eagle crowned and clutching a scepter and orb in its claws. One of only two examples known to exist, this coin is heavier than the other specimen. Undoubtedly, this carefully preserved ruble was created to be presented to an important individual as a gift of state and was struck to a gold weight of 13 ducats.

Strong, gifted, visionary, and exceptionally intelligent, Peter stands out in an era noted for its "enlightened despots." Concerned about his country's backwardness and its relationship to the West, he began his

Coin 114: piastra, Papal States
During the afternoon years of the Papal
State, its coinage achieved an artistry and
sophistication that made it among the most
handsome of all the Italian issues.

reign by devoting himself to modernizing Russia in every aspect: culturally, technologically, and especially militarily. Peter managed to implement these and other changes without borrowing money from the state. He merely taxed his citizens heavily instead.

Among Peter's great reforms was the transformation of Russia's old-fashioned coinage system into one of the most up to date in Europe. Initially, he inherited a system dominated by primitive little kopecks crudely struck on segments of silver wire, along with Russian-counter-marked foreign ducats, and talers. In 1704, Peter decreed the ruble to be the state unit of account and downvalued it to equal one taler. Even more remarkable, his was the first coinage to be ordered on the decimal system—dividing the ruble into 100 smaller units of copper kopecks.

In this period of war mongering and power politics the fanciful gold double ducat (coin 116) of Sweden's Karl XII (1697–1718) might serve as a parable for the luck and durability of the mighty and powerful. The humorous, almost naive-style, obverse die was by J. Memmius of Stettin. The king stands right in a fur-lined jacket with large bosses and buttons, hair upswept. In one hand he clutches a short baton or telescope, in his other a sword with a huge pommel. Some thought the young king mad—the remarkable coiffure and garish ensemble seen on this coin do seem suggestive. In the propagandistic tradition of the Romans, the reverse displays a lion standing left on a ledge between two pillars, toppling one, the second already broken. Inscribed below: CONCVSSIT VTRAMQVE. In effect, the inscription reads: "One Breaks, and So the Other." The reverse motif was most likely borrowed from the Biblical episode detailing Samson's destruction of the temple of the Philistines. This remarkable scene both boasts of Karl's accomplishments as king, and avows his future intentions.

Sweden had long been a significant regional power but during the 17th century, under King Gustavus II Adolphus, her importance increased dramatically. For his intervention on behalf of the Protestant states during Germany's Thirty Years' War, he was awarded both the important Baltic port of Stettin, and the eastern portion of Pomerania. Situated in northeast Germany, Pomerania stretched along the Baltic Sea from Mecklenburg, on the west, almost to modern-day Gdansk, in Poland. The land had a tumultuous history and had long been desired by Sweden and Denmark due to Stettin's access to the Baltic Sea. Whoever controlled Stettin also controlled

Coin 116: gold 2 ducats, Swedish Pomerania

Coin 115: novodel ruble, Russia
An exceedingly rare gold strike of Peter the Great's new silver ruble, dated 1705 in the Russian manner. It is said that Peter was so proud of his improved coinage that when the first ruble coins bearing Western-style Arabic dates were struck in 1707, it was Peter himself who was operating the coin press!

Coin 116: gold 2 ducats, Swedish Pomerania Karl's fanciful double ducat is a classic example of a ruler employing his coinage for propaganda and political posturing. The reverse refers to his success in felling one ruler (Poland), with an avowal of intent to do the same to another (Russia).

the very lucrative sea trade between Russia and western Europe. Throughout the 16th and 17th centuries, Sweden frequently clashed with its neighbors while empire-building in this area.

Karl XII succeeded his father as king of Sweden at the age of 15. His competitors sensed an advantage against the underage king, and an alliance was formed between Russia, Denmark, Norway, and Poland in order to try and re-take some of the Swedish territories. The alliance attacked in 1700, and so began the Great Northern War (1700–1721). Sweden received occasional aid from the Ottoman Turks throughout the conflict.

Initially Sweden achieved a string of victories, defeating the Russians and ousting the Polish king, August II. The latter victory is symbolized by the broken pillar on the Swedish two-ducat piece. Unfortunately for the headstrong Karl, he often passed up opportunities to arrange treaties with his adversaries on terms favorable to his country. When a treaty was eventually orchestrated in 1706, it proved to be of no advantage to Sweden.

The temporary cessation of hostilities allowed Russia's Peter the Great to rebuild his forces and navies (Peter was the intended second broken column depicted on the Swedish coin). When Karl attacked Russia directly he met with defeat, much in the manner Napoleon would experience a century later. Karl fled to the Ottomans and sought refuge there for several years. Sweden's defeat reverberated throughout Europe, and Russia was suddenly transformed into a significant power and noteworthy opponent.

When Karl returned to Sweden in 1714, he found himself at war against all of Northern Europe. He was fatally wounded on December 11, 1718, during the siege of Fredriksten in Norway, and his death ushered in the rapid fall of Sweden as a leading world power. Ultimately, the final treaty to the war deprived Sweden of its empire. By the 19th century, Sweden was considered one of the poorest countries in Europe. In politics, it seems nothing is forever, even for the mighty and powerful.

CHAPTER SIX

AN AGE *of* REVOLUTION 1776–1914

Richard G. Doty

REVOLUTION:

Noun. A turning over in the mind or in discussion; a winding or curving form of course.

That was how the world defined the word in the middle of the 18th century. It would shortly acquire other, expanded meanings and usages. My task is to show how all this took place, and what it meant for that most human of commodities, our money.

We shall examine a series of coins, struck between 1776 and 1914. Even in human terms (let alone geologic ones), this span of time is scarcely more than the blink of an eye; indeed, there were a few old men still living at the end of the period whose fathers were born near its beginning. But time, like size, sometimes matters and sometimes doesn't. And this was one of those occasions when it mattered very greatly.

We know where we are now. We know, vaguely at least, how we arrived here. But where did we start out? Where did our journey begin? It may be useful to provide a very quick sketch, in very broad strokes, of the world, and its money, before all the changes began.

Europe was at the center of everything—just ask any European! That continent was somewhat more at the center of events then than now, at least in political and economic terms, in comparison with the rest of the world. The Western Hemisphere was of economic importance, to be sure, but its political importance was negligible. Asia was immense. But Asia was very far away, looked inward, and occasioned little comment elsewhere. Africa was where you got people and products—otherwise a Dark Continent and likely to remain that way. Oceania was partly rumored, partly explored, but of no immediate importance to anyone except the locals.

That left Europe, or rather Western and Central Europe. Eastern Europe went on indefinitely until colliding with Asia; but it had an influence almost inversely proportionate to its size. Nothing much had ever happened there, so nothing much ever would.

Case in Point: Great Britain

Thus the world of the mid-18th century. Let's go in closer for a moment. Let's look at one country in particular, one for which we have a good deal of data. Let's look at Great Britain.

By 1775, the country was home to about nine million people. Most of them lived in the south and east—that's where the money and the jobs were. The largest city, then as now, was London, which dwarfed everyplace else with some 800,000 inhabitants. It had no real competitors, and the next tier would not appear on anybody's list today—Bristol came in second, then Norwich, then Newcastle, and so on down to a congeries of busy but tiny market towns. Places like Birmingham, Manchester, Hull, and Sheffield were not major players—not yet. Their time would come later, reflection of the revolution about to get under way.

The country was still predominantly rural—amazingly so, to our 21st-century eyes. Most people worked the land for themselves or for others, lived on small farms or in villages, from which they departed and to which they returned, day after day. And the days were long, running from "can to can't"—from the time when there was light enough to work outdoors to the time when there wasn't. Families were large in the country, somewhat smaller in the cities and towns; and if you were lucky, and healthy, you might live to see 60.

While Britons cherished their antient (that was often how the word *ancient* was spelled, back then) liberties (and were prone to annoy foreigners with their constant repetition), the fact was that Great Britain was ruled by a king (who had far more absolute authority than is commonly imagined) and an aristocracy (that enjoyed most of the powers denied to or overlooked by the king). The average man had little say in the running of things, and the average woman had none at all. But the man, at least, would have probably tugged on his forelock (women don't have forelocks; everybody knows that) and observed that it was all for the best anyway, and all part of God's plan.

In comparison with their Continental counterparts, Britons *were* marginally better off. They made slightly more money than did Frenchmen or Germans, a good deal more than Spaniards or Italians. And there were no bondsmen in Great Britain (except for African slaves, and there were stirrings even here); but there were still serfs in parts of Central and all of Eastern Europe. Political expression and power was even more jealously guarded on the mainland than it was on the islands, leading to an inevitable lack of what we would call Progress. The poet Heinrich Heine was speaking of his own land, but he might have been speaking of the whole of Europe. He claimed of Germany snoring:

She slept peacefully under the protection of her thirty-six monarchs. In those days, crowns sat firmly on princes' heads, and at night they just drew

their night caps over them, while the people slept peacefully at their feet.

So it was through the first two-thirds of the 18th century.

There is a last observation to be made. It will give us a final grounding on a number of points, and it will introduce us to the first of our visual witnesses, the first of a series of coins that will carry us from a world we have lost to a world that is still with us.

The coin is a taler, dated 1777 (**coin 117**). Talers were a logical outgrowth of the discovery of rich silver deposits in Middle Europe in the later medieval period. The dramatic increase in the amount of available silver inspired mints to create larger, more valuable coins. Some of the new pieces were created from silver from the fabulously wealthy Joachimsthal mine. The name *Joachimsthaler* ("from [St.] Joachim's Valley") was soon applied to this new coin, heralding its purity and value. But the name was eventually shortened to *taler* and applied to any silver coin with rough equivalence to the prototype. And from there, the coin, and its name, traveled west, and south, and eventually overseas, becoming the *daalder*, *daler*, *tallero*, and finally *dollar*.

Coin 117: silver taler, Germany

Our coin is a typical product of the 18th century. At first glance, we see a majestic portrait of a monarch on its obverse; a marvelously ornate crowned shield, with lion and unicorn supporters, on its reverse. But look more closely. This coin has much to say, and while some of its narrative will be found in its designs, rather more of it will be found in the words it contains, and proclaims.

The man on the obverse looks familiar, and the accompanying legend gives the game away. Translated, it reads "George III by the Grace of God King of Great Britain, France, and Ireland, Defender of the Faith." This is the monarch Americans loved to hate: wicked, mad King George.

The arms on the reverse look familiar too—at least, most of them do. There are the lions of England and Scotland, the harp of Ireland, and the lilies of France, this last still claimed by Great Britain. The lower-right quartering is a puzzle, but the reverse legend will solve it.

That legend continues the list of real estate begun on the obverse. In addition to being king of Great Britain, Ireland, and France, George III

Coin 117: silver taler, Germany

George III, most famous as the king of
England, was also the duke of Brunswick-
Lüneburg, and elector (and later king) of
Hanover. It is in his Continental role that
George appears on this silver coin, which is
not English but German.

is also "Duke of Brunswick-Lüneburg, Archtreasurer and Elector of the Holy Roman Empire." The mystery of the fourth quartering is explained: these are the symbols of Mad George's holdings in Germany.

We would call this coin a hybrid. It looks British, depicts a British king and British arms (and supporters: the lion and unicorn go to the heart of Merrie England), even bears a mostly British legend. But then again . . . it was minted in Germany and struck to German weights and standards. Exactly whose coin is it?

It's *George's* coin, of course, and that's the whole point. Prior to the Age of Revolution, monarchy was transnational. Monarchs were not necessarily attached to people; indeed, people could be transferred from one monarch to another, a species of intelligent, movable property. The ruler's transnationality was one of the first casualties of the Age of Revolution, and all the force and good intentions in the world would never revive it.

The German coin serves as our preface. Now let's get on with the story.

Themes in the Tapestry of Revolution

I want to examine what I consider the major threads or building blocks of an unsettled age; I want to do so through numismatics. My major components of the Age of Revolution are

- Revolutionaries: first hopes, immortal ideas
- Setbacks, or, the pendulum goes both ways
- Revolution, idealism, national identity
- Going global: new money in new places
- The industrialization of money, from one place to every place
- Modern money's worldwide sway—and what happened next.

A writer once referred to the revolutions of 1848 as the "springtime of the peoples." He was thinking of the birth of nationalism, but he was also thinking in terms of hope, of change, of possibility. Perhaps human history wasn't cyclical after all. Perhaps the race wasn't doomed to mindlessly repeat its mistakes until it guttered out at last. Perhaps things could actually get *better* for the planet and its suffering inhabitants.

Hope was the first and most important component of the Age of Revolution. There was almost something organic about it. It first sent out cautious shoots, so fragile and pale that they almost weren't there. Then it got a bit bolder—a bit more confident—and its strength and faith grew. The process continued, accelerating, deepening. And by the time it was finished, anything seemed possible.

It is said that success has many parents. So does hope, revolutionary hope. Most right-thinking inhabitants of the 18th century would have looked to Europe, perhaps to Great Britain (or to one of those countries with self-proclaimed enlightened monarchs) for the seeds of political change. They were most unlikely to look for them beyond Europe—and it is certainly true that the Age of Revolution could have easily begun someplace in the Old World. But it didn't. It began in the New World, among a group of colonies huddling along the Atlantic seaboard. Previously they had belonged to Great Britain. Now they would belong to themselves. And they would set wheels in motion towards a destination that even the most starry-eyed idealist could not imagine, because there was no way of imagining a future so different from all that came before. The human mind simply isn't equipped for that kind of activity.

We all know the basic account of the American Revolution: it used to get drilled into us from grammar school onward, and I can't imagine that today's students can dodge it entirely, even if they so desired. But I want to talk about one aspect of a great event that is *not* generally covered in school or anywhere else. I want to talk about hope, about ideas—and about their joint appearance on the first "American" coin, the Continental dollar.

As Thomas Jefferson later remarked, money is an attribute of sovereignty. Kings strike coins and states issue currency, in part, because it is their right to do so: centuries of tradition have established this prerogative, and whose it is and is not. Princes and states also provide money from necessity. The authorities may circulate money for the economic benefit of their subjects or citizens. But they may also provide it because their money tells the folks at home, and the world at large, that the regime or nation exists, that it's a going concern, and that it has the right to prosper and grow. This second reason for monetary production was far more important in earlier times than it is today, because the tools available for getting out the word were so much more limited then than they are now. Early money proclaimed identity quite as much as it fostered commerce.

In the case of the 13 American colonies (or *states*, as they began calling themselves shortly after the break with Britain), "money" generally meant "paper." The insurgents were heirs to a robust tradition of publicly issued and guaranteed currency going all the way back to 1690: Massachusetts, whose issues began in that year, circulated the first "official" paper money west of China. The other colonies soon followed suit, out of dire necessity. Their economies and populations were growing, but precious metals were in perpetually short supply. Paper money, acceptable in payment of taxes and all private transactions, was a godsend. This local currency had traditionally carried cautious messages of identity and sovereignty. With the bid for independence, the visual and verbal content of this money would be strengthened and expanded, intended to chip away at British resolve and reinforce American resistance.

Very early in the contest, a new player joined the state authorities. This was a loosely organized *national* entity, the Continental Congress. Its first paper money appeared a month or so after the clashes at Lexington and Concord. It was called *Continental Currency*. Continental Currency promised payment in "Spanish milled dollars," the 18th-century term for machine-struck pieces of eight. A wide range of denominations was printed—one- through eight-dollar bills (in an area devoid of coinage, you need odd denominations to make change), plus 20s and 30s. The designs were suggested by Benjamin Franklin, whose old printing house, now called Hall & Sellers, produced the notes. Dollar bills were issued through mid-1776; their production then ceased, not to be renewed until the beginning of 1779. One reason for the paper dollar's disappearance was the growing depreciation of the currency, as an American victory proved elusive: in time, the unit's purchasing power almost reached the vanishing point. But there was more to it than that.

The paper dollar was eliminated because its place would be taken by a *silver* dollar. By the middle of 1776, working contacts had been made with Britain's traditional enemy. French arms shipments were being arranged (though a bogus company called Rodrigue Hortalez et Compagnie, whose driving spirit was Caron de Beaumarchais, better known for his sparkling comedy, *The Marriage of Figaro*). The first volunteers were making the transatlantic crossing, pledging to do their bit to free one people and annoy another. And a loan of silver bullion was in the works, enabling the American insurgents to perform that most sovereign of activities—coin money with their name on it.

In anticipation of a done deal, unidentified patriots sought out a Freehold, New Jersey, engraver named Elisha Gallaudet. Gallaudet was then known for his ornamental cuts for a series of notes issued by the New York Water Works in the early 1770s. Now he was asked to pre-pare artwork for a new medium: he would create the dies for our first coin, the Continental dollar. The new entrant would perform two tasks. It would proclaim American sovereignty, of course. But it would also serve as the linchpin of the insurgent currency system, propping up the Continental notes, demonstrating to all and sundry that they were exactly what they said they were: promises to pay, redeemable in specie, coined money.

In anticipation of the new coin, Hall & Sellers was ordered to omit the paper dollar from its stack of denominations. Meanwhile, Gallaudet set to work engraving dies for the new coins (see **coin 118**).

He was not left to his own devices. He was told to follow designs suggested by Benjamin Franklin. The latter's contributions to the visual expression of ideas has been largely overlooked. But it was Franklin who came up with the first political cartoon in American history (a disjointed snake with the names of each of the colonies and the motto JOIN OR DIE—a reference to the need for unity during an earlier conflict, the French and Indian War). And it was Franklin who suggested the designs for the faces of Continental Currency, whose high-minded vignettes and Latin legends were intended to inspire (but probably did not). When it came to the designs for a new coin, the learned doctor had the inside track. He chose, and Gallaudet obeyed. If the result looked more like artwork for a note than for a coin, both men bore responsibility.

And the designs *had* appeared on paper currency earlier that year. In the late winter of 1776, Hall & Sellers had printed "fractional" currency with the same designs, cut by the same artist—notes worth a sixth, a third, a half, and two-thirds of a dollar. (Beyond attempting to meet the shortage of small change, the odd denominations suggest an attempt to meld an old standard with a new one: the new dollar was tariffed at six old shillings.) Franklin suggested, and Gallaudet engraved, two pictorial ideas, one for each side of the notes. The first was distinctly Franklinian, but the second was very much more.

Coin 118: Continental Dollar, United States of America (shown enlarged on page 209)

For the face of the notes (and the obverse of the coin to come), Franklin placed a sundial in the center, with the sun and the Latin FUGIO to the left, and the words MIND YOUR BUSINESS beneath. The whole is a rebus, a combination of pictures and words (of which the 18th-century wit was fond, none more so than Dr. Franklin); taken together, it means "Time flies [FUGIO], so mind your business." Shades of *Poor Richard's Almanac*! This design has Franklin written all over it.

For the notes' backs (and for the reverse of a coin in gestation), he picked another topic dear to his heart: unity in adversity. He had toyed with the concept by means of the political cartoon mentioned earlier. Now things came to full fruition. He devised a series of rings, each with the name of a state. But these rings were linked (unlike the poor snake, whose body lay in pieces). The point is obvious: these linked rings are immensely strong, far stronger than they would be if taken separately. Unity is essential if freedom is to be won. No one dares make side bets or accommodation with the common foe or the cause is lost. The outer design, then, may be taken as a warning.

The inner design expands on this idea, while making a statement for domestic and foreign consumption. Within a "glory"—a ring of light—we see two messages. An inner legend informs the world that WE ARE ONE, while a surrounding legend proclaims the existence of an AMERICAN CONGRESS. The latter deserves more than a passing glance. It could, and it probably did, refer to the new national governing body, the Continental Congress. But the 18th century would have attached another meaning, one of the utmost importance in time of war. "Congress" also meant a coming together and a blending together in need, and trust, in pursuit of a goal that could be met in no other fashion. So we may interpret this side of the note, or the coin, as a proclamation of strength, of resolve—and of a deep dedication to achieving those goals for which the rings, the states, have joined together. Here are the first concrete results of an Age of Revolution—the depiction of new aspirations and resolve on a new coin of a new realm.

But this first attempt was not the success it was intended to be, and there are many mysteries surrounding it that have never been solved. We assume that Gallaudet struck the new coin, but we don't know where. Numismatic historian Walter Breen thought the artist might have had a screw press set up at his home in Freehold, New Jersey—but if so, what

Coin 118: Continental Dollar, United States of America The *Guide Book of United States Coins* notes that "These coins were struck in pewter, brass, and silver. . . . Brass and silver pieces may have been experimental or patterns." The coin pictured is the "pewter" (or more likely tin) variety.

happened to a piece of machinery large enough to strike a crown-size coin? We don't know how many Continental dollars were struck. We assume that several hundred examples were minted in so-called pewter (actually tin, with perhaps five percent trace elements, especially antimony; an early scholar got the composition wrong and the mistake stuck), a few more in copper and brass, and fewer than half a dozen in silver. We do not know why the various metals were used, and we don't know why, or for what purpose, the pewter strikes were made. It has been hypothesized that all of the pieces in all of the metals were for congressional consideration. If that were the case, it would have made sense for Gallaudet to make most of his coins in the softest of the three metals, for the sake of the dies and the safety of his press. Pewter makes a poor circulating medium. But it does take a lovely impression with a minimum of effort.

> *By 1780 it took 40 paper dollars to buy one Mexican silver dollar. . . .*

All of Gallaudet's efforts went for naught, and it would be nearly two decades before Americans would see another American dollar. The key to everything was the anticipated French bullion. It never arrived, and a realistic attempt to coin could not be pursued. And even if the silver had come to our shores, and Gallaudet had managed to turn it all into dollars, the new coins would soon have gone into hiding—because war's uncertainty began driving down the value of Continental Currency by the autumn of 1777. Depreciation worsened through 1778 and 1779, and by the spring of 1780, it took 40 paper dollars to buy one piece of eight, or Mexican dollar—that is, if you could find anyone gullible enough to agree to the swap. Hard money—specie coinage—cannot survive and circulate under these circumstances. So the Continental dollar stands as the opening salvo in the Age of Revolution, and no more. But that was enough: the Americans won their struggle (with much help from their friends), and the new way of looking at things, at what got put on money and why, at the relation of Man to the King or to the State, at the nature of life and time themselves—all these had time to take root, to grow, and to spread. At home, the return of peace allowed the savaged American monetary system to recover, reform, and expand. An experiment with extreme federalism under the Articles of Confederation led to a backlash and to a new constitution, one shifting many of the bases of power away from the states and towards the national government. One of the rights taken away from the states was the right to make and circulate money, either in the form of coins (several of the states had been doing just that over the past decade) and currency, or "bills of credit," in the words of the 1787 constitution. Of course, that prompted a question: if the states were now out of business, what was left?

The answer was twofold. For the circulation of paper, private banks were allowed in—a few at first, many hundreds in the years to come. And for coinage, the new national government would come to the rescue. Under Alexander Hamilton's prodding, a Mint Act was passed in the spring of 1792. It prescribed the construction of a mint in the federal capital, established the range of denominations and their relation to each other, and had something to say about what would go on the new coins. And with this last, the messages of hope, unity, and a new order received permanent, metallic expression.

The Mint Act stipulated that "an impression emblematic of liberty" grace the obverse of every United States coin—along with the actual word LIBERTY, to underscore the point. The act allowed more latitude for the reverse, traditionally the less important face of a coin. For copper, the denomination within a wreath would do. But for precious metals, an American eagle was mandated. During the first decade of America's federal coinage, both Liberty and her eagle were presented in a number of guises, reflections of our aspirations—and of larger events.

Our first ten-dollar gold piece **(coin 119)**, or *eagle*, is laden with new imagery. On the obverse, a bust of Liberty faces right, her name above, the date below. She wears a conical cap, meant to represent the cloth bonnet given to freed slaves in Roman times: America, then, has a new freedom and a new hope. To her right and left are a total of fifteen stars, one for each of the states. An eagle adorns the reverse—but a special kind of eagle. Unlike the bellicose, heraldic birds that had already dominated European coins for half a millennium, this bird has his wings completely outstretched, his breast exposed: this is a peaceable bird, signifying a country with peaceable intentions. The symbolism concludes with an olive wreath, representing a hopeful plea for peace, clutched in

Coin 119: gold eagle, United States of America (shown enlarged on page 213)

the eagle's beak, and a palm branch, traditional symbol of honor, victory, excellence, upon which the eagle stands. Around the bird, in letters large enough for all to see, is the name of the new country. Optimism, pride, hope: components of this new age, put there for all to see.

And to these elements on American money another would soon be added: a nervous nationalism. Consider a second coin (**coin 120**), struck a few years after the first. Liberty dominates the obverse, but the goddess now seems in tune with contemporary fashion, with her faintly revealing drapery and cleavage. The number of stars has been reduced to thirteen, it being realized that, if a new star were consistently added for each new state, at the rate the country was growing there would soon be room for nothing *but* stars. The rest of the obverse follows standard procedure: Liberty's name above, date beneath. But it is the reverse that claims our attention now, as it was intended to then. Here is no pacific mascot: this bird is defiant, willing to take on all comers, and he wants to tell the world. He first appeared on our precious-metal coinage in 1796, and his sway had become universal by the time this dollar was struck, in 1802. What was going on? America, and her coinage, was reacting to larger events overseas. Ironically, the country itself bore much of the responsibility: once you initiate an Age of Revolution, you cannot be certain where it will go next. The Americans started something, and the French carried it forward.

In backing the Americans in their war for independence, the French had beggared themselves. The Crown ran up deficits year after year, and a series of ingenious reforms and reformers only served to worsen the situation. Had the current king been a tyrant like his great-great-great-grandfather, the imperious Louis XIV, or a roué like his grandfather, Louis XV, he might have ridden roughshod, bribed left and right, and survived. But Louis XVI was neither: he seems to have been a genuinely nice man who happened to be living atop a volcano. Guess what the smart money said. . . .

Louis XVI gave, then tried to take back, then had to give some more, then tried to flee, then was brought back, demoted, and finally executed—all this in the three and one-half years between the summer of 1789 and the winter of 1793. All of this was reflected on French coinage—and something more, something that appeared fairly early and forecast the European course of events over the next century.

Coin 120: silver dollar, United States of America

Coin 119: gold eagle, United States of America Two major types exist of this coin: one with 13 leaves below the eagle, and one with nine leaves. Combined, their mintage was fewer than 5,600 pieces.

Coin 120: silver dollar, United States of America It didn't take long for the eagle on the new country's coinage to take a bold, defiant form.

You have to look closely to see it. Through the middle of 1792, the coins of Louis XVI bear an abbreviated legend—in Latin—proclaiming him king of France and Navarre (a small principality huddling between France and Spain). This was the way matters had always been, both here and throughout the rest of Europe: kings ruled geographical areas. But then Louis' coinage changed. The Latin is gone, and the legend is in the national language. More to the point, it proclaims Louis king of the *French*. The king is now identified with his people, his fortunes linked to theirs. Later members of the House of Bourbon made their best efforts to turn back the clock, but they never succeeded for very long. The other peoples of Europe observed the changing state of affairs, and their monarchs trembled accordingly. The shift from monarchs-and-real-estate to monarchs-and-peoples was well under way by 1800, firmly established in many places after 1850. The change in how kings and subjects viewed each other and their relations and obligations to each other was another step forward, away from the past and towards the future, another of those steps contributing to the Age of Revolution.

The reverses of Louis' coins changed too, reflecting the new state of affairs. The changes there resembled what we just saw: gone were the Latin legends and the lilies of the ruling house. They were replaced by new legends and new images, the latter with a mix of classical and national motifs. And that brings us to our next coin (**coin 121**).

Coin 121: 24 livres, France

It is the equivalent of the old louis d'or (but now called *24 livres*: the king had just been guillotined, and keeping the old name seemed in questionable taste). The coin's designs were a complete departure from what had gone before. A simple wreath with the value dominates the reverse, with the name of a new regime (the French Republic) and a new way of reckoning the date (Year Two: the new revolutionary calendar began with the proclamation of the republic in September 1792). Coins would bear both revolutionary dates and Christian ones for another few months, then shift entirely to the new system—and then back again, a decade of so later under a new set of circumstances.

Greater surprises await us on the obverse. The legend refers directly to the Reign of Law, a deliberate comparison with the evils of the Ancien Regime, when the law was whatever the king said it was. A winged angel dominates this side of the coin. He is a *genius*, a spiritual representation of the French Republic. He was adopted from ancient Roman coinage,

Coin 121: 24 livres, France Struck in 1793, this revolutionary coin replaced the louis d'or, whose royal namesake had been executed that January.

where he often served as *Genio Populi Romani*—Guardian of the Roman People—and for a new regime that liked to think of itself in terms of classical virtue, he was the fittest image imaginable. He is writing on a tablet, inscribed CONSTITUTION: the divine protector will permanently enshrine the fruits of revolution; permanently cloak them in the glory of the Law.

Two subsidiary devices round out the obverse design. To the left, we see the fasces, surmounted with a Liberty cap. The fasces acquired sinister connotations in the 20th century; in the 18th, it was simply a shorthand way of symbolizing popular, collective strength and will. The rooster on the right symbolizes France itself.

By the time this coin was issued, the country was at war with most of the rest of Europe. One senses that the European monarchs put up with and even supported the American Revolution because it weakened Great Britain, the country everyone loved to hate, and because what went on across the Atlantic couldn't conceivably threaten anyone back home. But the French Revolution was back home: France stood at the center of the continent, was large, very populous, and at the moment very, very red—at least in the eyes of neighboring rulers. By mid-1792, France was at war with Austria and Prussia, and the execution of Louis XVI brought other nations into the fray. One was Britain; and while the military genius of an upstart named Buonaparte came extremely close to total victory on several occasions, even he was never able to defeat this island power, who apparently didn't know when to quit.

Buonaparte and a New Revolution in Money

The French Revolution and the rise of Napoleon took coinage much farther into the Age of Revolution. It affected European money in a number of interesting ways. But one of its most curious effects took place across the seas, in the New World. Do you remember that silver dollar with the Screaming Eagle? Why do you suppose this bird replaced its peaceable predecessor? Could there have been any connection between numismatic depiction and larger events?

Recall that France and Britain were at war by early 1793. Consider that this was a *world* war, one that would last, through starts and stops, all the way down to 1815. Now ponder this: France was a land power, while Britain ruled the seas. France could survive indefinitely on her own and neighboring resources, while Britain could not. Finally, add in the fact that the French and the Americans had concluded a formal treaty of alliance in 1778, and that the French now wanted us to make good on our word, as they had on theirs.

The result was a festering quasi-war between France, Great Britain, *and the United States*, wherein each of the Europeans attempted to gain the services of the American merchant marine, the largest unaffiliated carrier of goods. If the Americans assisted their old enemy, they would adversely affect the success of the Gallic war effort. If they aided their new friends-by-treaty, they might threaten the survival of Great Britain herself.

In other words, the stakes were high, and the two sides attempted to cajole or harass the United States into line. Ships were stopped and searched on the high seas. Seamen were removed, claimed as deserters from the British or French navies. A meddlesome diplomat named Edmond Genêt did his best to damage or end America's proclamation of neutrality, eventually sending President Washington into a state bordering on apoplexy. Genêt was threatened with deportation, but he made a plausible case for being allowed to stay on (the government that had appointed him had been overthrown, and he would have faced the guillotine had he gone home). He moved to New York, married an American heiress, and we heard no more about him.

It was within this climate of opinion that the reverse eagle on America's gold and silver changed from friendly to feisty. Meanwhile, public perception and public policy swung back and forth. Americans fought an undeclared naval war with France between 1798 and 1801 (that explains the U.S.S. *Constitution*, which is still afloat today); they eventually went on to fight a much larger war with Great Britain. They did rather better in the first conflict than the second.

It would have been unrealistic to expect that revolution, counterrevolution, and war would not have affected Europe's money. It was modified in a number of ways, some temporary, others more permanent. And the latter would speak to other, greater events, ones that would carry Europe into modern times.

Some of the more ephemeral changes surrounded the fortunes of a professional soldier named Napoleon Buonaparte (or *Bonaparte*: he changed his name to something more French as his star began to rise). Napoleon first came to popular attention in 1795, when he helped save

Coin 122: 6 lira, Cisalpine Republic

Coin 123: 5 francs, France

the Directory, that moderate successor to Robespierre and the other fanatics behind the Reign of Terror. Partly as a reward (and partly to get him out of the country, just in case he harbored political ambitions), Bonaparte was sent to liberate Italy, then largely ruled by Austria and the Papacy. He succeeded brilliantly, and in his wake he left a string of Italian republics, all dependent on continued French assistance for their continued existence. They issued their own coinage, featuring designs borrowed from classical art, bearing high-minded legends and inscriptions. A scudo or six-lira piece from the Cisalpine Republic (**coin 122**) is fairly typical. We see a seated figure representing France (the Gallic rooster on her helmet is a bit of a giveaway), accepting the thanks of a standing Cisalpina for her liberation. The obverse legend repeats the message. The reverse expresses the coin's value and gives the date in a conscious imitation of the French Revolutionary calendar (*Pratile* was the Italian equivalent of *Prairial*, the sixth month of the year). French-supported mini-states were set up from the Swiss border to Naples, and while none of them lasted very long (and while Bonaparte eventually swept all of them together into a new Kingdom of Italy, with himself as head), they did provide food for thought. The temporary states had been set up on the properties of traditional, legitimate monarchs. While the latter might indeed return to power after the defeat of France, they might be sent packing again, this time by the Italian populace itself. And the course of events, especially the temporary creation of a French-backed Kingdom of Italy, inspired dreams of a new, permanent, unified country embracing the entire peninsula. In other words, what happened as an outgrowth of the French wars helped unleash one of the most potent ingredients in the entire Age of Revolution. It helped make nationalism acceptable and desirable, and whatever happened next, there would be no turning back.

Closer to home, Napoleon's victories in the field were matched by his tightening grip on political power. During the second half of the 1790s, France had been ruled by an oligarchic-if-republican regime called the Directory. Late in 1799, Napoleon and his supporters unceremoniously ejected the members of the old government and installed a new one—the Consulate, with the rising star as First Consul. A five-franc silver coin (**coin 123**) dated Year XI (1802/3) shows things in motion. We see a youthful-looking conqueror, his unadorned portrait facing right. As if to

Coin 122: 6 lira, Cisalpine Republic
Napoleon cobbled together the Cisalpine Republic from what had been the duchies of Milan and Modena, the Piedmont province of Novara, the Papal Legations, and other territories comprising some 16,000 square miles and a population of more than three million people. Here, "Cisalpina" thanks France for her liberation.

Coin 123: 5 francs, France In the early years of the new century, Napoleon was First Consul of France—but he would soon wear the mantle of emperor. This coin's date is shown as Year XI of the Revolution.

Coin 124: 5 francs, France

Coin 125: taler, Grand Duchy of Berg

underscore the fact that this was still a government of laws and not of princes, he is referred to by his surname; his job title is spelled out in full, however, as is the name of the issuing authority on the reverse. Within a few years, much but not all of this would change. Napoleon overthrew his own government in 1804, proclaiming the French Empire on the body of the French *Republic*. The obverses of his coins now used his *given* name (princes customarily did so, after all), called him *Emperor* in no uncertain terms—but waffled on the reverses, where the regime remained the French Republic for the next three years. I know of no similar case elsewhere in the annals of numismatics.

In time, the discrepancy was attended to, and Napoleon's obverses and reverses jibed. Our next coin **(coin 124)** is one of the emperor's final issues, created during the famous "Hundred Days" (March–June 1815), when he dramatically returned from exile on the islet of Elba (where he had been relegated by a coalition of outraged European princes: one suspects that they hated him as much for being an upstart as for being a threat to the natural order of things). Except for the date, this is an ordinary French coin of the day, another five-franc piece, with the emperor's laureate head on the obverse (someone once observed that Napoleon had a profile that cried out to be seen on coinage; he did, and it was) with a simple title, the name of the regime, the denomination, and the date on the reverse. Note that the date is again expressed in the traditional fashion. The revolutionary calendar had gone the way of much other baggage from a discredited era.

One of the keys to Napoleon's downfall lay in his loyalty to family. He made a brother-in-law grand duke of Berg, in western Germany. When Berg was absorbed into a new creation, the kingdom of Westphalia, the dispossessed relative was given the kingdom of Naples by way of compensation. A taler from Düsseldorf **(coin 125)** shows him in his first iteration. This is Joachim Murat, who had married Napoleon's sister Caroline. He would have been advised to remain in Germany: they eventually shot him in Italy.

Nor did the emperor forget his blood relatives. To his older brother Joseph he awarded the kingdom of Naples (before it went to Joachim Murat), having dislodged the original, and very tenacious, ruler, Ferdinand IV. This Italian venture did not pan out, and Joseph was shifted elsewhere: when Napoleon invaded Spain in 1808, he brought this

Coin 124: 5 francs, France By the time of Napoleon's post-Elba Hundred Days, the revolutionary calendar had lost its place on French coins: here, 1815 is shown in traditional Arabic numerals.

Coin 125: taler, Grand Duchy of Berg Being Napoleon's brother-in-law brought many benefits to Joachim Murat. The army officer was named Marshall of France, grand duke of Berg (as seen on this coin), and, later, king of Naples.

Coin 126: 120 grani, Kingdom of the Two Sicilies

Coin 127: 320 reales, Spain

brother along and installed him in Madrid. That was one of the emperor's greatest miscalculations: the Spanish people rose up against him, his feckless brother, and the Grande Armée, and a dirty, guerrilla conflict (the word *guerrilla* means "small war," and it was actually invented to describe the endless hit-and-run techniques adopted by the Spanish insurgents) ensued for the next half-dozen years. Decisions made in 1808 anticipated the final defeat in 1815.

Joseph appeared on some Italian coins, and on rather more Spanish and Spanish-American ones. A silver piastra of 120 grani from the Naples mint **(coin 126)** bears his head on the obverse (the family resemblance is striking), with an elaborate, crowned, and supported coat of arms on the reverse. The triskelis (three-legged) design represents Sicily, but the crowned imperial eagle in the center shows where the real power reposed. A gold onza (technically, it's a 320-real piece; but no one called it that at the time and no one has since) from Madrid, struck in 1810, shows Joseph in his later assignment **(coin 127)**. Again, the familial resemblance is striking. The reverse carries over traditional Spanish elements—except for one. Earlier coins had depicted the three lilies of the House of Bourbon (*Borbón*, in Spain) at the center of the shield. New ones showed the Napoleonic eagle.

Another brother, Louis Bonaparte, was awarded Holland. A reluctant and unsuccessful prince, Louis inadvertently succeeded in uniting the fractious Dutch states—against him and his more famous brother. He did leave a splendid legacy in the form of a magnificent silver rijksdaalder of 1809 **(coin 128**, page 225). The following year saw the annexation and occupation of Holland by France, which did little to endear the latter to the former.

Finally, there was brother Jerome, for whom Napoleon carved out a new realm in those portions of Germany bordering on France: the kingdom of Westphalia. The country's first coinage appeared in 1807, its last a half dozen years later, after which, with its architect safely in exile, it was returned to its original owners. Jerome's coinage began with traditional German denominations and designs, but it quickly shifted in another direction. The franc had been one of the lasting creations of the French Revolution, dating from a reform enacted in 1794. Five-franc silver pieces were introduced during the following year, and the unit itself a few years later. Where French armies conquered, French coinage often followed: the new Italian lira was the exact equivalent of the franc, as was the frank, a

Coin 126: 120 grani, Kingdom of the Two Sicilies Napoleon made his brother Joseph a king, but he wears no crown in this portrait; instead, the imperial French eagle is crowned on the coin's reverse.

Coin 127: 320 reales, Spain Out with the old, and in with the new: this Spanish coin dispenses with the lilies of the deposed House of Bourbon, and introduces the imperial Napoleonic eagle (reverse, center).

Coin 128: rijksdaalder, Netherlands

Coin 129: 20 franken, Westphalia

new German coin appearing in Westphalia in 1808. Just as elsewhere, there were multiples of the frank in silver and in gold. A 20-franken coin struck in the yellow metal **(coin 129)** might have borne legends in German, but it was effectively a French concept, and looked it.

Here is an irony. Of all the dramatic innovations of the French Revolution and its Napoleonic successor, very little endured in anything like its original form. But the money proved an exception: for the next century, French monetary concepts would hold sway in Europe and much of the remainder of the world, to an extent incomprehensible to those who had introduced them. In the process, this revolution in money, featuring coins that were interchangeable across countries and continents, would drive the Age of Revolution forward quite as much as anything taking place on the battlefield.

As we saw in the case of Italy, the temporary success of French arms, the temporary overthrow of the traditional order, led to a growth in national sentiment, or nationalism. Once people's attention had been directed to the fact that they lived under the sway of foreigners, whose major occupation seemed to be the keeping of various branches of the same families separate from each other; and once people saw that an upstart from nowhere, armed with a new idea and an iron will, could defeat the odds and keep defeating them for the better part of 20 years—well, then, perhaps there was hope for the future. Perhaps things *didn't* have to go on as they always had. Perhaps nations could be created and survive, based not on the identity of the ruler, but on the homogeneity of the ruled.

The Rise of National Sentiment

The years after 1815 saw these ideas undergo intense scrutiny and direct action. In the process, several new nation-states came into existence—most notably Belgium, Greece, Italy, and Germany. The new guests at the European table (and the way in which they had arrived, and the chairs they occupied) would occasion jealousy, fear, and a desire for emulation. And all of this would one day lead to global war. But that was unimaginably distant. For now, the future held possibility and hope.

The Belgian story predated the others. During the age of the Old Order, you'll recall that tracts of land and their inhabitants were traded back and forth; this generally occurred at the conclusion of wars. In 1713, most of what is now Belgium was ceded to the Holy Roman

Coin 128: rijksdaalder, Netherlands

Louis Bonaparte took his job as king of Holland seriously, learning the Dutch language and going by the name *Koning Lodewijk I*. His brother Napoleon found Louis too independent, and forced him from the throne. Later, Louis' son would carry the Bonapartist torch as Emperor Napoleon III.

Coin 129: 20 franken, Westphalia

For Napoleon's brother Jerome, an entirely new kingdom was created: Westphalia, in Germany, bordering on France.

Empire, Austria. The locals were not consulted, and when Vienna's attention had been distracted by worsening tensions with France, they mounted an armed insurrection and struck money to proclaim the new order and pay for it. Their revolt was eventually suppressed, but some evocative coins remain. One of them is a lion d'or dated 1790 (**coin 130**). On this coin, only about the size of an American quarter dollar, the Belgians placed an immensely dense set of images, incorporating hopes, solidarity—and sense of nationhood.

The Lion of Brabant rears up on the obverse. He is armed and defiant. He holds a shield with the simple inscription LIBERTAS—Liberty. The date (1790) marks the start of the insurrection and the actual year of issue. In fact, coins were only struck during that first year. The obverse legend, DOMINI EST REGNVM, is the proclamation of a new order of things. This land and its people don't belong to any earthly power. They belong to God ("The Earth is the Lord's").

The reverse borrows an idea seen a decade and a half earlier on the other side of the Atlantic. A sun at the center sheds beneficent light on 11 shields that touch each other. They are the 11 provinces in revolt against Austria, joined in this common struggle. The legend ET IPSE DOMINABITVR GENTIVM completes the declaration begun on the obverse. Taken together, the legends mean "The Earth is the Lord's and He Shall Have Dominion over the Nations." The Lord. Not the Holy Roman Emperor. Not the king of France. *Are not the people as legitimate caretakers of the Lord's domain as self-styled emperors or kings?*

Brave thoughts. But the insurrection was soon suppressed and the undemocratic swap of real estate went on for a few decades longer. France occupied the country in 1795, and it was unceremoniously welded onto the Kingdom of the Netherlands at the end of the Napoleonic Wars. But the damage had been done. This people had discovered its identity and would not consent to rule by others. A revolt took place in 1830 (on the heels of a larger affair in France), and Belgium formally gained its independence the following year.

It was joined by Greece, whose revolt against the Turks had attracted the compassion and support of some extremely high-profile individuals, among them Lord Byron, who died in the struggle. Bitter warfare consumed most of the 1820s, but by 1828, this nation, too, was striking its own coinage. It chose a phoenix for its main design—the mythical bird

Coin 130: lion d'or, Belgium

Coin 130: lion d'or, Belgium
This gold coin roars its defiance. The Lion of
Brabant is shown with a shield and sword,
ready to defend Belgium—with violence, if
necessary. The Belgians were protesting the
Holy Roman Empire's claim on their lands.

Coin 131: 100 drachmai, Greece

consumed by fire, only to rise from the ashes. There could be no more potent, and no more appropriate, symbol for a reborn nation. But the reality was frequently at variance with the ideal, both here and elsewhere. New nations don't come into being fully formed; neither do old nations, now reborn. Compromises have to be made. Old ties have to be maintained (especially old economic ties) or new ones established. Skilled personnel may have to be imported to establish new institutions, such as factories or even improved farming, deemed to be in the national interest. In other words, exalted nationalism may result in a new country, one representing a distinct people, but it will take much work, more than a little luck, and a host of outside contacts to make it a going and growing concern.

Greece is a case in point. Its first coins were struck on Aegina and in Athens. Then precious-metal coinage was largely outsourced, while copper coinage was retained for the Athens mint (which was acceptable: this was a very poor country, and copper coinage was the money most frequently seen and used by its inhabitants). In time, copper was outsourced too: by 1865, all of Greece's coinage came from abroad. This is somewhat ironic, in that the Greeks had essentially invented coinage in the first place, some thousands of years before. In any event, a magnificent, and extremely rare, hundred-drachmai gold coin of King George I (ruled 1863–1913) shows the process at work **(coin 131)**. Only 76 of these coins were ever struck, the largest Greek gold coins in history. It shows the ruler, his titles, and the date on the obverse; the name of the country, the denomination, and a splendid draped and crowned shield of the new nation on the reverse. But look closely at that side. The tiny bee and anchor flanking the denomination are the privy marks of the Paris Mint. Now look at the obverse, near the truncation of the neck. There's a prominent letter A, emblem of the Paris Mint, and the word BAPPE under the neck, adjacent to the date. That's *BARRE*, rendered in the Greek alphabet: this coin was designed by Albert Desiré Barre, son of the most prominent engraver in mid-19th century France.

The Italian and German stories are better known, and they need not long detain us here. The Italian amalgamation occurred about a decade prior to the German, and both left a good deal of unfinished business that would linger on into the 20th century. France acted as midwife in the birth of modern Italy. Prussia forced the birth of modern Germany,

Coin 131: 100 drachmai, Greece

George I, King of the Hellenes, was actually born a prince of Denmark, the second son of King Christian IX. He was elected to the Greek throne in 1863, after the overthrow of the unpopular Otto I (himself a Bavarian prince). George's 50-year reign was the longest in modern Greek history. This outstanding gold coin is neither Greek nor Danish in design: it was made by Barre, a talented engraver of the Paris Mint.

by defeating those German states that got in its way—and the French for good measure: the German Empire was proclaimed at Versailles, former locus of French power. The insult could not have been more deliberate. The French remembered and looked forward to a time when they could return the favor.

Colonialism and Global Coinage

The Age of Revolution moved towards the present with accelerated speed. One of the ways in which countries that had been slighted, were of recent vintage, or were stung by defeat could get ahead, restore respect, was by occupying those portions of the globe where the writ of Europe did not yet run. The British had already been doing so for 10 generations. One of the benchmarks of their earlier successes had been coinage minted in London for the Gold Coast—today's Ghana—in 1796 and 1818. A large silver ackey of the latter year **(coin 132)** will repay a close look. George III (would he *ever* die?) appears on the obverse, a coat of arms with supporters on the reverse. Two African men support an elaborate shield with an elephant crest (shades of the tiny beast that once appeared on British coins made from gold from the region!). The shield itself has a cornucopia and a beehive at the top, symbols of wealth and industry, while a trading ship dominates the bottom two-thirds of the shield. The marvelous scrollwork and the entire layout suggest the 18th century, and the coin must have been designed by an artist who had heard mention of the place and its people but had never seen it, or them.

Coin 132: ackey, Gold Coast

The ackey is important because of what it portends. Soon other nations will be making other coinage for other colonies they will establish. The coins will first be made in the mother countries, later in the new lands themselves. And in the process, coinage, and coinage of a particular type, will become *global*. The Age of Revolution, which began with myriad small towns, states, and customs, will end, at least in one instance, with a universal object.

Several coins will show us the process at work. It occupied several stages, steps occurring almost but not quite simultaneously. First, regions that had had a distinctive coinage of their own began adopting money of a recognizably Western pattern. Second, places that had never previously had a coinage were now introduced to one, again on Western models. Third, in a direct response to expanded overseas commerce, various coun-

Coin 132: ackey, Gold Coast The *ackey* denomination was derived from the name of the large, poisonous akee seed, which originated in western Africa. Unripe arils of the akee fruit are toxic, but when exposed to air (after they ripen and split) they become edible.

Coin 133: gold piaster, Viet Nam
(shown enlarged on page 234)

Coin 134: gold tael, China (shown enlarged on page 234)

Coin 135: 5 shillings (Holey Dollar), New South Wales, Australia (shown enlarged on page 234)

tries began producing *trade coins*—and this event played its own role in the spread of a particular type of money. Finally, the way in which coinage was manufactured changed, modernized, and mandated money of a particular type, in order to get the most out of the new methodology.

Two gold coins, one from Viet Nam and the other from China, show the first process at work. The Vietnamese gold piaster **(coin 133)** includes recognizably traditional elements, including the nien-hao or reign title of the current emperor, Thieu Tri (reigned 1841–1847), and a beneficent dragon on the reverse. But the traditional elements stop there: this coin lacks the square hole peculiar to Far Eastern coinage, it's made of gold rather than copper or brass (another distinctly unusual feature), has denticles like a Western coin, and seems to have been struck on a Western-style screw coining press. Another gold coin carries the process through to its logical conclusion: a 1906 gold tael **(coin 134)** of the Chinese emperor Kuang Hsu (reigned 1875–1908) may have an obverse dragon and a reverse legend in Chinese, but in terms of fabric (the workmanship, style, and general "feel"), this is a Western object, not an Eastern one.

During the last century of the Age of Revolution coinage became truly global: places that had never used coinage before used it now, and what they used was coinage on a particular model. Introduction sometimes took place in stages. In Australia, the first locally produced coinage only appeared in 1813, and it was a very simple, but very distinct, affair **(coin 135)**. A large hole was punched into a Latin American peso or piece of eight, yielding two coins. The ring was valued at five shillings, while the center plug or *dump* was valued at 15 pence. This simple money was created in Sydney, and it comes as no surprise that a prisoner transported for counterfeiting was tapped for the job. (After all, he had the experience. . . .) By the middle of the century, huge deposits of gold had been found in Ballarat and elsewhere. A local coinage was produced at Adelaide, capital of South Australia, in 1852 **(coin 136)**. Strictly speaking, this coinage was illegal, and it was one of the factors moving the government in London to authorize official branch mints on the southern continent. Three were set up—at Melbourne, Sydney, and eventually Perth—and the final stage in the Australian story took place: gold coins, exact counterparts of homeland issues in terms of weights, finenesses, and designs, coins that revealed their origin only if you looked very closely for a tiny mintmark, an M, S, or P.

Elsewhere, the new money was introduced all at once. The Belgian Congo (or Congo Free State, as it was then called) was treated to its first coinage in 1887 **(coin 137)**. It was struck in Belgium, had a completely European appearance (the five-franc piece of 1887 is typical)—and the only concession to local sentiment was the placing of holes in the lowest-value coins, so that they could be strung and transported from one place to another by people lacking pockets. A 20-mark gold coin **(coin 138)**, struck in Berlin for German New Guinea, falls into the same category. The bird of paradise was emblematic of the new colony, but otherwise, this coin was a completely Western object.

Since ancient times, some coins had been more popular than others, achieving an international popularity. The Athenian tetradrachm was one such object in antiquity. The medieval silver penny was another, holding sway across Europe a thousand years ago. The piece of

Coin 137: 5 francs, Belgian Congo (shown enlarged on page 235)

Coin 136: pound, South Australia (shown enlarged on page 235)

Coin 138: 20 marks, German New Guinea (shown enlarged on page 235)

Coin 133: gold piaster, Viet Nam

Coin 134: gold tael, China

Coin 135: 5 shillings (Holey Dollar), New South Wales, Australia

Coin 136: pound, South Australia

Coin 137: 5 francs, Belgian Congo

Coin 138: 20 marks, German New Guinea

Coin 139: trade dollar, United States of America

Coin 140: trade dollar, Great Britain

eight was yet another, dominating much of the world's trade for more than two centuries. Increased international trade and tension led to an increase in the number of coins minted specifically for foreign commerce. There was competition and pride at work. Sometimes there were additional reasons: one explanation for creation of the ill-starred United States trade dollar **(coin 139)** was that it would use up some of the mountains of silver that were coming to light in Nevada, Montana, and other Western states and territories.

Introduced in 1873, the "trades" were only struck for commerce for five years. Their commercial intention was obvious: we see Lady Liberty seated beside the ocean, surrounded by objects ready for trade. The reverse depicts the obligatory eagle, but it also states the coin's exact fineness and silver content, so that suspicious foreign merchants would know exactly what they were getting. But the merchants wanted Latin American pieces of eight: they were accustomed to them, respected their purity, and saw no reason to accept new money with strange designs. And so production for commerce was halted after only five years. The relative failure of the coin is suggested by the fact that, while many Mexican dollars bear bankers' and merchants' marks (called *chop marks*), far fewer United States ones do. A British version **(coin 140)**, introduced in 1895 and struck in London, Bombay, and several other places, had greater success, in part because it was penetrating places with less competition.

The final step in the globalization of money was the *industrialization* of money. Unless coinage of the new type could be mass produced in enormous quantities (growing every year, as economies expanded and comfort with and confidence in the new medium grew apace), then this component of the Age of Revolution would remain an aspiration rather than a reality; and the progress of the planet would be retarded, perhaps even reversed.

Fortunately, money's industrialization took place at the precise moment when it was most urgently required. One aspect of the Age of Revolution that has not been discussed is its industrial phase, wherein those concepts we now take for granted (mass production, factories, the progressive nature of the manufacturing process, even mass advertisement) were all devised, buttressed each other, and opened the door to Modern Times.

Coin 139: trade dollar, United States of America U.S. trade dollars are sometimes seen "chopmarked"—punched with the identifying stamps of 19th-century Oriental merchants who tested them for the purity of their silver.

Coin 140: trade dollar, Great Britain The British trade dollar was struck from 1895 through 1935. It was a great success as a trade coin, especially compared to the earlier (1873–1885) attempt of the United States.

Coin 141: Bank of Ireland dollar (6 shillings), Ireland

Coin 142: gold sovereign, Great Britain

The Industrialization of Money

What follows is a gross simplification, but what roughly took place was this. Factories sprung up in areas where water, fuel, and raw materials were plentiful. Sometimes these areas were near or in towns and cities, but more often they were not. Workers were needed to run the new machines. But traditional methods of labor and payment (obligatory work, payment in kind) wouldn't work in new areas, where no one had previously lived. So payment had to be made in *wages*, in the form of coins. But those coins had to be copper—low-value, because wages were low. And there would have to be more and more of them with each passing year, as additional factories dotted the land. The British government's reaction to all of this was to ignore it, and the same could be said of the other pioneer areas of the Industrial Revolution. But that inspired forgers to take up the slack: writing in 1791, an English correspondent estimated that 98 percent of circulating coppers were fakes!

Most of the British counterfeits were made in Birmingham. But a local magnate named Matthew Boulton decided to do something about it: to create good, and safe, copper money for the laboring poor (and incidentally achieve lasting fame for himself). Boulton, working with one of partner James Watt's steam engines, set up the world's first modern factory to strike coins—the world's first modern mint. It did excellent work, as a lovely proof Irish dollar of 1804 **(coin 141)** will attest. The piece is perfectly round, and all portions of it are perfectly clear, something very difficult to achieve with the old, hand-operated coining presses. (This coin was made from fresh silver, for collectors. Ordinary examples of the series were overstruck on what Boulton called "resurrected" pieces of eight, and they usually exhibited faint traces of the original coins. Boulton claimed that this was a guarantee of purity. What it actually was was an admission that even *his* coining presses were inadequate for the job.) The British government did its best to keep him at arm's length, but it finally allowed him to provide it with a new Royal Mint, which went into full operation a few months after the Battle of Waterloo. Its capabilities are suggested by a superb Proof gold sovereign of 1818 **(coin 142)**, one of the rarest, and most spectacular, British coins ever produced.

The machines created by Boulton and his successors produced major effects, some obvious and others less so. They could expand the quantities of coinage produced, especially large and heavy pieces, although

Coin 141: Bank of Ireland dollar (6 shillings), Ireland This Proof coin is a showcase of Matthew Boulton's modern minting techniques.

Coin 142: gold sovereign, Great Britain A classic theme of British coinage—St. George on horseback, slaying a dragon—is illustrated on the gold sovereign of King George III, as designed by Benedetto Pistrucci. The first rendering of the motif, which in effect sold its use for the coin, was on a large hardstone cameo by Pistrucci, a gem engraver.

their improvements here were not as dramatic as we often believe. But they could indeed mass-produce coins and, shortly, coin *dies*. And when every coin looks like every other coin, the work of the forger is increased exponentially. The creation of an unforgeable coin was what Matthew Boulton was after, and he essentially achieved it.

The new methodology had negative aspects as well. Due to the much greater downward force of the press, coins would henceforth have to be struck in one-piece collars. This essentially meant that you could have anything you wanted on the edge of the coin—providing you wanted it plain or reeded. And the greater power meant that the glorious high relief, seen on coinage from the days of the ancients to the dawn of the Age of Revolution—that relief was a thing of the past. You could still achieve it on special strikings, such as the beautiful five-pound British gold pattern of 1839 (**coin 143**). But you couldn't have it on a normal coin, struck for normal trade. As with most of the events we call Progress, there were losses to balance the gains.

> *Bolton, working with one of James Watt's steam engines, set up the world's first modern mint. . . .*

Coin 143: pattern 5 pounds, Great Britain

The Journey's End

Let's consider where we are, where coinage has arrived, as a result of our journey through the Age of Revolution. Let's pick a year: 1914.

The world is far more crowded than it was when last we looked. Cities that were wide spots in the road in 1770 are centers of world power in 1914. Europe still dominates, but the United States is gaining on it. Europe has divided up much of the Third World, but two non-Continental powers have empires too. They are the United States and Japan, and a few pessimists are already foreseeing a clash between the two.

But any war is far more likely to originate somewhere in Europe. As a result of a half-century of clever statecraft, the continent is now divided into two heavily armed camps, each nervously eying the other. War's possibility is a natural outgrowth of the Age of Revolution, which, as we

Coin 143: pattern 5 pounds, Great Britain On this legendary coin, the young Queen Victoria is shown as Una, a mythical character representing Truth and Purity, from Edmund Spenser's *The Faerie Queen*. She leads her loyal companion and protector, a lion representing Britain.

have seen, has encompassed nationalism and national aspirations. But so far, despite crises on an almost annual basis, the world, or at least the business end of it, has always stepped back from the brink.

And the business of the world is business in 1914—industry beyond the ability of previous generations to comprehend, export agriculture, mass marketing, inter-oceanic trade on a scale never previously achieved. All of this takes money, of course: coins and currency. We've seen some of the ways in which coinage passed through a revolution of its own. We can expect its continued improvement, a richer global economy, continued peace, uninterrupted progress.

And then an unfortunate event takes place in a town no one ever heard of. The town is Sarajevo.

CHAPTER SEVEN

LATIN AMERICAN COLONIAL COINAGE

Ana Lonngi de Vagi

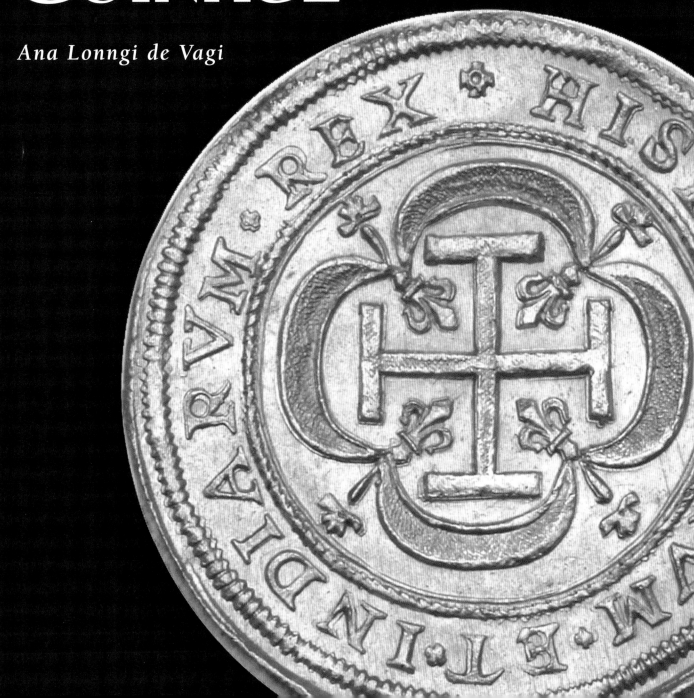

During the 15th century Spain and Portugal devoted many resources to maritime explorations, which were mainly directed to finding a sea route to the Orient. In doing so, they hoped to end the monopoly of Italian and Ottoman middlemen over the lucrative trade in spices and other luxury products.

Columbus' "discovery" of America in 1492 was an accidental result of such efforts. In Spain, two other major events took place that same year: the final defeat of the Moors in Granada and the expulsion of the Spanish Jews. During the reign of the Catholic monarchs Ferdinand of Aragon and Isabella of Castile (ruled 1479–1516), national unity was realized particularly by combating common enemies (infidels). The cost, however, would be very high for Spain, which lost its most economically important population.

The first half of the 16th century saw the creation of the administrative and governmental structure in the Spanish empire in America. The sweeping powers granted initially to expeditionary leaders such as Columbus, Cortés, and Pizarro would soon be revoked or limited. Institutions would progressively assure a centralized political control, which mirrored Spain's own absolutist and centralized regime.

The most important institution in the government of the Spanish colonies in America was the *Consejo de Indias* (Council of the Indies), chartered in 1524. Its role was to handle Spain's imperial affairs in all matters, administrative, political, legal, religious, and military. It worked only under the king, and amongst its functions was the nomination of the high colonial officials to the king.

In the colonies the main authorities were the viceroys, the captains-general, and the members of the *audiencias* (high courts). The main difference between the functions of viceroys and captains-general was the size and importance of the territories under their jurisdiction. Though captaincies-general were subdivisions of viceroyalties and theoretically were dependant upon them, they were virtually autonomous. The audiencias governed smaller subdivisions called *presidencias*.

The first two viceroyalties were New Spain (1535), which comprised the territories north of the Isthmus of Panama, and Peru (1544), including all of South America except Brazil and the coast of Venezuela.

The most important administrative organ for the Indies was the *Casa de Contratación* (House of Trade), founded in Seville in 1503. Its role was to keep a centralized control over trade coming to and from the Indies, to maintain Spain's monopoly. It established many protectionist measures such as forbidding trade between the colonies, establishing the fleet system, and restricting products.

Together with the military conquest of the lands and peoples of America came the introduction of the European monetary system, specifically the one used at the time in Spain, based on gold and silver coins. During the first phase of the Spanish conquest and settlement, the Crown made some shipments of coinage to meet the needs of the New World. However, these flows were insufficient, and Spaniards had to resort to making their own ad hoc "coins," which in some cases were marked with a royal seal to make them official.

Even with these emergency currencies the demand for money for trade was not totally covered and Spaniards had to get acquainted with the indigenous means of exchange such as cocoa beans, coca leaves, cotton cloth, and jade beads. Some of these currencies coexisted with coinage throughout the colonial period, and even well in the 19th century.

As more cities were founded, commerce increased, and rich mines were discovered, it became necessary to establish mints in the New World. We will follow the path of the coins in this collection to unveil some interesting aspects of their history and features.

Establishment of Spanish Colonial Mints

The order to found a mint at Mexico City was received in 1535 at the same time that the Viceroyalty of New Spain was officially established. Though the exact date when the Mexico City mint began operations is not known, it is thought that dies began to be engraved in March 1536 and that the first coins were probably struck in April that same year.

The first coins produced in Mexico were in the names of Charles I (ruled 1516–1556; he was the emperor Charles V of Germany) and his mother and joint ruler, Johanna. These coins were hammer-struck and, although the technique used was quite crude, their general appearance is nice, their thickness is regular, and they are round.

On the obverse they bear the crowned arms of Spain with the names of Charles and Johanna in the surrounding Latin inscription. The reverse consists of the crowned Pillars of Hercules, which represent the Straits of Gibraltar. Between the Pillars, the motto PLVS VLTRA (More Beyond) is a clear reference of how the Spaniards had reached the New World. The inscription reads: HISPANIARVM ET INDIARVM REGES (Monarchs of Spain and the Indies). There are two series of Charles and Johanna coins, which may be easily distinguished because the later one has waves between the Pillars of Hercules.

The standard denominations issued in the early series consisted of 1/4, 1/2, 1, 2, 3 and 4 reales in silver, and of 2 and 4 maravedíes in copper. The 3-reales coins ceased to be produced because they were very similar to 4 reales in weight and diameter, which caused confusion. Also the copper issues were abandoned, due to a general rejection by the natives.

Curiously, the production of 8 reales was also tested for a brief period in 1538, but they were abandoned because of the technical difficulties involved in their manufacture. This collection includes a remarkable example of the test-strike 8 reales of the Charles and Johanna early series (coin 144). The assayer's initial (R) corresponds to Francisco del Rincón, who was the first assayer at the mint, where he worked from 1536 to mid-1538.

The inscriptions on the early series appear in Latin or Gothic characters, while the denominations are sometimes represented by dots or bars, and other times by Arabic numerals. On this coin we find Gothic and Latin characters: the mintmark (M) to the left of the Spanish coat of arms on the obverse is of the Gothic style, while the assayer's initial (R) below the pillars on the reverse is Latin-style. The cross potent above the pillars on the reverse, in lieu of the 8 of the value, suggests that this coin was a trial strike not intended for circulation.

This is one of the very first coins struck at the mint in Mexico City and it is one of only perhaps three or four known. Not only is it a fabled rarity of early coinage in the Americas, but it is a wonderful example of the first crown-size coins struck in the New World. The overstrikes visible on the coin are probably a sign of the actual process that was used and of the amount of work involved in producing such a piece.

The Mexico City mint would continue to strike coins in the name of Charles and Johanna well into the reign of Spain's next king, Philip II (ruled 1556–1598), until the type was changed in 1572. This remarkable fact helps to demonstrate the inefficiency of the bureaucracy and communications at the time.

Coin 144: 8 reales of Charles and Johanna, Mexico City

Coin 144: 8 reales of Charles and Johanna, Mexico City Considered by many to be the first dollar-size coin struck in the New World, this has become a fabled rarity. The debate continues on whether it was a coin or a trial piece, constituting one of the mysteries of the early years of the mint in Mexico City.

War was a constant ingredient of the reign of Philip II, whose imperial policies did not correspond to the resources at his disposal. The shipments of silver from the New World inspired the king's confidence in a perennial supply of treasure to pay his debts, but his campaigns in Europe consumed far more than what arrived from America.

His attempt to crush a Protestant outbreak in the Netherlands would turn into the Eighty Years War (1568–1648). In the Mediterranean, though the Spanish fleet defeated the Turks at Lepanto in 1571, its superiority would not last even a decade. Philip II took possession of the throne of Portugal in 1580 and he is especially known for his Invincible Armada, which failed to conquer England in 1588.

The first coins issued in the Indies in the name of Philip II were produced in the viceroyalty of Peru, at Ciudad de los Reyes (Lima). A royal decree of 1565 had authorized the coinage of silver with the same design that had been introduced earlier at the Mexico City mint, but the mintmark was to be the letter P, for Peru.

Operations at the mint began sometime in 1568, but they would not last long. In fact, coinage at Lima ceased in 1571 and the mint was transferred the following year to Ciudad de la Plata, and then to Potosí.

This collection includes an example of the 8 reales (**coin 145**) struck at Lima sometime between 1568 and 1570, of which only a few pieces were produced, perhaps as an experiment. It represents the first crown-size coin struck in South America and it is undoubtedly the finest of the seven to ten known examples.

The Latin inscription on both sides of the coin reads: PHIL(I)PVS II D HISPANIARVM ET INDIARVM REX (Philip II, King of Spain and the Indies by the Grace of God). The obverse bears the crowned arms of Castile and Leon, with a pomegranate at the lower tip. The reverse shows two crowned pillars over waves; between the pillars is the motto PLVS VLTR(A), with the mintmark (P) above, and the denomination (8) below.

The assayer's initial (R) on the obverse to the left of the arms corresponds to Alonso Rincón, who is thought to have worked previously at the Mexico City Mint. This is an exceptional piece, because it bears the name of Philip II, while maintaining the style of the Charles and Johanna pieces. In fact, all the other issues bearing Philip II's name are of the "cob" type, which we will describe below.

Coin 145: 8 reales of Philip II, Lima, Peru

Coin 145: 8 reales of Philip II, Lima, Peru The earliest coins from Peru were struck in the name of Philip II. They borrow the familiar designs of Charles and Johanna (later series): the crowned coat of arms on the obverse and two crowned pillars above waves on the reverse. The motto PLVS VLTRA, meaning "More Beyond," would become a standard feature on later coins.

Consolidation of the Empire and Cob Coins

The second coin type to be produced in Spanish America is known as "cob." Cobs are coins which have irregular shape and thickness; however, due to their content of precious metal they were accepted widely.

The main factor that contributed to the involution in the workmanship of coins in the later part of the 16th century was the opening of the sea route from the port of Acapulco in Mexico (on the Pacific) to the Asian continent and the Pacific Islands, which caused a rise in demand for Spanish American coins. This increased demand could be met thanks to the abundance of metal in the Americas but, as production rose, the coining techniques remained the same and thus the coins became crude.

Already in 1566 a royal decree of Philip II ordered a change in the coin design: coins were to bear the arms of Spain on the obverse and a cross with castles and lions on the reverse. However, the punches for this type were not received in the Indies until 1572, when the new type was introduced.

In that same year the 8-reales denomination was officially added, since by then the technical difficulties of striking such large pieces were overcome. The 8 reales would be the most famous Spanish American coin and it became an international currency.

During the period of cob coinage, which extended for nearly 170 years, some extraordinary coins were struck. They are called *royals* or presentation pieces. They were struck with special dies on round planchets, thus allowing the full display of the inscriptions and other elements which are rarely complete on regular-issue cobs. Many believe that royals were made to show the fine production of the mints to the authorities in the Indies and most probably also in Spain.

Coin 146: royal 8 reales of Philip III, Mexico City

The first example of a royal in this collection is a beautiful 8 reales from the mint of Mexico City (**coin 146**), issued in the name of Philip III (ruled 1598–1621). On the obverse it bears the crowned Spanish coat of arms, which reflected the extent of the Habsburg rule in Europe, for it comprises the arms of Castile and Leon, Aragon, Naples and Sicily, Granada, Austria, New Burgundy, Old Burgundy, Brabant, Flanders, and Tirol.

The mintmark (an M with an O above) and the assayer's initial (F), which could correspond to Esteban Franco, are to the left of the arms. The value in this case appears as an Arabic 8 to the right. The surrounding Latin inscription reads PHILLIPPVS III DEI GRATIA (Philip III by the Grace of God).

Coin 146: royal 8 reales of Philip III, Mexico City During the long period of "cob" coinage in Mexico, special presentation pieces, such as this coin, were struck. Numismatists refer to them as royals, since it is believed that they were produced as samples to be given to officials in the New World as well as in the Spanish Court.

The reverse design consists of the quartered castles and lions of Castile and Leon, enclosed by a tressure with eight lobes. This piece illustrates an anomaly that commonly occurred on coins, the misspelling of the king's name or of the HISPANIARVM ET INDIARVM REX. On this coin we see two such mistakes: first in the monarch's name, which appears as PHILLIP-PVS instead of PHILIPPVS, and second on the reverse in the king's titles, which reads INDIARVN instead of INDIARVM.

In the viceroyalty of Peru the mines of Potosí were discovered by the Spaniards in 1545, and the city of the same name was founded the following year. A mint began operating there in the spring of 1574, striking silver coins of the cob type, but it was not until the year 1617 that coins from Potosí began to be dated. This collection includes the finest known Potosí royal of the mid-17th century, an 8 reales struck in 1650.

At the time the mint faced a tremendous scandal that nearly closed it, due to the confirmed suspicions about its production of debased coins. The first claims about the high content of copper in silver bars and coins from Potosí reached Spain as early as 1626, and a report of 1641 not only mentioned the low-silver alloy but also indicated that some officers were becoming rich quite rapidly.

In 1646 a further report to the Council of the Indies from Viceroy Mancera confirmed the fraud, and in late 1647 Francisco Néstares Marín was directed to investigate the matter and to eradicate the problem. After closing the mint for a few months so the due verifications could take place, he confirmed a fraud committed by the assayer Felipe Ramírez de Arellano and a silver merchant, Francisco Gómez de la Rocha. The debased coins had been produced with silver that Gómez had supplied the mint, and the fraud amounted to 472,000 pesos.

Néstares' solution was proportional to the severity of the faults, and the law prescribed the death penalty for such felonies. A total of 48 people directly involved in the mint and another 38 from the region were convicted. Some, including Gómez and Ramírez, were executed, and others were imprisoned or exiled.

To allow the mint to continue working, assayer Juan Rodríguez de Rodas and an assistant, Antonio Ovando, were sent from Spain. They worked at the mint from 1649 to 1651/2. Following Néstares' recommendations, Philip IV (ruled 1621–1655) directed in mid-1650 that the debased coins be withdrawn from circulation. A second decree, of early

1651, ordered that the bad coins should be melted so that a new coin design could be issued to restore the integrity to the coinage and thus the confidence of users.

Coin 147, which bears the initial of assayer Rodríguez de Rodas (an O with a dot inside), belongs to the previous type and perhaps the fact that it is a royal saved it from being melted. The obverse shows the crowned Spanish coat of arms, with the mintmark (P, for Potosí) on the left, while the assayer's initial appears both to the left and right of the shield.

The inscription on both sides reads: PHILIPVS IIII D G HIS-PANIARU(M) ET INDIARVM REX followed by ANO 1650 (Year 1650). In 1651 Rodríguez de Rodas would also be replaced for not being able to provide the silver fineness demanded by Néstares, whose investigations continued for some time.

In 1653 a devaluation was ordered for all coins minted in Potosí during the previous 25 years. This affected only pieces of 4 and 8 reales, since the lower denominations were re-melted. The coins were devalued according to their content of silver, with some pieces being reduced to half their face value.

The new cob type was introduced in 1652. It consisted of a cross quartering castles and lions on the obverse and the Pillars of Hercules on waves on the reverse. This type was then extended to the mint at Lima and became distinctive of the viceroyalty of Peru.

Toward the end of the 17th century, still under the Habsburgs, Spain faced a profound economic crisis caused by continuous wars and the loss of territories in Europe, and, in the New World, by the loss of treasure-laden ships to pirates and storms. The situation affected the colonies because the needs of the mother country were reflected in protectionist measures such as restricting production and commerce in the Americas, even to the point of abandoning some mines.

Although Charles II (ruled 1665–1700) was married twice, he had no descendants. Thus before his death he appointed as his successor Philip, duke of Anjou and grandson of Louis XIV of France. This caused the War of the Spanish Succession (1702–1713), after which Spain was left with a smaller empire, consisting of the kingdom of Castile and Aragon and the Indies. It was possible then to start implementing a reform program.

During the 18th century Spain experienced a clear recovery, indebted to three kings of the House of Bourbon: Philip V (ruled 1700–1746) and his

Coin 147: royal 8 reales of Philip IV, Potosí, Bolivia (shown enlarged on page 255)

Coin 148: royal 8 escudos of Philip V, Mexico City

Coin 149: royal 8 reales of Philip V, Mexico City (shown enlarged on page 257)

sons, Ferdinand VI (ruled 1746–1759) and Charles III (ruled 1759–1788).

The production of gold coinage at the Mexico City mint began in 1679, and this collection includes a royal 8 escudos **(coin 148)** struck there in 1714 in the name of Philip V. The inscription on the obverse is abbreviated PHILIPPVS V DEI G (Philip V by the Grace of God) to leave enough room for the date.

That year the design of the coat of arms was modified so that the Bourbon crest covered completely the lower-right castle on the obverse, while the reverse displays a quatrefoil (four-lobe) tressure which, along with the cross potent, would remain the basic design until gold cobs stopped being produced at the Mexico City mint.

To the left of the crowned coat of arms is the mintmark and the assayer's initial (J), which corresponds to José Eustaquio de León y Losa. The denomination is indicated in Roman numerals (VIII), which seems to have been the common practice in gold pieces, while denominations of silver coins were expressed with Arabic numerals.

In 1714 Philip V made Isabella Farnesio from Parma his second wife and queen, to whom he would trust many governmental responsibilities. Through Isabella and her Italian chief minister, French influence in Spain would be progressively weakened in favor of Italian interests. The superb 1723 royal 8 reales of Mexico City in this collection **(coin 149)** comes from this period. The workmanship on this piece is outstanding, and it is struck on a perfectly round flan. This coin has been called by some "the finest royal of any Spanish king."

The piece displays in great detail every feature of the design on both obverse and reverse. As in some presentation pieces, this one has small rosettes below the assayer's initial and above and below the denomination. This style began to be produced in 1717 and is recognizable in that, apart from having the Bourbon crest completely covering the lower-right castle on the obverse, the tressure on the reverse is foliated and with several dots in the leaves facing inwards. Another ornament consists of the balls at the ends of the cross.

Under Philip V the spelling of his name on coinage appears systematically with a double P, as we can see from this piece, which is inscribed PHILIPPVS V DEI G, followed by the year, 1723, and on the reverse, it continues: HISPANIARVM ET INDIARVM REX.

Coin 147: royal 8 reales of Philip IV, Potosí, Bolivia The standards of Potosí coinage were so poor that the king decreed a change of designs the year after this issue.

Coin 148: royal 8 escudos of Philip V, Mexico City This coin was perhaps among the gifts distributed to celebrate the king's marriage to Isabella Farnesio in 1714.

In January 1724, Philip V abdicated in favor of his son, Louis I, who died in late August, only a few months after being proclaimed king of Spain. The news of Louis I's enthronement must have reached the New World quite late, probably after he had already died, as coins were struck in his name in Mexico from 1724 to 1725, at Lima in 1725, and at Potosí from 1725 to 1727.

This collection has an extraordinarily rare piece **(coin 150)**, struck in the name of Louis I at Potosí in 1727. On this royal 8 reales the name of the monarch appears as LVIS PR (Louis I; PR stands for *Primero* or First), and the mint name is EL PE(RU) POTOSI. The date, 1727, appears in three different places, both on the obverse and reverse.

The design is crude, yet the devices are perfectly identifiable: on the obverse, the crowned Cross of Jerusalem with the castles and lions between its arms; on the reverse, the crowned Pillars of Hercules over waves. The assayer at the time was Diego de Ybarbouru, as shown by the initial Y.

There is documentary evidence that the news of the death of Louis I had arrived to Cuzco by July 1725, so it must have reached Potosí more or less at the same time. Why the mint continued striking coins in his name for so long remains a mystery.

Bourbon Reforms and Milled Coinage

During the 18th century Spain would experience a true recovery thanks to the reforms the Bourbon kings would put to work in the administrative, economic, and industrial fields. Colonial reform had to be implemented cautiously, since the most powerful sectors were identified with the status quo. The goal was to centralize colonial administration even more than it was and to make it more efficient. The commercial reforms were meant to attack smuggling while strengthening the exclusive trade ties between Spain and its colonies.

A major reorganization occurred with the separation of the northernmost region of the viceroyalty of Peru, which became the Viceroyalty of New Granada (present-day Colombia, Ecuador, and Venezuela). This change was intended to better protect the Caribbean coast and to respond to the rapid growth of the population in central Colombia. Venezuela was given the title of captaincy-general within the new viceroyalty, yet it remained virtually independent.

Coin 150: royal 8 reales of Louis I, Potosí, Bolivia

Coin 149: royal 8 reales of Philip V, Mexico City The former duke of Anjou and grandson of Louis XIV, Philip V introduced French institutions and ideas to Spain.

Coin 150: royal 8 reales of Louis I, Potosí, Bolivia Louis I had one of the shortest reigns of all Spanish kings, but it was long enough for him to be named on coins.

Another modification was the creation in 1776 of the Viceroyalty of the Río de la Plata, separating the provinces of La Plata from the viceroyalty of Peru. The new viceroyalty included Upper Peru (present-day Bolivia). Noticeably, the monarchs were concerned about the problems of communication and government caused by the great distances separating the different provinces.

But changes under the Bourbons came also from a numismatic point of view, as Philip V tried to improve coinage with technological advances; just as the mints in Spain had done for some time, the Spanish-American mints started producing milled coins.

With the introduction of the screw press in mid-1732 the mint in Mexico began to produce a new coin known as the "Pillar" (*columnario*) type due to the Pillars of Hercules which appear on the reverse, flanking two crowned globes above waves. On each of the pillars a ribbon bears a portion of the motto PLUS ULTRA.

The design was perhaps the most fortunate of the ones used in Spanish colonial coinage in its balance and beauty. The largest denomination, 8 reales, was also called a Pillar dollar, and it was to become the most popular coin of the age in international trade.

Coin 151: 8 reales of Philip V, Mexico City

This collection includes a beautiful example of the first-year Pillar dollar struck at the Mexico City mint (**coin 151**). The obverse presents a new version of the crowned arms of Castile and Leon, the center of which is occupied by the Bourbon escutcheon consisting of three fleurs-de-lis. The surrounding Latin inscription reads: PHILIP V D G HISPAN ET IND REX (Philip V, King of Spain and the Indies by the Grace of God).

On the reverse the inscription reads: VTRAQUE VNUM (Both [Worlds] Are One). The mintmark (M°), which appears twice, and the date (1732) are a part of this circular inscription. In the field on the obverse, next to the Spanish arms, both the assayer's initial and the denomination are accompanied by decorative rosettes above and below. The initial F, to the left of the arms, corresponds to the assayer Felipe Rivas de Angulo.

The next coin takes us to Brazil, the only territory in the Americas colonized by the Portuguese. At first money for circulation in Brazil was provided by coins shipped from Portugal and by Spanish colonial issues that were overstamped. Following a decree of 1694 a mint was established at Bahia, then in 1699 the mint was transferred to Rio de Janeiro, which was identified by the initial R.

Coin 151: 8 reales of Philip V, Mexico City The introduction of milled coins in all the territories under Spanish rule was meant to prevent the edges of coins from being trimmed or filed. This improvement greatly changed the appearance of the coins, which now had a design on their edge and which were round, rather than irregularly shaped. Consequently, the coins were more appealing.

Coin 152: 12,800 réis of Joao V, Minas Gerais, Brazil

Towards the end of the 17th century the first important gold mines were found in the region of Minas Gerais. These ore sources made Brazil the primary gold producer in the 18th century. During the reign of John V (1706–1750) the abundant shipments of gold gave Portugal a period of splendor, economic as well as cultural and artistic. But soon the gold riches passed to England to pay the trade imbalance between the two countries, which was unfavorable to Portugal.

With the production of coins made of Brazilian gold the mint at Bahia was reopened (1714) and another mint was founded at Villa Rica (1724), the capital of the province of Minas Gerais. Coinage from Brazilian mints increased and some was also exported to Portugal.

In 1727 a new series of coins was created, which for the first time bore the bust of the Portuguese monarch on the obverse. The denominations were in réis ("kings") (3,200; 6,400; and 12,800), and in escudos (400; 800; and 1,600). Some varieties exist, depending on the mint, especially in the type of arms (oval and italic) that appears on the reverse.

This collection includes a gorgeous example of the gold 12,800 réis **(coin 152)** struck in 1732 at the mint of Minas Gerais (M). The obverse bears a laureate royal portrait with long curly locks. The Latin inscription that surrounds it reads IOANNES V D G PORT ET ALG REX (John V, King of Portugal and Algarve by the Grace of God). Below the portrait are the mintmark and the date.

The reverse consists of a crowned Italic coat of arms, which we may appreciate in full detail. The standard gold coin of the series was the 6,400-réis, and apparently its double-denomination, the 12,800 réis, was not well received. In fact, it was issued only between 1727 and 1733.

Now we shift to Chile, which was not settled by Spaniards as fast as the northern regions of South America. Chile was part of the Viceroyalty of Peru until it separated in 1778 and became a captaincy-general. The city of Santiago was founded in 1541 and repeated requests were made by the city authorities to the Council of the Indies to establish a mint there in order to alleviate a chronic money shortage.

These requests had been made since the late 16th century, yet a mint was not authorized until the fall of 1743 and was not opened until 1749/50 to strike gold and silver. Thus, the first coins produced there were milled coins of the types then being struck in the other Spanish American mints.

Coin 152: 12,800 réis of Joao V, Minas Gerais, Brazil The rich gold ores found in the region of Minas Gerais greatly increased the Brazilian economy. A side effect was an increase in the African slave population, responding to the need of labor to work the mines. The demand for this labor was so high that agriculture was nearly abandoned in some areas.

Coin 153: 8 reales of Ferdinand VI, Santiago, Chile

Coin 154: countermarked 8 reales of Ferdinand VI, Lima, Peru (Jamaica counterstamp)

Gold coins dominated the first years of the operation of the Santiago mint, and silver ones would increase slowly but steadily until they leveled up with gold coins (during the first decade of the mint's operation silver coinage was produced only in 1755 and 1758). Since 8 reales were struck only in this period, they are extremely rare. In fact, fewer than ten examples are known of the Santiago silver dollars. One of them, struck in 1758, is included in this collection, and it is considered the finest of the known specimens **(coin 153)**.

Chilean silver dollars were the only Spanish American coins to spell out the full name of Ferdinand, as we see in the Latin inscription on the obverse, which surrounds the Spanish/Bourbon arms: FERDINANDUS VI D G HISPAN ET IND REX. To the right of the coat of arms is the value of the coin and to the left is the assayer's initial, J, which corresponds to José Larrañeta.

On the reverse the mintmark (S°) is included as part of the inscription and appears on both sides of the date (1758). Although it is quite late compared to some of the coinage produced at other Spanish American mints, this is certainly a wonderful example of the early silver coinage from Santiago, especially considering the scarcity of its production of silver coinage.

Pillar coinage produced throughout the Spanish domains in America followed the tradition of Spanish American cob coinage in that it was internationally accepted. Pillar dollars circulated throughout North, Central, and South America, the Caribbean, Great Britain, Australia, Portugal and its colonies, and in Asia, especially in the Philippines and China.

Many different countermarks were used to control the money in circulation in each location, so numerous 8-reales pieces (or cut sections of them) bear a visible sign of their worldwide circulation. In China, instead of using a countermark, coins were checked to verify their alloy and then marked with small symbols called *chopmarks*.

An example of a Pillar dollar from the Peruvian mints in this collection is an 8 reales struck in the name of Ferdinand VI in 1757 at Lima **(coin 154)**. But the important thing about this coin is that it was countermarked in Jamaica.

After having been under Spanish rule from 1494 to 1655, Jamaica passed to British hands. During the second half of the 16th century,

Coin 153: 8 reales of Ferdinand VI, Santiago, Chile Apparently, Ferdinand VI succumbed to madness after his wife died in 1758—the year this fabled rarity was struck.

Coin 154: countermarked 8 reales of Ferdinand VI, Lima, Peru (Jamaica counterstamp) With no coinage of its own, the Jamaican government counter-marked Spanish Pillar dollars to make them legal tender.

the voyages of Sir John Hawkins and Francis Drake made it clear that England had become the rival for Spain regarding its empire in the Americas. England would try to demonstrate its superiority by seizing Spanish treasure ships, attacking Spanish colonial towns, and circumnavigating the globe for the second time.

During the 17th century, piracy and smuggling were accompanied by efforts to found European colonies on the American mainland as well as in the Caribbean. The Dutch, French, and English would, respectively, establish their bases in Curaçao, Saint-Domingue (in the northwest of Hispaniola), and Jamaica.

In the last quarter of the 17th century piracy was leaving its place to contraband trade, which had been steadily increasing for two centuries. So the European establishments in the Caribbean became bases for contraband trade with the Spanish colonies. Jamaica was to become the main naval and military base for England's West Indies and it served as a center for processing bullion. Its prosperous economy was based on sugar, slaves, rum, and, of course, piracy.

In November 1758, the Jamaican Council determined that gold and silver coins should be marked with a counterstamp to indicate official issues. The countermark, consisting of the floriated initials GR, for George III Rex, was applied to silver coins of the Pillar type and to contemporary gold issues from Lima, Mexico, and Popayán. The used of countermarked coins solved the problem of the many underweight coins which were circulating at the time.

Back to the mainland, another South American region that was part of the Viceroyalty of Peru until the Bourbon administrative changes was New Granada, today Colombia. As early as 1550 gold and silver mines were discovered in four provinces and a century later gold was found in the region of Chochó.

In fact, the first gold coins struck in the New World come from the *Nuevo Reino de Granada* (New Kingdom of Granada) and their mintmark would be NR, for *Nuevo Reino*. Though the official authorization to strike gold coins in the Indies did not occur until 1675, the mint at Bogotá began to produce gold coinage long before, in 1633.

The first coins struck at the mint of Bogotá were of the cob type with the Spanish coat of arms on the obverse and the cross quartering castles and lions on the reverse. This type remained unchanged for gold coins until the introduction of milled coinage in 1756. However, due to the aforementioned Potosí mint scandal, silver cobs from Bogotá had to adopt the pillars-and-waves type from the end of 1651.

During the 18th century there were several attempts to organize the viceroyalty in the region, but only in 1740 was the Viceroyalty of New Granada founded, with its capital at Santa Fe de Bogotá.

We are fortunate that this collection contains a real treasure from this era—the finest known example of the 8 reales issued in the name of Ferdinand VI (coin 155). It is Colombia's only Pillar dollar issue, for they were struck only in 1759. The obverse bears the crowned coat of arms of Castile and Leon with the three Bourbon fleurs-de-lis in the center. The Latin legend reads: FERDND VI D G HISPAN ET IND REX. The assayer's initials JV are to the left of the shield, while the denomination (8) is to the right.

The reverse bears the crowned Pillars of Hercules, bannered with the motto PLUS VLTR(A), with two worlds under a crown in the center, and everything over waves. The surrounding inscription reads VTRAQUE VNUM, and it includes the year of issue (1759) and to the sides, the mintmark N° R°, for Nuevo Reino.

The design of the Pillar coins was so attractive and recognizable that it became a model for other contemporary foreign coins, such as the Greenland piastres issues of 1771 and 1777 by Christian VII of Denmark and Norway (ruled 1766–1808). As we observe on the beautiful example in this collection (coin 156), it is very similar to a Pillar dollar in overall composition, though it ingeniously alters the details.

It is known that the 1771-dated issue was struck at the Copenhagen mint both that year (in which only 543 pieces were struck) and in 1774, when the bulk of the production (close to 45,000 pieces) was made. These were in reality Danish trade coins, which were not meant principally for Greenland. The obverse bears the crowned arms of Denmark, Norway, and Sweden, with a surrounding Latin inscription with the titles of Christian VII: CHRISTIANUS VII D G DAN NOR VAN GOT REX.

The reverse shows two crowned pillars with the motto PLVS VLTRA on the banners surrounding them; between the pillars, instead of the two worlds, there are two circles with the arms of Norway and Denmark under a royal crown. Underneath, the waves have three islands with the names ISLAND GRÖNLAND FERŌ. The Latin inscription reads: GLORIA EX AMORE PATRIAE (Glory Comes From the Love of the Fatherland).

Coin 155: 8 reales of Ferdinand VI, Colombia (shown enlarged on page 267)

Coin 156: Greenland piastre of Christian VII, Copenhagen, Denmark (shown enlarged on page 267)

Very few of these pieces have survived, and the two mintages can only be distinguished by analyzing the die combination. Of the 1771 strikes only five specimens are known. This piece corresponds to the 1774 strike, of which 20 specimens are known, half of which are in museum collections. It is certainly a piece of historical relevance since it illustrates the influence of Spanish American coinage over foreign currency in the 18th century.

When milled coinage was introduced in Spanish America, along with the Pillar type for silver, a bust type was used for gold coinage. From 1732 gold coins bear the monarch's bust on the obverse and the crowned arms on the reverse. The first type of bust was armored and had long and curly hair.

The denominations struck in this metal were of 8, 4, 2, and 1 escudos. Gold coins went through a number of modifications under the Bourbons, especially regarding their inscriptions and portrait styles. Under Charles III there were three different types in gold, but these variations did not change the main structure.

It was under Charles III that reform, both in the colonies and in Spain, reached its peak. Progressive measures were taken to eliminate the restrictions to trade both within the colonies and between them and Spain. In 1778 a free-trade decree allowed all qualified ports in Spain to conduct trade with most of the American provinces; Mexico and Venezuela, which the decree excluded, were included in that of 1789.

During the 18th century there was a strong recovery of silver mining in Peru and Mexico, but the Mexican mines were more productive. There were continuous efforts from the Crown to encourage mining, for example by the reduction of taxes and the dispatch of mining experts to Mexico and Peru.

This collection contains a beautiful 8 escudos (**coin 157**) struck at the Mexico City mint in 1763 in the name of Charles III illustrates the second type of gold coinage of this monarch. The bust is quite large; the monarch wears a wide cloak, his neck is covered, and he has the Golden Fleece on his chest. His hair is tied, with small curls falling down his back. The surrounding Latin inscription reads CAROLUS III D G HISP ET IND REX, and is completed with the year of issue, 1763.

The reverse bears a Spanish coat of arms in which the Castile-Aragon and Granada arms are in the center, with the Bourbon arms superimposed. The crown above the arms is higher than on the first type, the

Coin 157: 8 escudos of Charles III, Mexico City (shown enlarged on page 269)

Coin 155: 8 reales of Ferdinand VI, Colombia Unlike the abundant Pillar dollars from other mints, this one-year issue is a classic Latin American rarity.

Coin 156: Greenland piastre of Christian VII, Copenhagen, Denmark This Danish Pillar dollar amply demonstrates the impact of Spanish-American coinage throughout the world.

mintmark is on the left, and the assayers' initials on the right. In this case, there were two assayers working in conjunction at the mint; their initials, MM, correspond to Manuel de León and Manuel Assorín. A specific feature of the 8-escudos is the Order of the Golden Fleece around the arms. The inscription reads: IN UTROQ(UE) FELIX AUSPICE DEO (Happy in Both Worlds With the Auspices of God).

A similar bust style, sometimes called the "rat nose," appears on the 8 escudos struck in the Chilean mint of Santiago in 1764. The example in this collection (**coin 158**) has survived in outstanding condition and is the finest yet known. From the initial (J) we know that the assayer was José Larrañeta, who worked at the mint from 1749 to 1767.

Although the region of Chile became a captaincy-general in 1778, it continued to be practically isolated from the rest of the viceroyalty and the empire, and immigration was not encouraged. There was a totally different type of settlement from that introduced in Mexico and Peru, and the Indian population resisted the Europeans well beyond the Spanish colonial period.

Coin 158: 8 escudos of Charles III, Santiago, Chile

Decline of the Spanish Empire and Bust Coinage

Regardless of the Bourbon reforms, Spain was unable to free itself from some of its harmful and inefficient traditions. American silver helped to sponsor the Bourbon wars in Europe, but modifications in commercial policies were not able to supply either the mother country or its colonies with the tools required to compete with the European powers.

Competition from cheap foreign wares caused a decline of colonial manufacturing toward the end of the 18th century. Although Spain adopted mercantilist measures, they had little effect in supporting large-scale manufacturing. The main problems were the lack of investment capital, the preference to invest in land and mining, and a semi-servile labor system that was harmful to workers and to productivity.

Under Charles III some successive measures were taken to reduce the alloy in gold and silver coinage. There was a secret decree in 1771 to change the gold alloy from 22 karats (.916 fine) to 21-1/2 karats and 21-1/2 grains (.904 fine), and the silver alloy from .916 fine to .903 fine. Then, in 1786, a new confidential reduction was ordered, taking gold coins to .875 fine and silver pieces to .896 fine.

These modifications in the alloy forced a change in the coin designs used in Spanish America. In silver coins, starting in 1772, the mints

Coin 157: 8 escudos of Charles III, Mexico City Charles III led two wars against England, by which Spain lost Florida in 1763 and recovered it and Menorca in 1783.

Coin 158: 8 escudos of Charles III, Santiago, Chile Probably only a tale, it is said that Charles III secretly ordered the murder of the engraver of this "rat-nose" portrait.

Coin 159: 8 reales of Charles III, Guatemala City

Coin 160: 8 reales of Ferdinand VII, Popayán, Colombia

went from the Pillar type to the Bust type, which bears on the obverse the royal portrait, and on the reverse the Pillars of Hercules to the sides of the crowned Spanish arms. Also from that year the royal bust on gold coinage abandoned the wig and adopted a version similar to the one used on silver issues.

This collection includes an 18th-century Bust 8 reales (**coin 159**) struck at the Guatemala City mint in 1787. The Captaincy-General of Guatemala consisted of all Central America except Panama. Since the old capital city of Santiago de los Caballeros (Antigua Guatemala) was destroyed by an earthquake in 1773 (which also destroyed the mint facility), a new city was established at Guatemala City, with a new mint at which coining resumed in late 1776 and continued until 1821. Its mintmark, NG, stands for *Nueva Guatemala* (New Guatemala).

The obverse bears the laureate, cuirassed, and draped portrait of Charles III, facing right, surrounded by the Latin inscription CAROLUS III DEI GRATIA. Below the portrait appears the year of issue (1787).

The reverse bears a neo-Classic design of the Pillars of Hercules with banners around them with the motto PLUS VLTRA; the pillars flank the crowned arms of Spain with the Bourbon arms in the center. The monarch's titles are stated in the inscription: HISPAN ET IND REX, which is followed by the mintmark (NG), the denomination (8R), and the assayer's initial, M, which may correspond to Manuel Eusebio Sánchez.

The beginning of the 19th century saw the rise of the French empire guided by Napoleon Bonaparte, who in 1808 invaded Spain and absorbed it into his empire by forcing both Charles IV (ruled 1788–1808) and Ferdinand VII (ruled 1808 and 1813–1833) to abdicate. Then, Napoleon appointed his brother Joseph as king of Spain. The American colonies, so far as they were protected from the chaos in Europe, did not recognize Napoleon's appointee and continued to issue coinage in name of Ferdinand VII until the end of the Independence war in 1821.

A Bust 8 reales in this collection (**coin 160**) struck in the name of Ferdinand VII in 1811 at Popayán (in Colombia) comes from that particular period. The city was founded in 1538, and it was a rich mining center due to the gold mines of Chochó, Barbacoas, and Almaguer. Though a mint was established there thanks to the authorization given by Philip V in mid-1729, the first coins known from Popayán are from 1732.

Coin 159: 8 reales of Charles III, Guatemala City This reverse design combines elements of both the obverse and reverse of the previous type: the coat of arms and the Pillars of Hercules.

Coin 160: 8 reales of Ferdinand VII, Popayán, Colombia Though issued in the name of Ferdinand VII, this coin bears the portrait of the previous monarch, his father Charles IV.

Due to the vicinity to these abundant gold supplies, the mint's production was mostly in that metal. Since silver was obtained only by extraction from gold ores, silver coinage was scarcer and of a low-grade alloy. Silver coinage would begin during the reign of Charles III, when coinage became more regular and abundant, and it used the types and denominations adopted by all Spanish American mints.

On many occasions long distances within the viceroyalties and slow communications with the mother country made it such that when a monarch died and another took his place the new bust design was not immediately available. For this reason there are many cases in which coins were struck in the name of one monarch but bore the portrait of the previous one.

We have an excellent example of this phenomenon in the aforementioned 8 reales of 1811 from Popayán. The royal portrait on the obverse is that of Charles IV, Ferdinand VII's father. A second portrait type which is very rough, this time of Ferdinand VII himself, would appear only in some pieces struck in 1817. Silver coinage from the Popayán mint is quite scarce in general, yet more pieces have survived of the Bust type than of the Pillar type.

Apart from the date, all the specific information on the coin appears on the reverse: the mintmark (P), followed by the denomination (8R), and the assayers' initials, which in this case are J and F.

Ferdinand's reign was characterized by European wars and internal problems in Spanish America. The French invasion would contribute substantially to encourage the movement for independence that began in 1810 and would be generalized in all the viceroyalties, since *criollos* (locals of Spanish descent) seized the chance to fight for better opportunities. These movements for independence would end Spanish domination in the Americas and would open a new chapter in history with the emerging republics.

CHAPTER EIGHT

COINS *of the* LATIN AMERICAN REPUBLICS

Ana Lonngi de Vagi

Though far removed from Spain and its neighboring nations, the Americas were nonetheless affected by developments in Europe. Thus, when Napoleon assumed control of Spain in 1808 it had a profound effect on the territories in the New World. Enlightened ideas from the French and the American Revolution influenced political movements that progressively took more radical positions: from allegiance to the Spanish monarchy to complete independence. The struggle gave rise to new nations, which have survived in one form or another to the present day.

From New Spain to Independent Mexico

The movement for independence in Mexico began in September 1810 with priest Miguel Hidalgo's uprising. The war made shipping precious metals to Mexico City more difficult and insecure, and made it necessary to establish provisional mints near the mining centers. Eight such mints operated between 1812 and 1821. Official dies often did not reach the mints in time, resulting in a variety of different coinages.

In general, their production was mainly of silver and copper coins, which bore inscriptions demonstrating allegiance to the Spanish monarch, Ferdinand VII (ruled 1808 and 1813–1833), or at least stating they were issued by a royalist authority or institution, such as the Royal Funds.

Since the mining centers were in royalist hands, the insurgents suffered money shortages and depended upon forced loans and money they could capture from their opponents. Thus, they resorted to producing their own coinage to pay the troops. Insurgent issues were made with rudimentary means, and they were mostly struck in copper. Very few silver pieces were made, of which, even fewer have survived.

Hidalgo appointed José María Morelos, another priest, to organize an army in the south of the country. So when Hidalgo was captured in 1811, Morelos took the lead of the armed movement and he was the first to proclaim independence from the Bourbon monarchy.

Morelos ordered the striking of coins in denominations of 8, 2, 1, and 1/2 reales. His copper pieces were basically payment promises: they were meant to be exchanged for their face value in gold and silver coins once the movement triumphed. Thus, they represented the first fiduciary coinage in Mexico.

Another important leader to emerge after Hidalgo's capture was Ignacio López Rayón, who at Zitácuaro in mid-1811 established the Supreme

National American Junta, which was meant to govern in the name of the ousted Spanish king Ferdinand VII. The Junta produced coins to substitute Spanish ones; the first issues were cast and quite crude, while subsequent ones were struck.

This collection contains a wonderful example of an 8 reales (**coin 161**) struck in 1811 under López Rayón. It encloses an interesting mix of concepts. On the obverse we find the name of the Spanish monarch in the Latin inscription FERDIN VII DEI GRATIA (Ferdinand VII by the Grace of God), because the Junta was considered his constitutional representative, yet all of the motifs in the design are Mexican.

In fact it was on the coinage of the *Junta de Zitácuaro* that the vernacular elements which would become representative of the Mexican nation appear for the first time: the eagle on the cactus, as opposed to the monarch's bust on the royalist coins.

The obverse bears an early version of this motif, which would become the national emblem, only in this case the eagle is crowned and it appears over a bridge. The date, 1811, is part of the surrounding inscription, while we find the denomination (8. R.) in the field to the sides of the main device.

The reverse bears several symbols of the struggle for liberty and independence: a hand clasping a bow and arrow, a spear, an arrow, a quiver, and a sling. The inscription is in Spanish and reads PROVICIONAL POR LA SUPREMA JUNTA DE AMERICA (Provisional [Issue] by the Supreme Junta of America).

Besides the several royalist and insurgent issues, many original varieties were produced from countermarking coins taken as booty by both bands. The countermarks were meant to revalidate their own coins or to legalize the ones taken from their enemies. The Junta of Zitácuaro also applied to circulating coins from royalist mints a counterstamp with a small representation of the obverse and reverse types of the Junta coins.

After the death in 1815 of Morelos, who had been the leading figure of the insurgency, the movement for independence declined into a guerrilla war between the many rival leaders. Royalist armies gradually extinguished the remaining centers of insurgent resistance.

But the regional crisis was to be shaped further by events in Spain, when in 1820 the reinstated King Ferdinand VII faced a revolution that defended a constitutional regime. Consequently, the elites in Mexico

Coin 161: 8-reales Insurgent issue, Zitácuaro, Mexico (shown enlarged on page 277)

(conservative clergy, merchants, and army officers) feared they would lose their privileges and so they planned to separate from Spain and establish independence.

To do this, they used Agustín Iturbide, a *criollo* (local of Spanish descent) officer who had fought against the patriots and now offered a settlement to Vicente Guerrero, the chief rebel leader. Iturbide's plan was advantageous to both sides since it sanctioned independence, while it secured conservative interests through monarchy and the official recognition of the Roman Catholic Church. Civil equality was only achieved for criollos and Spaniards. The joint forces of Iturbide and Guerrero crushed royalist resistance.

Once the war was over, in mid-1822 a National Congress proclaimed Iturdibe Emperor Agustín I of Mexico. This put an end to the brief life of the regency that had provisionally governed the new nation. But the economic situation was far from attractive: mining had been practically abandoned, commerce had stopped, and much of the capital had been withdrawn from the country.

With Iturbide's coronation it became obvious that a monarchic system needed substantial resources to be sustained. So Iturbide immediately decreed the issuing of banknotes in the name of the Mexican Empire as a way of getting resources for the government. However, these banknotes were rejected by the population, which was accustomed to metal coins. The issue of such banknotes contributed to the fast discredit of the empire, and to its fall.

A commission was established to choose the design for imperial coinage; meanwhile, the mints continued to strike the colonial types without changing the date of 1821 until June 1822, when the new dies would be ready. A decree of June 1822 authorized the issue of silver, gold, and copper coins, which were to bear on the obverse Iturbide's portrait and an emblem with a crowned eagle on a cactus on the reverse.

Coinage of Iturbide followed the colonial in the denominations and in that the motifs elected were a bust for the obverse and the arms for the reverse. Because of how short the empire's life was, only gold and silver coins were issued. This collection includes a superb example of the 8-escudos piece (**coin 162**) struck at the Mexico City mint in 1822. The obverse bears the portrait of the emperor, surrounded by the Latin inscription AUGUSTINUS DEI PROVIDENTIA, the mintmark, and the year.

Coin 162: 8 escudos of Iturbide, Mexico City

Coin 161: 8-reales Insurgent issue, Zitácuaro, Mexico Though struck in the name of the Spanish king, this coin has an early version of the national emblem, an eagle on a cactus.

Coin 162: 8 escudos of Iturbide, Mexico City The short-lived empire of Iturbide annexed the provinces of Central America, but had no resources to support itself.

The reverse bears an emblem formed by a crowned eagle on a cactus augmented with war clubs and quivers containing arrows, and the continuation of the inscription—MEX I IMPERATOR CONSTITUT—the denomination (8s), and the assayer's initials (JM, which correspond to José García Anzaldo). The legend on both sides would translate as "Agustin I Constitutional Emperor of Mexico by the Providence of God."

This coin corresponds to the first type issued. A different type was used for 8 and 4 escudos struck in 1823, in which the bust of the emperor is larger and the eagle on the reverse appears in an oval frame.

The Mexican Empire included the annexed territories of the former Captaincy-General of Guatemala (what today is Guatemala, El Salvador, Honduras, Nicaragua, and Costa Rica). Some rare coins of Augustin I were struck in Honduras in 1823. But his abdication in the spring of 1823 immediately nullified the annexation. The rest of his coins were produced in Mexico City because the other mints in Mexico never received the imperial dies.

In 1823, after the collapse of Iturbide's empire, the Mexican Republic was established amid a financial crisis that would last for decades. Political instability required the foundation of several mints throughout the territory to reduce the risks of shipping precious metals from the mining centers to Mexico City. It also was meant to generate profits since the mints in the country were leased to private owners until the government recovered their administration toward the end of the century.

Coin 163: 8 escudos, Mexican Republic

New designs, inspired in republican ideals, were introduced. The common obverse was the national emblem and the surrounding legend in Spanish: REPUBLICA MEXICANA (Mexican Republic). The first type, with a "hook-necked" eagle, was struck in gold only in 1823 at the Mexico City Mint, and in silver at only two other mints. A beautiful example of this gold one-year type is included in this collection (**coin 163**). The obverse bears the eagle facing left, with a snake in its beak, and the inscription REPUBLICA MEXICANA on a semi-circle above joined branches of laurel and oak. The reverse bears a hand holding a liberty cap on a staff over an open book, which has the word LEY (law) on it, and the surrounding legend LA LIBERTAD EN LA LEY (Liberty in Law).

The rest of the elements to appear in this case are the denomination (8 E), the mintmark (M°), the year (1823), the assayer's initials (JM), and the alloy (21 karats). It is worth mentioning that Mexican republican

Coin 163: 8 escudos, Mexican Republic Some say that engravers at the Mexico City mint prepared dies with the portrait of the first president of the republic, but that he rejected them as a sign of monarchy. In 1823 a decree established that all Mexican coins should bear the national emblem, and this hook-necked eagle was struck in gold in Mexico City only in that year.

Coin 164: 8 reales, Durango, Mexican Republic

Coin 165: 8 reales, San Luis Potosí, Mexican Republic

coinage stated the fineness of its alloy, on both gold and silver coins. The assayer's initials correspond, as in the previous piece, to José García Anzaldo, assayer at the Mexico City mint from 1822 to 1832.

This is the first gold coin issued by the new republic in Mexico. The fact that it is a one-year type makes it all the more rare, especially when it is found in such remarkable condition as the example shown here.

Some of the provisional mints that had emerged during the war for independence would also become republican mints. This is the case with Durango, which started striking republican coins in mid-1824 and continued to operate until 1895.

Although dies were supposed to be sent from Mexico City to the other mints spread throughout the country, the difficulty of delivery resulted in some design varieties.

This collection also contains a second example of the hook-necked eagle issues: a silver 8 reales (**coin 164**) struck in Durango in 1824, when the mint was run by the government of the State of Durango (1824–1829). This was the only year that Durango produced hook-necked eagle 8 reales, and although the obverse design is similar to the previous coin, the Durango pieces have a period between the two words REPUBLICA and MEXICANA.

It bears on its reverse a liberty cap inscribed with the word LIBERTAD, with rays behind it. This type, known as "Cap and Rays," was the one used in silver. Surrounding the device is all the information about the coin: denomination (8 R), mintmark (D°), year of issue (1824), assayer's initials (RL), and fineness (10 dineros and 20 grains = .9027 fine).

Unlike Durango, where a provisional mint had existed during the War for Independence, at San Luis Potosí a mint was established to issue republican coinage. It began to operate in the fall of 1827 and for most of its life was leased to private foreign companies. It produced silver coins in the denominations of 8, 4, 2, 1, and 1/2 reales, as well as copper 1/4 reales. The 8 reales of 1827 from San Luis Potosí in this collection (**coin 165**) is an example of the mint's very first production; we know it started striking Cap and Rays 8 reales in late 1827, and continued to produce them until 1893. When this coin was struck the mint was under the administration of the government of the State of San Luis Potosí (1817–1835).

Interestingly, the type of the obverse design on this coin is not the profile, hook-necked eagle, but a facing eagle with spread wings (only its

Coin 164: 8 reales, Durango, Mexican Republic The first issue from the mint of Durango, this coin bears another hook-necked eagle.

Coin 165: 8 reales, San Luis Potosí, Mexican Republic This classic rarity belongs to the first year that the Republican type was struck at San Luis Potosí.

head shown in profile). Since the decree which established the national emblem as the common obverse for all republican coinage did not specify details such as the position of the eagle and its size, it left room for different interpretations and varieties. These make coinage of the Mexican Republic all the more interesting.

The reverse is the Cap and Rays type, yet the style is different than on the Durango piece: the liberty cap is larger and the incuse word LIBERTAD is in non-cursive, capital letters and is followed by a period. Next to the denomination appear the mintmark (Pi, for San Luis Potosí), the year (1827), and the assayer's initials, JS, which correspond to Juan Sanabria. Only about a half a dozen specimens are known, and this is one of the two which survive in superior condition.

> *When the Mexican Empire collapsed, the Republic of Central America broke away . . . .*

Events in Mexico had a strong influence in the neighboring region of Central America. As an echo of the declaration of Mexican independence, Central America declared its independence from Spain in 1821 and proclaimed the *República del Centro de América* (Republic of the Center of America). However, concerns about the capability of the country to defend itself led to its annexation to the Mexican Empire under Iturbide early in 1822.

This only aggravated the confrontations between the different factions: the city of Guatemala was in favor of the annexation, moderate sectors in the provinces supported the union with Mexico but were against the dominance of the Guatemalan elite, whereas the province of San Salvador and a few more radical cities were totally opposed to the annexation.

When the Mexican Empire collapsed in 1823 this annexed region separated from Mexico and became an independent nation: the Republic of Central America. The foundation of the country was characterized by faction-struggles and the lack of a central government able to reconcile the local interests of each province with those of the Federation.

The Federation started striking coins in 1824 at three different mints: Guatemala (NG), Tegucigalpa in Honduras (T), and Costa Rica (CR). The main type of the Central American coinage bears on the obverse a radiate sun over five mountains, while the reverse bears a native *ceiba* tree.

This collection includes a beautiful first-year 8 escudos struck in Guatemala (**coin 166**). The five peaks on the obverse represent the five member-states of the Federation: Guatemala, El Salvador, Honduras, Nicaragua, and Costa Rica. The surrounding inscription reads: REPUBLICA DEL CENTRO DE AMERICA, and the year of issue, 1824.

The tree on the reverse, the ceiba, is a tropical species and is the largest to grow in the region's forests. The denomination appears in the field to the sides of the tree (8. E.), and the surrounding inscription reads LIBRE CRESCA FECUNDO (Free May it Grow Fecund), followed by the mint-mark (NG, for New Guatemala), the assayer's initial (M, which corresponds to Manuel Eusebio Sánchez), and the fineness of the alloy (21 karats).

As mentioned above, since the birth of the Central American Republic there were many interests pulling the member states in different directions. This shows from the fact that from 1824 to 1825 each separate state promulgated its own constitution. The Federation dissolved in 1838–1840, giving way to the present-day nations.

The Struggle for Independence in South America

The movement for independence in South America was in good part a consequence of events in Europe, since the Spanish involvement as an ally of France in 1796 had given England cause to engage in trade with the Americas, by which communications were reduced between Spain and its colonies.

Coin 166: 8 escudos, Guatemala (Republic of the Center of America) (shown enlarged on page 285)

The great distances separating the different regions, along with their strong cultural and economic isolation, resulted in a lack of unity in the movements for independence in South America.

As early as 1806 the citizens of Buenos Aires had experienced autonomous power, when a volunteer army expelled an English fleet that had captured the city. A second British invasion was also rebuffed, forcing the British commander to evacuate both Buenos Aires and Montevideo.

Once the criollos—who had led the defense of the city on both occasions—tasted power, they were not willing to relinquish it. Santiago Liniers, the hero of the defense, was proclaimed viceroy, but soon he was deposed because of his Napoleonic tendencies.

The detonator of the independence movement in Argentina was Napoleon's intervention in Spain, beginning in 1808. To respond to it,

Coin 167: 8 escudos, Argentina (Provinces of Río de la Plata)

an autonomous government (*Junta*) was established in May 1810 at Buenos Aires to rule in the name of the ousted Spanish king Ferdinand VII. As revolutionary ideas spread to the rest of the viceroyalty of Río de la Plata, the Junta sent expeditionary armies to Upper Peru, known to be a royalist bastion.

After the patriot victory there in early 1813 the Argentine Auxiliary Army, led by General Manuel Belgrano, occupied the city of Potosí from June to November that same year. The patriots took control of the mint and struck gold and silver coins in the name of the *Provincias del Río de la Plata* (Provinces of Río de la Plata), which was the original name of Argentina.

A wonderful example of this coinage is included in this collection. It is an 8 escudos (**coin 167**) struck by the Argentines in the summer of 1813 at occupied Potosí. An interesting fact is that since most of the mint workers had left when the city was evacuated, some people who did lesser tasks were promoted to the main offices. This was the case with the substitute smelter José Antonio de Sierra, who was promoted to assayer at age 67 and whose initial (J) appears on this piece.

The designs on this coin reflect the rupture with the colonial power. The obverse bears a beaming sun with a human face. The reverse bears the new arms of the republic surrounded by the inscription EN UNION Y LIBERTAD (In Union and Liberty), followed by the mintmark, which is a monogram formed by the letters PTS, for Potosí, then the assayer's initial, the denomination, and the date.

The city of Potosí was taken back by the royalist forces late in 1813, and fortunately the patriot plan to blow up the mint failed. During 1814 the Argentine coins were withdrawn from circulation in Upper Peru and melted to produce royalist pieces. A similar episode occurred in 1815 when the Argentine forces occupied Potosí again and produced coins for the independent provinces.

Next we go to Chile, where the struggle for independence began in the fall of 1810 and continued until 1824, even though independence was declared by generals José de San Martín and Bernardo O'Higgins in early 1818.

O'Higgins was the first ruler of independent Chile and, though he drafted constitutions in 1818 and in 1822, his belief that the only way to establish order in the country was through a dictatorship caused him to lose popularity rapidly. He was forced to leave power early in 1823.

Coin 166: 8 escudos, Guatemala (Republic of the Center of America) The five mountain peaks represent Guatemala, El Salvador, Honduras, Nicaragua, and Costa Rica, the states of the Republic.

Coin 167: 8 escudos, Argentina (Provinces of Río de la Plata) This type, Argentina's first independent coinage, was struck in Upper Peru, the last royalist bastion of the viceroyalty of Río de la Plata.

Coin 168: peso, Chile

After three years of relative order under his successor Ramón Freire (1823–1826), a period followed which is known as "the five years of anarchy." It is from this period that one of the classic Latin American rarities comes to us: the 1828 Coquimbo silver peso (**coin 168**).

While the colonial mint at Santiago continued to work, now striking coins in the name of the new country, another mint was established in Coquimbo by president Francisco Antonio Pinto (ruled 1827–1829). This mint worked only for the year 1828–1829, and produced silver pesos in 1828.

The piece bears on the obverse a rare volcano type that is artistically superior to the regular type struck in the Santiago mint. The smoking volcano is amid mountains and a lake, above which is a wreath enclosing the denomination (UN PESO). The inscription reads CHILE INDEPENDIENTE (Independent Chile) and it describes its place of origin, Coquimbo, at the bottom.

The reverse bears a column surmounted by a globe, above which is a star and a banner inscribed LIBERTAD (Liberty). The surrounding inscription reads UNION Y FUERZA (Union and Strength), the assayer's initials, T.H., and the year of issue, 1828.

The year 1828 is important for the Constitution of the Republic of Chile, which was decreed in August. It divided the country into eight provinces—Coquimbo, Aconcagua, Santiago, Colchagua, Maule, Concepción, Valdivia, and Chiloé—and it established Catholicism as the exclusive national religion. Amongst the responsibilities of the Congress was "to establish the weight, fineness, value, type and denomination of coins."

The coastal region of Coquimbo would only begin developing by the mid-19th century, when copper foundries were established and, in 1862, the railroad finally linked the mines with the ocean.

Reaching Stability

In most of the new Latin American countries the first years of independent government were characterized by economic crises, an extended dispute between conservative and liberal parties, differing views on the type of government they should adopt, and friction between supporters of centralist and federalist regimes.

In the case of Argentina, although the government in Buenos Aires tried to maintain the original extent of the viceroyalty of Río de la Plata,

Coin 168: peso, Chile Though a mint was founded in Coquimbo by president Francisco Antonio Pinto (in what probably was an attempt to develop that coastal region of Chile), it only operated for a year. True economic growth did not begin until the mid-19th century, when copper foundries were established.

it faced fragmentation through the independence of Paraguay in 1814, Bolivia in 1825, and Uruguay in 1828, as well as through the internal disputes between Buenos Aires and the rest of the provinces.

Although the country had enormous riches derived from its export trade in grains, hides, meat, and wool, it would struggle to transform its wealth into a stable economic and monetary system.

Several liberal reforms were introduced under Bernardino Rivadavia (ruled 1826–1827), such as giving access to instruction to women and supporting agricultural development and foreign immigration, but his attempt to establish a centralist constitution only led to his fall.

Rivadavia was succeeded by the ruthless General Juan Manuel de Rosas (ruled 1829–1852), the first military dictator of Argentina. He supported a loose federal confederation and was against the believers of a unified state dominated by Buenos Aires. With a strong hand, he was the arbiter of a very delicate balance of groups of influence.

Under Rosas coinage bore the new name of the country, *República Argentina Confederada* (Confederate Argentine Republic). This collection includes an example of a very rare provincial issue (**coin 169**) which bears on its obverse a portrait of the dictator Rosas in military uniform, with his name below. The inscription calls him RESTAURADOR DE LAS LEYES (Restorer of the Laws).

This gold 8 escudos is a one-year type struck at the mint of La Rioja in 1842, of which fewer than ten specimens are known. The reverse shows the republican oval shield (clasped hands holding a liberty cap on a staff) surrounded by a wreath, flags or banners, and arms, and topped by a radiant sun with a human face. The inscription reads: REPUB. ARGENT. CONFEDERADA, followed by the mintmark (R), the denomination (8E), and the year (1842).

Rosas proclaimed himself "ruler anointed by God" in 1835, and it would be 17 years until José de Urquiza defeated him in the battle of Caseros in 1852, forcing him to leave power.

Further north, in Ecuador, the independence of the *audiencia* of Quito was proclaimed in the spring of 1822, along with its integration into the Republic of Gran Colombia (formed by Colombia, Ecuador, and Venezuela). The union did not even last ten years, yet it originated the conflicts of boundaries between Ecuador, Colombia, and Peru.

Coin 169: 8 escudos, Argentina (Confederate Argentine Republic)

Coin 169: 8 escudos, Argentina (Confederate Argentine Republic)

The strong divisions between the provinces of Argentina made it possible for several leaders to rule at the same time. Juan Manuel de Rosas, originally the governor of Buenos Aires, who is portrayed on this rare gold coin, extended his power and influence during 17 years of a military regime that brought stability to the nation.

Ecuador separated from Gran Colombia in 1830 and the Congress of Riobamba drafted the first constitution, which gave the country its name and established its capital at Quito.

Only in 1836, however, did coinage begin to be issued in the name of the *República del Ecuador* (Republic of Ecuador). On 4-reales pieces of 1844 the bust of Simón Bolívar, one of the icons of the independence movement, appeared, as well as the arms of Ecuador. Then, in 1846 the 8 reales was introduced and a Liberty head was adopted for all the silver denominations.

An example of the first crown-size coin of republican Ecuador is also included in this collection: the 8 reales (**coin 170**) struck in Quito in 1846. The obverse bears a draped bust of Liberty wearing a liberty cap with the word LIBERTAD incuse on its border. The inscription surrounding the device reads EL PODER EN LA CONSTITUCION (Power in the Constitution). The year of issue (1846) and the fineness of the alloy (10 dineros, 20 grains = .9027 fine) also appear.

Coin 170: 8 reales, Republic of Ecuador

Ecuador's first crown-size coin declared the power of the constitution . . . .

The reverse bears an oval shield containing a radiant sun on astrological course, over a mountain and a steamship on water; the shield is supported by fasces, to the sides of which are flags and a wreath, while an opened-wing condor stands above. The inscription names the issuer, REPUBLICA DEL ECUADOR, the mint (Quito), the assayer's initials (GJ), and the denomination (8 Rs).

Ecuador was ruled at the time by Vicente Ramón Roca (1845–1849), and soon after, in 1851, a revolution brought the military to power under José María Urbina. The following decades were characterized by the confrontation between militarist and liberal sectors.

We now go to Bolivia, which was founded as a nation in 1825 when General Antonio José Sucre, one of Simón Bolívar's lieutenants, detached Upper Peru from the Provinces of Río de la Plata. Bolivia took its name from Bolívar, who was declared "Father of the Country" and appointed its first president.

Coin 170: 8 reales, Republic of Ecuador Ecuador separated from the republic of Great Colombia, which also had included Venezuela and Colombia. The capped bust of Liberty on this 8 reales—the first crown-size coin of Ecuador—resembles the contemporary Liberty bust on coins of the United States of America, though the inscription on the cap, LIBERTAD, is rendered in Spanish.

Nevertheless, Bolívar delegated power to Sucre, who was confirmed as the constitutional president and governed from 1826 to 1828. A revolution then put power in the hands of Andrés de Santa Cruz (ruled 1829–1839), who tried to bring order to the country and established a confederation to reunite Bolivia with Peru in 1836. Chile and Argentina felt threatened by this development and a Chilean army defeated Santa Cruz in 1839 and forced him into exile.

Chaos followed and in 1841 there were three simultaneous governments. Peru tried to take advantage of the situation by invading Bolivia, but was repelled by José Ballivián, whose triumph sealed Bolivia's independence for good.

Coin 171: 8 escudos, Bolivian Republic

Ballivián ruled in calm from 1841 to 1847, when he was deposed by a rebellion. A new period of reordering began in 1848 under Manuel Isidoro Belzú (ruled 1848–1855), whose authoritarian regime quelled several uprisings.

The famous mint of Potosí continued to work, striking the new republican coinage, which followed the colonial system of denominations, weights, and fineness. This collection includes an example of the rarest of the Bolivian portrait gold 8 escudos (**coin 171**). It was struck at Potosí in 1852 and only six specimens are known. The obverse bears the laureate portrait of Bolívar facing left and the inscription LIBRE POR LA CONSTITUCION (Free by the Constitution).

The reverse is a synthesis of the country's riches: it bears a radiant sun above a mountain, an alpaca, and a wheat sheaf. They represent respectively mining, wool production, and agriculture. The coin was issued by the Bolivian Republic, as we may read on the inscription REPUBLICA BOLIVIANA surrounding the device.

At the bottom, beneath a curved row of nine stars representing the principal regions of the country, is the mintmark (a monogram made of the letters P T S, of Potosí), the denomination, 8 E(scudos), the year of issue (1852), the assayers' initials (F P), and the fineness of the alloy, 21 karats.

Our next stop takes us further north. After the dissolution of the Gran Colombia one of the countries to emerge was the Republic of New Granada, proclaimed by the constitution in 1832. Francisco de Paula Santander was the first president (ruled 1832–1837).

The first properly independent coinage of Colombia had retained the denominations and alloys of the Spanish colonial system. However, the economic and political crisis forced a reduction in purity by the 1830s,

Coin 171: 8 escudos, Bolivian Republic Ironically, the mountain of Potosí, portrayed on this coin as the symbol of Bolivia's riches, had by the mid-19th century become quite poor after two centuries of intense exploitation. Indeed, by this time tin had replaced silver as the chief mining product.

when the silver alloy fell to .666 fine, while the gold seems to have maintained its original properties.

In 1847, the silver purity was re-established by the adoption of the French system. The debased 8 reales became the new 10 reales, weighing 25 grams and being .900 fine, which was equivalent to the 5 francs of the Latin Monetary Union. So the peso was issued along with its fractions, first in reales, then in décimos, and finally in centavos.

Though in 1849 gold coins of 2 and 16 pesos (paired to the French 10 and 80 francs) appeared, more natural denominations of 1, 5, 10, and 20 pesos followed. This collection includes an example of the 20 pesos one-year type of 1859 (**coin 172**). The obverse bears a Liberty head facing left, with a ribbon bearing the word LIBERTAD. The inscription surrounding the device reads: CONFEDERACION GRANADINA (Granadine Confederation), followed by the year of issue, 1859.

The reverse consists of a condor above the bannered arms of Colombia. The inscription gives us all the information about the piece: denomination (VEINTE PESOS), weight (32.258 grams), fineness of the alloy (.900), and the mint where it was struck (BOGOTÁ).

The constitution in force had been promulgated in 1858 under Mariano Ospina Rodríguez, and it had established a federal government and had called the country *Confederación Granadina*. Then, in 1863 a new federal constitution established the *Estados Unidos de Colombia* (United States of Colombia) until a centralist regime was established in 1886 and the country was given the name of *República de Colombia* (Republic of Colombia).

Now we jump back to the south of the continent, to the small republic of Uruguay, whose first antecedent lies in a revolt led in 1811 by José Artigas in the *Banda Oriental del Uruguay* (east bank of the Uruguay River). With the support of most rural sectors, Artigas proposed a federation with the provinces of Río de la Plata. But the Buenos Aires oligarchy felt threatened by his liberal views and sent forces to crush him in 1816.

After a period of Portuguese-Brazilian intervention (1817–1828), the independence of Uruguay was recognized in August 1828. A constitution was approved in July 1830 and the country had to test its validity. Coinage was not issued in the name of the *República Oriental del Uruguay* (Eastern Republic of the Uruguay) until 1840 and even then, it consisted only of copper pieces of low denomination.

Coin 172: 20 pesos, Colombia (Granadine Confederation) (shown enlarged on page 297)

The first decades of independence were marked by uprisings in the interior and civil war (1839–1851) between the opposing factions led by Fructuoso Rivera (the *Colorados* or "Reds") and Manuel Oribe (the *Blancos* or "Whites"). During this period, the Blanco party controlled the interior while the Colorado party had control of Montevideo. According to their own interests, foreign powers intervened: England and France on the side of the *Colorados*, and Argentina on the side of the *Blancos*.

It is remarkable how such a small territory was coveted by so many different parties. In fact, Montevideo was called New Troy because of the protracted siege it suffered from 1843 to 1851, in the war between forces of Oribe and the Argentine dictator Rosas.

> *It is remarkable how such a small territory was coveted by so many . . . .*

These confrontations were an obstacle to national unity, and they often urged the involvement of Uruguay in the affairs of Argentina and Brazil, such as Uruguay's participation in the War of the Triple Alliance (1865–1870) on the side of Argentina and Brazil against Paraguay. Between 1870 and 1872 the country was plunged into civil war, especially thanks to President Lorenzo Batlle's policy of total exclusion of the Blanco party.

This collection contains an extraordinarily rare silver peso (**coin 173**) struck in 1870, at the outset of the civil war, of which only two specimens are known. The obverse shows an oval shield with the arms of Uruguay, with a rising sun atop, surrounded by a wreath with crossed cannons and banners behind.

The reverse consists of the value (1 PESO) within a wreath and the year of issue at the bottom. The inscription on both sides of the coin describes the REPUBLICA ORIENTAL DEL URUGUAY, LIBRE Y CONSTITUIDA (Free and Constituted Eastern Republic of the Uruguay).

That year of 1870 also marked the beginning of a wide European immigration to the country. Uruguay would finally be unified under Lorenzo Latorre (president 1876–1879), a dictator who combined a strong power with some modernizing reforms that resulted in an important economic growth.

Our next stop is Venezuela. After the disintegration of the Gran

Coin 173: peso, Republic of Uruguay (shown enlarged on page 297)

Colombia, Venezuela became an independent nation in 1830. The separation of Venezuela from Colombia had resulted from the rivalry between Bolívar's lieutenants, José Antonio Páez and Francisco de Paula Santander.

Páez became the country's first president from 1830 to 1835; he was in power again from 1839 to 1843, and once more between 1861 and 1863. His death was followed by a period of revolts during which a federal system was established in Venezuela.

In 1870 Antonio Guzmán Blanco (ruled 1870–1877, 1879–1884, and 1886–1888) took power. For practically two decades he was in command as a dictator who stopped militarism and was particularly concerned with promoting education.

The area had lacked a mint under the colonial government and when it was a part of Gran Colombia. The earliest independent Venezuelan coins are coppers struck in 1843 in London, followed by other issues produced in 1852 and 1858 in Paris and Birmingham. A small issue of silver coins was also struck in Paris in 1858, in denominations of 5, 2, 1, and 1/2 reales.

The Venezuelan government was unable to provide sufficient coinage for the country, so it was normal to have foreign money in circulation, which caused disparity and confusion. To combat this, Venezuela adhered to the Latin Monetary Union in 1871, and beginning in 1873 issued coinage based on the silver venezolano (Venezuelan), equivalent to five French francs.

This collection includes an example of the short-lived venezolano (**coin 174**). Although it was the main unit of the new monetary system, it was struck only in 1876, in Paris. On the obverse it bears the portrait of Simón Bolívar facing left, identifying him as the *Libertador* (Liberator). The anchor and bee are signs of the engraver and director of the Paris mint, while the A identifies the production. The engraver was Albert Desiré Barre, whose name also appears below the portrait.

The reverse bears the arms of Venezuela, flanked by branches, beneath crossed cornucopias laden with produce. On the ribbon below the shield we find incised the words: INDEPENDEN.[CIA] – LIBERTAD – 5 DE JULIO 1811 – 28 DE MARZO 1864 – DIOS Y FED.[CN] (Independence and Liberty – July 5, 1811 – March 28, 1864 – God and Federation). The device is surrounded by the main legend: ESTADOS UNIDOS DE

Coin 174: Venezolano, United States of Venezuela (shown enlarged on page 299)

Coin 172: 20 pesos, Colombia (Granadine Confederation) The constitution of 1858 established a federal government and named the country the Granadine Confederation.

Coin 173: peso, Republic of Uruguay The fate of Uruguay in its early years was often determined by the interests of its neighbor countries.

VENEZUELA (United States of Venezuela). As in other cases, the coin describes its weight (25 grams) and alloy (.900 fine) to the sides of the date, which appears in the bottom.

The dates on the ribbon refer respectively to the first declaration of independence from Spain, and to the promulgation of the constitution incorporating federalist principles. Venezuelan regular coinage would progressively substitute foreign currencies, covering the demand for circulating money, until finally in 1886 foreign coins were declared illegal.

We now return to Central America, where, after the collapse of the Federation of Central America from 1838 to 1840, its five member-states separated and each had to organize its own government and economy, as well as its own monetary system. Interestingly, they had three independences: first from Spain, then from Mexico, and finally from the Federation.

> *In Guatemala, Rufino Barrios was yet another example of the "liberal dictator."*

Guatemala declared its third independence in 1839. Similar to the other states, apart from taking care of its government and economy, it produced its independent coinage, for which it chose characteristic motifs and legends.

Although the earliest gold and silver coins of independent Guatemala still followed the Spanish colonial denominational system, in 1869 to 1871 there was an attempt to introduce a decimal coinage based on a silver peso of 25 grams and a gold 20 pesos of 32.26 grams, which were equivalent respectively to the 5 francs and 100 francs of the Latin Monetary Union.

A good part of Guatemalan history of the later quarter of the 19th century was related to the government of Justo Rufino Barrios, who came into power after the liberal revolution of 1871 and was president from 1873 until his death in 1885. He is yet another example of the "liberal dictator": with a personal and strong power he promoted cultural and economical reforms, proclaimed liberty of cult, established total separation between the State and the Church, and secularized the goods of the Church.

Barrios imposed his influence over the other governments in the region, but his mistake was in being a believer in the Central American Federation, which he tried to re-establish by force. His attempts failed

Coin 174: Venezolano, United States of Venezuela Venezuela's dictator Antonio Guzmán Blanco may be credited with abolishing militarism. But this advance was reversed with the coup of General Joaquín Crespo, who restored a militarist form of government. With Crespo's regime came political stability, but also an incompetent administration and a loss of civil rights.

and he not only was defeated, but fell in battle at Chalchuapa.

This collection includes an example of a rare two-year issue of the Barrios-era coinage of Guatemala (**coin 175**). The type bears on the obverse a laureate head of Liberty facing left surrounded by the inscription REPUBLICA DE GUATEMALA (Republic of Guatemala) and the denomination VEINTE PESOS (Twenty Pesos).

The reverse consists of a scroll on crossed arms (two swords and two rifles) in a laurel wreath. A quetzal stands atop the scroll, which has an incuse inscription in four lines: LIBERTAD – 15 – DE SET.^{E} DE – 1821 (Liberty, September 15, 1821). This date refers to the first declaration of independence, that from Spain, which had little of a nationalist character. The fineness of the alloy (.900 fine) is stated on the bottom, followed by the assayer's initial (F) and the year of issue (1878).

Coin 175: 20 pesos, Republic of Guatemala

The Mexican Revolution and its Coinage

Just as in the war for independence in Mexico (1810–1821), an immediate consequence of the Mexican Revolution early in the 20th century was the disappearance of coins from circulation. Gold and silver coins were hoarded and often sent abroad.

Paper money issues multiplied, both from the Federalists and the revolutionary forces, none of which had reserves to back them. This created an unprecedented inflation in the country. Once again, necessity issues emerged in an attempt to meet the needs of the population and of the belligerent parties. This makes the Mexican Revolution one of the most varied and interesting epochs to study from the numismatic point of view.

The revolutionary movement in Mexico began as an opposition to the possible sixth re-election of Porfirio Díaz (ruled 1876, 1877–1880, and 1884–1911), even though he had ruled according to the Laws of Reform, promoted industry, and had given the country a period of stability. The 1910 elections were approaching and by then Díaz would be 80; he had been in power for more than 30 years, so the question of who would take his place was in the air. Díaz himself had announced that he welcomed an opposition party and that the country was ready for democratic elections.

In response to the dictator's invitation, Francisco I. Madero was the presidential candidate for the Anti-Reelection Party. He was arrested and jailed in June 1910. Just around that time, Díaz's reelection was announced

Coin 175: 20 pesos, Republic of Guatemala Guatemalan president Justo Rufino Barrios had his own ideas on progress. His chief economic plan was to grow and export more coffee, which involved constructing railroads and outfitting ports for greater exportation. In the process, the native communities lost their lands and their people were forced to work on the coffee plantations.

and it was clear that the only way to change things was an armed revolt.

Madero was freed on bail in October 1910 and went to the United States of America. From there he designed his revolutionary plan calling for an armed uprising on November 20. His *Plan de San Luis* was synthesized in the motto "effective suffrage, no reelection." But instead of mass uprisings, when the date arrived there were only a few isolated guerrilla bands. When they combined, however, they started defeating Federalist forces in the State of Chihuahua.

The echo of the military victories in the north caused mutinies against Díaz in the capital, forcing him to resign and leave the country. The elections of 1911 declared Madero president. However, he had to face constant attacks from revolutionary leaders who were disappointed about not having access to power, and by counter-revolutionaries who conspired against the new government.

Only 20 days after Madero had assumed power Emiliano Zapata rose with his own view of what the revolution should achieve, especially the claim that land should be owned by those who worked it. The economic elites felt threatened, as did foreign investors. In February 1913, after the *Decena Trágica*, ten days of cannoning the heart of Mexico City, the old army and the counter-revolutionary sectors took power and murdered Madero.

Coin 176: peso de Bolita, Hidalgo del Parral (Chihuahua), Mexico

The usurper, Victoriano Huerta (ruled 1913–1914), promised peace but spread repression and violence. To respond to Huerta, the revolutionaries instinctively regrouped. Led by Venustiano Carranza, they directed their efforts to restore constitutional order. Finally Huerta's resistance was defeated and he left power in July 1914.

Coins of the revolution were produced mostly by the forces of Zapata and Francisco (Pancho) Villa. There were also issues by the *Estado Libre y Soberano de Oaxaca* (Free and Sovereign State of Oaxaca), which seceded from the rest of the country, unwilling to accept Huerta. The materials used to produce revolutionary coins were not only gold, silver, and copper, but anything available, such as iron, nickel, and even clay.

Villa's issues were produced in the states of Chihuahua, Durango, Jalisco, and Aguascalientes. The most famous are the *Muera Huerta* (Death to Huerta) and *Bolita* (small ball) pesos. It is known about the first that Huerta ordered that anyone holding such a coin was to be shot.

The latter, of which this collection includes the finest-known exam-

Coin 176: peso de Bolita, Hidalgo del Parral (Chihuahua), Mexico
Railroads had been built in Mexico by dictator Porfirio Díaz in an effort to link different regions of the country. They were seen as the key to progress and order. Ironically, Francisco Villa used these railways in the Revolution to transport his soldiers and horses, as well as the women in charge of feeding the troops.

Coin 177: peso, Constitutionalist Army, Mexico

Coin 178: 2 pesos, Suriana, Mexico

The coin features the motto "Reform, Liberty, Justice and Law."

ple (**coin 176**), was struck at Hidalgo del Parral, in the state of Chihuahua, as we may confirm from the inscription on the obverse: H DEL PARRAL. The date, 1913, and a wreath appear below. On the reverse the denomination, 1 PESO, is superimposed on a central ball, from which the type takes the name of Bolita.

This collection also contains another example of Villa's issues from the State of Chihuahua, a silver peso (**coin 177**) struck in 1914 in the name of the Constitutionalist Army. While copper coins of this type are common, this piece is the only specimen known in silver.

The motifs on obverse and reverse repeat the ones used in the republican coinage: the cap and rays and the scales of justice. The inscription on the obverse reads REPUBLICA MEXICANA, and states below the place it was produced, E. DE CHIHA. (State of Chihuahua). On the reverse we find the issuer, EJERCITO CONSTITU-CIONALISTA (Constitutionalist Army); the value, UN PESO (One Peso); and the date, 1914.

Zapata's issues were produced in Mexico City as well as in the states of Morelos, Guerrero, and Mexico. This collection includes one of the top rarities of the revolution, a 2-pesos coin (**178**) produced with metal from a mining camp known as Suriana in Guerrero, of which only two examples are known. The other one is in the Banco de México collection. This piece is certainly the finest of the two, for the quality of the planchet, the strike, and the amount of wear.

The coin is of the general type with the motto "Reform, Liberty, Justice and Law" in the surrounding inscription. It shows two mountains, a smoking volcano, and a sun with a human face on the reverse, beneath which is SURIANA, the name of the mining camp.

The obverse consists of the national emblem (the eagle with a snake on its beak, on a cactus), and the inscription REPUBLICA MEXICANA, followed by the denomination, DOS PESOS (Two Pesos), and the place and date of issue, G^{RO}. (Guerrero), 1915.

The struggle between the different revolutionary forces, however, was far from over. The revolutionary Carranza succeeded in bringing

Coin 177: peso, Constitutionalist Army, Mexico Though long considered a numismatic myth, this silver issue is a unique item of the Mexican Revolution.

Coin 178: 2 pesos, Suriana, Mexico Zapata fought on behalf of the rural poor, convinced that the land should belong to those who worked it

under control the agrarian insurrections led by Zapata and Villa, and ten years after the beginning of the war, a new era of stability and reconstruction was emerging.

Notwithstanding the eventual revolts spread in the country, a new, strong power that went beyond the presidency was able to lead the nation in the transformations that the revolutionary movement had announced. The Banco de México, founded in 1925, would have an important role in putting the financial and monetary situation back in order. Finally, it was established by law as the Banco's exclusive prerogative to issue coins and banknotes in the country.

Market values compiled by Ira and Larry Goldberg, in three grades
(Very Fine, Extremely Fine, and Uncirculated), and in Proof where appropriate.

COIN	PAGE	DESCRIPTION	VERY FINE	EXTREMELY FINE	UNCIRCULATED	PROOF
\multicolumn{7}{c}{CHAPTER ONE: ANCIENT GREEK COINAGE}						
1	3	Lydia. Croesus, 561-546 B.C. Gold stater	$3,500	$8,000		
2	5	Aegina. Aegina, c. 480-457 B.C. Silver stater	1,500	5,000		
3	5	Corinth, c. 520-515 B.C. Pegasus, curled wing, left / Swastika. Silver stater	2,750	5,000		
4	7	Athens, after 449 B.C. Head of Athena / Owl right. Silver tetradrachm	1,250	3,500		
5	9	Peloponnesos. Elis, c. 432 B.C., the 87th Olympiad. Silver stater	12,500	35,000		
6	11	Caria. Islands off of Rhodes, c. 404-385 B.C. Silver tetradrachm	10,000	25,000		
7	11	Thrace. Island of Thasos, c. 485-410 B.C. Silver stater	1,500	3,500		
8	13	Macedon. Abydus, c. 323-319 B.C. (under Philip III). Gold stater	2,250	5,000	$7,500	
9	13	Macedon. Alexander III (336-323 B.C.). Amphipolis, c. 324-318 B.C. Rare dies. Gold distater	13,000	22,500	35,000	
10	15	Macedon. Demetrios Poliorketes (305-284 B.C.). Amphipolis, c. 290-289 B.C. Silver tetradrachm	2,500	5,000		
11	15	Thrace. Lysimachos (323-281 B.C.). Pella, c. 286/5-282/1. Gold distater	2,750	5,000	9,000	
12	17	Ptolemaic. Berenice II (247-221 B.C.). Gold octadrachm	17,500	30,000		
13	19	Bruttium. Caulonia, c. 520 B.C. Silver stater	7,500	15,000		
14	19	Bruttium. Rhegium, c. 320 B.C. Silver tetradrachm	12,500	30,000		
15	21	Sicily. Messana, c. 412-408 B.C. Silver tetradrachm	4,000	12,500		
16	21	Sicily. Syracuse, c. 510-490 B.C. Silver tetradrachm	7,500	15,000		
17	23	Sicily. Syracuse, c. 404-400 B.C. Signed by Cimon. Silver decadrachm	30,000	75,000		
18	23	Sicily. Syracuse, c. 405-390 B.C. Style of Euainetos. Silver decadrachm	15,000	35,000		
19	27	Siculo-Punic. Machanat series, c. 330-325 B.C. Silver tetradrachm	3,500	9,000		
20	27	Carthage, c. 260 B.C. Gold trihemistater	7,500	15,000	20,000	
21	29	Celts. Danube region, c. second century B.C. Imitating Philip II of Macedon ("Reiterstumpf"). Silver tetradrachm	1,000	2,500		
22	29	Bosporos. Pharnakes II (63-47 B.C.). Panticapaeum, c. 53/52 B.C. Gold stater	10,000	25,000		
23	31	Pontos. Mithradates VI, 120-63 B.C. Silver tetradrachm	2,500	5,000	9,500	
24	31	Achaemenid. Darius I / Xerxes II, c. 485-420 B.C. Gold daric	1,500	3,500	5,000	
25	33	Bar Kochba (132-135 A.D.). Year Two, struck 133/134 A.D. Large bronze	17,500	30,000		
26	33	Bactria. Eukratides (c. 171-135 B.C.). Merv. mint. Heroic bust. Silver tetradrachm	2,750	7,500		
27	35	Persis. Bagadates I (c. 220-180 B.C.). Silver tetradrachm.	7,000	20,000		
28	35	Kushans. Kanishka I (c. 127-152 A.D.) / Shiva. Gold dinar	1,500	3,000	5,000	
\multicolumn{7}{c}{CHAPTER TWO: ANCIENT ROMAN COINAGE}						
29	39	Rome. Julius Caesar (d. 44 B.C.). Jan-Feb 44 B.C. M Mettius. Denarius	5,000	12,500		
30	39	Rome. Brutus (d. 42 B.C.). Struck summer/autumn 42 B.C. Gold aureus	75,000	250,000		
31	43	Rome. Marc Antony / Octavian. Ephesus (?), 41 B.C., M Barbatius Pollio. Gold aureus	10,000	30,000		
32	43	Rome. Sextus Pompey (d. 35 B.C.). Sicily, 42 B.C. Gold aureus	27,500	65,000		
33	45	Rome. Octavian (44-27 B.C.). Ephesus (?), 28 B.C. Crocodile. Denarius	2,500	9,500		
34	45	Rome. Tiberius, 14-37 AD. After 16 AD. Livia (?) as Pax, enthroned. Aureus	2,750	4,500	9,500	
35	45	Rome. Caligula (37-41 A.D.). Head of Germanicus. Gold aureus	10,000	35,000		

COIN	PAGE	DESCRIPTION	VERY FINE	EXTREMELY FINE	UNCIRCULATED	PROOF
36	47	Rome. Caligula (37-41 A.D.). C. 37-38 A.D. "Three Graces" brass sestertius	$10,000	$25,000		
37	47	Rome. Claudius (41-54 A.D.) C. 41-42 A.D. Sear II 1831. Gold aureus	6,000	20,000		
38	49	Rome. Nero (54-68 A.D.). C. Oct-Dec 54 A.D. Agrippina, RIC 1 variety. Gold aureus	7,500	20,000		
39	51	Rome. Galba (68-69 A.D.). Late 68 A.D. Sear II 2091. Gold aureus	10,000	40,000		
40	51	Rome. Vitellius (69 A.D.). Aug-early Dec 69 A.D. Calico 571 (this coin). Gold aureus	17,500	55,000		
41	53	Rome. Vespasian (69-79 A.D.). C. 71 A.D. Judaea Capta. Sear II 2327. Sestertius	10,000	30,000		
42	55	Rome. Domitian. Germania as mourning captive. Gold aureus	6,000	17,500	$30,000	
43	57	Rome. Trajan (98-117 A.D.). C. 109 A.D. "Arabia" gold aureus	5,000	12,500		
44	57	Rome. Hadrian (117-138 A.D.). C. 130-138 A.D. Jupiter Victor. Sear II 3397. Gold aureus	4,500	9,500	17,500	
45	59	Rome. Marcus Aurelius, Caesar (139-161 A.D.). 148-149 A.D. Fides. Sear II 4768. Gold aureus	4,000	8,000	15,000	
46	59	Rome. Lucius Versus (161-169 A.D.). C. 163-164 A.D. Verus on platform, with king of Armenia. Aureus	4,500	9,500	15,000	
47	61	Rome. Didius Julianus. 193 A.D. Rome mint, Togate Didius. Sear II 6071. Gold aureus	25,000	50,000		
48	63	Rome. Septimius Severus (193-111 A.D.). C. 198 A.D. Victory walking left. Gold aureus	6,000	15,000	25,000	
49	63	Rome. Julia Domna (193-217 A.D.). 201 A.D. Domna / child Caracalla and Geta. Fr-409. Gold aureus	15,000	25,000	40,000	
50	65	Rome. Elagabalus (218-222 A.D.). C. 218 A.D. Victory striding right. Gold aureus	7,000	15,000	25,000	
51	67	Rome. Severus Alexander (222-235 A.D.). 223 A.D. Colosseum. Sear II 7825. Gold aureus		200,000		
52	67	Rome. Gallienus (253-268 A.D.). 263 A.D. Legend, wreath. RIC 41. Gold "heavy aureus"	7,500	15,000		
53	69	Rome. Postumus (260-268 A.D.). Colonia Agrippinensis, c. 260-268 A.D. Postumus seated left on platform. RIC 276. Gold aureus	15,000	35,000		
54	69	Rome. Diocletian (284-305 A.D.). C. 285-286 A.D. Jupiter frontal, nude. Gold aureus	3,000	5,000	8,500	
55	71	Rome. Licinius I (308-324 A.D.). C. 321-322 A.D. Facing bust / facing enthroned Jupiter. Fr-821. Gold solidus	12,000	25,000	40,000	
56	73	Rome. Constantine I (307-337 A.D.). Antioch, c. 335-336 A.D. Victory advancing left with trophy. Fr-840 variety. Gold solidus	4,000	7,500	10,000	
57	73	Rome. Romulus Augustus (475-476 A.D.). Military bust frontal / Victory left holding cross. RIC 3404. Gold solidus	30,000	60,000		

CHAPTER THREE: COINS OF THE MIDDLE AGES

COIN	PAGE	DESCRIPTION	VERY FINE	EXTREMELY FINE	UNCIRCULATED	PROOF
58	79	Rome. Marcian (451-457). Constantinople, c. 450-453. RIC 510. Gold solidus	400	700	1,000	
59	81	Persia. Sasanian. Xushro II (591-628). C. 611 or 613. MACW 1107. Gold dinar	4,500	8,000		
60	85	Aksumite Kingdom. Anonymous, c. 450-500. Munro-Hay 81. Gold unit	1,500	2,000	3,500	
61	91	Byzantine Empire. Justinian II, second reign (705-711). Bust of Christ (second type). SBC 1414. Gold solidus	1,250	2,500	3,500	
62	91	Byzantine Empire. Basil I (867-886). Struck 868-879. SBC 1704. Gold solidus	450	900	1,200	
63	93	Lombardic Kingdom. Liutprand (712-744). Milan. Fr-942 (Pavia). Gold tremissis	2,000	3,500		
64	95	Carolingian. Charlemagne (768-814). Milan (?). RX - F, Cf. MEC 730, 731. Denarius	3,000	6,500		
65	99	Britain. Mercia. Offa (757-796). Canterbury. North 301; S-905. Silver denarius (penny)	9,000	17,500		

COIN	PAGE	DESCRIPTION	VERY FINE	EXTREMELY FINE	UNCIRCULATED	PROOF
66	99	Britain. Wessex. Alfred (871-899). London. North 646; S-1062. Silver penny	$4,000	$10,000		
67	101	Hiberno-Viking. Anlaf Guthrithsson (939-941). North 537; S-1019. Silver penny	7,500	15,000		
68	101	British Kings. Hardicnut (1040-1042). Taunton. North 811; S-1168. Silver penny	4,000	10,000		
69	103	British Kings. Harold II (1066). Lewes. North 836; S-1163. Pax type. Silver penny	1,500	3,000		
70	103	Britain. Norman Kings. William I (1066-1087). Hastings mint. North 839; S-1250. Cross fleury type. Silver penny	1,000	2,500		
71	109	Germany. Erfurt. Henry I of Harbourg (1142-1153). Cf. Peus Bonhoff Sale 293, no. 1085. Silver denar	500	1,000	$2,500	
72	111	Crusaders, Rhodes. Order of St. John H. de Villeneuve (1319-1346). Silver grosso gigliato	300	750	1,500	
73	113	Frankish Greece. Andrea Dandolo, Venice. Imitation from Chios. Cf. Fr-38a (Italy, Achaea). Gold ducat	500	1,500	2,500	
74	117	Britain. Edward III. Calais. S-1521. Fourth Coinage. Post-Treaty. Gold noble	2,000	3,500	6,000	
75	117	Anglo-Gallic. Aquitaine. Edward III (1327-1377). Fr-4 (Aquitaine). Leopard d'or	2,500	5,000		
76	121	England. Black Prince. Pavilion d'or	5,500	12,500	17,500	
77	121	Spain. Castille and Leon. Pedro I (1350-1368). Seville. Fr-108. Gold dobla	2,500	4,500		
78	123	Flanders. Louis de Maele (1346-1384). Ghent. Fr-163. Chaise d'or	1,500	2,750	4,000	

CHAPTER FOUR: COINS OF THE EUROPEAN RENAISSANCE

COIN	PAGE	DESCRIPTION	VERY FINE	EXTREMELY FINE	UNCIRCULATED	PROOF
79	133	Austria. Maximilian and Mary of Burgundy. C. 1497. Only two known. Gold 7 ducats	–	500,000	–	
80	133	Spain. Ferdinand and Isabel (1469-1504). Fr-125. Gold 4 excelentes	12,500	25,000		
81	135	Spain. Enrique the Weak (1454-1474). Gold enrique	2,000	4,500	7,500	
82	137	Britain. Mary Tudor. 1553 (Roman numeral). S-2488. Gold sovereign	13,000	25,000		
83	137	Italy. Milan. Philip II of Spain. 1578. Gold doppia	1,250	2,500	4,000	
84	141	Britain. Elizabeth I (1558-1605). Milled coinage, no date. S-2543. By Mestrelle, curly Z. Gold half pound	5,000	12,500		
85	141	Britain. Henry VII. S.2187. Gold angel	1,750	3,000	5,000	
86	143	Low Countries. Philip the Good (1419-1467). Bruges. Fr-185. Lion d'or	1,500	3,000	5,500	
87	143	Austria. Wolf Dietrich v. Raitenau. Fr-569. Gold 10 ducats	15,000	25,000		
88	145	Switzerland. Zurich. 1512. Dav-8771. Silver guldiner	2,500	5,000	10,000	
89	147	Austria. Counts of Schlick (1505-1526). No date (Joachimsthal). Dav-8138. Taler	2,000	5,000		
90	147	Austria. Sigismund (1446-1490). 1486. Dav-8087. First dated dollar. Guldiner	5,000	10,000		
91	149	Spanish Netherlands. Philip II (1555-1598). No date. Delm-88. Double taler	7,500	15,000		
92	149	Germany. Saxony. Friedrich III. Hall, no date (1512). Dav-9699. Guldengroschen	4,000	12,500		
93	151	France. Lorraine. Antoine I (1508-1544). 1544. Boudeau 1514. Testone	900	2,500		
94	151	Italy. Milan. Giovanni Galeazzo Maria Sforza. Fr-693 variety. Gold doppia ducato	10,000	25,000		

CHAPTER FIVE: 1600-1750: THE AGE OF REASON?

COIN	PAGE	DESCRIPTION	VERY FINE	EXTREMELY FINE	UNCIRCULATED	PROOF
95	155	Spain. Philip IV (1621-1665). 1635-R (Seville). Dav-LS567. 50 reales	20,000	37,000		
96	159	Austria. Leopold I. 1661. Fr-174. 5 ducats	5,000	11,000	18,000	
97	161	France. Louis XIII. 1642-A (Paris). Dav-3796. 60 sols	2,000	4,500	10,000	
98	163	Germany. Nuremberg. Leopold I. 1698. Fr-1873. Peace of Rijswik. 5 ducats	5,000	11,000	15,000	
99	165	Germany. Nuremberg. Charles VI. 1733. Dav-2480. Reichstaler	3,000	7,500		

COIN	PAGE	DESCRIPTION	VERY FINE	EXTREMELY FINE	UNCIRCULATED	PROOF
100	167	Germany. Regensburg. Fr-2558. 8 ducats	$10,000	$20,000	$45,000	
101	169	Germany. Brunswick-Wolfenbuttel-Luneburg. Rudolf August. 1685. Dav/Sond-110a. 3 talers	4,000	8,000		
102	173	Britain. Charles I. Oxford, 1644-OXON. S-2729. Small "elan." Triple unite	20,000	45,000		
103	173	Britain. Charles II. 1644. S-3341; Fr-288. Second bust. Guinea	15,000	35,000	55,000	
104	175	Britain. William III. 1701. S-3457. "Fine Work" 2 guineas	5,000	10,000	18,000	
105	179	Britain. Anne. 1703. S-3561. VIGO. 5 guineas	30,000	75,000	125,000	
106	181	Britain. George II. 1746. S-3689; Dav-1350. Old Head. DECIMO NONO edge. LIMA crown	1,250	4,500	10,000	
107	181	Massachusetts Colony. 1652. Large Planchet. Noe 1; Crosby 12-I. 72.2 gns. R-2. Pine Tree shilling	5,000	12,500	35,000	
108	183	Netherlands. Holland. 1684. Dav-4953 (Rarity-2). Dies by Drappentier. Provincial 3 gulden	300	750	1,500	
109	183	Netherlands. Utrecht. 1648. Dav-4863. Lionthaler	150	500		
110	185	Netherlands. Netherlands East India Company. 1645. (Batavia.) Dav-415. Kroon		85,000		
111	187	Austrian Netherlands. Maria Theresa. 1749. Dav-1280. Ducatone	300	750	1,500	
112	191	Italy. Genova. Biennial doges. 1639. Dav-555. Scudo largo	3,500	8,000		
113	191	Italy. Tuscany, Livorno. Cosimo III di Medici. 1704. Dav-1498. Tollero	900	2,500		
114	195	Italy. Papal States. Innocent XII (1691-1700). No date (1693). Dav-4103. Piastra	1,500	3,500	1,750	
115	197	Russia. Peter I. Moscow, 1705. Fr-76. Novodel ruble			350,000	
116	197	Sweden. Pomerania. Karl XII (1697-1718). Fr-2118. 2 ducats	5,000	12,500		

CHAPTER SIX: AN AGE OF REVOLUTION, 1776-1914

COIN	PAGE	DESCRIPTION	VERY FINE	EXTREMELY FINE	UNCIRCULATED	PROOF
117	203	Germany. Brunswick-Luneburg-Calenberg-Hanover. George III (of Britain). 1777. Dav-2107. Taler	900	2,000	3,500	
118	209	United States of America. 1776. Breen 1089; Newman 1-C. Pewter, CONTINENTAL CURENCY. Continental dollar	15,000	25,000	50,000	
119	213	United States of America. 1795. Capped Bust, Small Eagle type. Gold eagle	22,500	35,000	75,000	
120	213	United States of America. 1802. B-6 (R-1); BB-241; URS-12. Narrow date. Silver dollar	2,500	5,000	20,000	
121	215	France. Convention coinage. 1793-A (Paris). Fr-478. 24 livres	3,000	5,000	11,000	
122	219	Italy. Cisalpine Republic. Anno VIII (1800). Dav-199. 6 lira	1,000	2,000	4,500+	
123	219	France. Napoleon Bonaparte, First Consul. AN-XI-A. Dav-82. 5 francs	250	800	1,500+	
124	221	France. Napoleon Bonaparte. 1815-A (Paris). Dav-85. "100 Days" issue. 5 francs	700	1,500		
125	221	Germany. Berg-Casa. Joachim Murat (1806-1808). 1807. Dav-625. Taler	1,250	3,500	7,500	
126	223	Italy. Kingdom of Naples. Joseph Napoleon. 1808. Dav-165. 120 grani	850	2,500		
127	223	Spain. Joseph Napoleon. 1810-RS (Madrid). Fr-300. 320 reales	10,000	25,000		
128	225	Netherlands. Napoleonic Kingdom. Louis Napoleon. 1809 (Holland). Dav-230. Rijksdaalder	6,000	12,000	25,000	
129	225	Germany. Westphalia. Jerome Napoleon Bonaparte. 1808-J (Paris). Fr-3517. 20 franken				$7,000
130	227	Belgium. Insurrection, Brussels (1790-1792). Fr-402. Lion d'or	2,500	5,500	9,500	
131	229	Greece. George I (1863-1913). 1876 A (Paris). Fr-13. 100 drachmai		75,000	150,000	
132	231	African Gold Coast. George III. 1818. Dav-36; KM-9. Ackey	650	1,250	2,500	
133	234	Annam (Viet Nam). Thieu Tri (1841-1847). No date. Fr-3. Piaster	3,500	7,500		
134	234	China. Kuang Hsu (1875-1908). 1906 (Tientsin). Fr-1. 1 K'uping tael		60,000	100,000	
135	234	Australia. New South Wales. 1813. KM-213. 5 shillings (Holey Dollar)	50,000	95,000		

COIN	PAGE	DESCRIPTION	VERY FINE	EXTREMELY FINE	UNCIRCULATED	PROOF
136	235	South Australia. Victoria (1837-1901). Adelaide, 1852. Type 2. Fr-3. Pound	$17,500	$40,000	$60,000	
137	235	Belgian Congo. Leopold II (1865-1909). 1887. Dav-10. 5 francs	750	1,250	2,500	$5,000
138	235	German New Guinea. 1895-A (Berlin). Fr-1. "Bird of Paradise." 20 marks				35,000
139	237	United States of America. 1876. Trade dollar	100	150	1,500	2,500
140	237	Great Britain. 1934-B. KM-Tn5. Trade dollar	150	200	500	3,500
141	239	Ireland. George III. 1804. Dav-101. Bank of Ireland dollar (6 shillings)	300	800	1,500	2,500
142	239	Britain. George III. 1818. S-3785A; Fr-371. New Coinage. Gold sovereign	1,100	2,100	6,000	15,000
143	241	Britain. Victoria (1837-1901). 1839. "Una and the Lion." S-3851; Fr-386. Five pounds				50,000

CHAPTER SEVEN: LATIN AMERICAN COLONIAL COINAGE

COIN	PAGE	DESCRIPTION	VERY FINE	EXTREMELY FINE	UNCIRCULATED	PROOF
144	247	Mexico. Charles and Johanna. No date (1538). Mint M. Assayer R. 8 reales		500,000		
145	249	Peru. No date (c. 1568-1571). WR-16. Assayer R. First Peru dollar. 8 reales	100,000	275,000		
146	251	Mexico. Philip III (1598-1621). No date. WR-2. Royal 8 reales	25,000	50,000		
147	255	Bolivia. Philip IV (1621-1665). 1650. WR-4. Royal 8 reales	20,000	35,000		
148	255	Mexico. Philip V. 1714-Mo-J. Fr-- (cf. Krause/Mishler, *World Coins, 1700-1800*, p. 753). Royal 8 escudos			100,000	
149	257	Mexico. Philip V (1700-1746). 1723-MO-J. WR-5. Royal 8 reales	25,000	50,000		
150	257	Bolivia. Louis I (1724). 1727 P-Y. WR-10. Royal 8 reales	50,000	100,000		
151	259	Mexico. 1732 Mo-MF. Pillar dollar. 8 reales	20,000	35,000	55,000	
152	261	Brazil. Joao V. 1732-M (Mina Gerais). Fr-55. "Gold Joe." 12,800 reis	1,500	3,500	6,500	
153	263	Chile. 1758 So-J. Eliz.-8. 8 reales	30,000	50,000		
154	263	Jamaica. George II. No date (1758). Prid-4 type. Countermark GR monogram on Peru (Lima) Pillar dollar, Ferdinand VI	1,000	2,000		
155	267	Colombia. 1759 NoRo-JV. 8 reales	40,000	85,000		
156	267	Greenland. Copenhagen, 1771 (1774). Dav-411a. "ISLAND" variety. Specimen strike. Pillar dollar (piastre)		40,000	75,000	
157	269	Mexico. Charles III. 1763-Mo-MM. Fr-29. 8 escudos	4,500	9,000	24,000	
158	269	Chile. Charles III. 1764 So-J. Fr-11. "Rat-nose" 8 escudos	6,000	10,000	25,000	
159	271	Guatemala. Charles III. 1787NG-M. Eliz-41. 8 reales	900	2,000	10,000	
160	271	Colombia. Ferdinand VII. 1811 P-JF. Eliz.-3. 8 reales	6,000	12,500		

CHAPTER EIGHT: COINS OF THE LATIN AMERICAN REPUBLICS

COIN	PAGE	DESCRIPTION	VERY FINE	EXTREMELY FINE	UNCIRCULATED	PROOF
161	277	Mexico. Insurgent coinage, Zitacuaro. 1811. Eliz.-MX120. 8 reales		60,000		
162	277	Mexico. Iturbide. 1822-Mo-JM. Fr-59. First portrait type. 8 escudos	4,500	9,000	20,000	
163	279	Mexico. 1823-Mo-JM. Fr-3. Type II. 8 escudos	12,500	20,000	35,000	
164	281	Mexico. Durango. 1824-Do-RL. Hubbard & O'Harrow Die pairings no. L9-N5. DP-Do01; KM 376. 8 reales	2,000	4,000		
165	281	Mexico. Republic. 1827-Pi-JS. WR-63; Eliz-801. 8 reales			25,000	
166	285	Guatemala. Republic of the Center of America. 1824-NG-M (New Guatemala). Fr-26. KM-8. 8 escudos	20,000	60,000	150,000	
167	285	Argentina. Provincias del Rio de la Plata. 1813 PTS-J (Potosi). Fr-1. 8 escudos	25,000	60,000	100,000	
168	287	Chile. 1828. Un peso		50,000	75,000	
169	289	Argentina. Republic. 1842-R. Fr-10. 8 escudos	30,000	50,000		
170	291	Ecuador. Republic. 1846-GJ. WR-1; Eliz-1. Liberty type. 8 reales	4,000	9,000	17,500	
171	293	Bolivia. Republic. 1852-FP. Fr-33. Laureate head type. 8 escudos	12,500	24,000	40,000	
172	297	Colombia. Granadine Confederation. 1859. Fr-87. 20 pesos	6,000	10,000		
173	297	Uruguay. Republic. 1870. Cf. WR-2 (not this date). Peso				30,000
174	299	Venezuela. Republic. 1876. Eliz.1. Venezolano	500	3,500	15,000	

COIN	PAGE	DESCRIPTION	VERY FINE	EXTREMELY FINE	UNCIRCULATED	PROOF
175	301	Guatemala. 1878 F. Fr-44. 20 pesos	$14,000	$20,000	$35,000	
176	303	Mexico. Revolution. Chihuahua, 1913. WR-R2; Eliz-MX191. GB-78 (plate coin); KM-610 (plate coin). "La Bolita" peso	6,000	10,000		
177	305	Mexico. Revolution. Constitutionalist Army. 1914. Cf. KM-Pn-3. Silver peso			30,000	
178	305	Mexico. Revolution. Zapata Issues. Suriana, Guerrero, 1915-GRO. WR-R5; Suriana, "DOBE." 2 pesos	22,000	35,000		

Abbreviation Key

B	Bolender	**Dav/Sond**	Davenport/Sondegaard	**MACW**	Mitchiner
BB	Bowers/Borckardt	**Eliz**	Elizondo	**RIC**	*The Roman Imperial*
Dav	Davenport	**KM**	Krause/Mishler		*Coinage* (Mattingly, et al.)

Bibliography

Bolender, M.H. *The United States Early Silver Dollars From 1794 to 1803* (third edition), Iola, 1982 (reprinted 1987).

Boudeau, E. *Monnaies Francaises Provinciales* (revised edition), Maastricht, 1970.

Breen, Walter. *Walter Breen's Complete Encyclopedia of U.S. and Colonial Coins*, New York, 1988.

Crosby, S.S. *The Early Coins of America*, Boston, 1875 (reprinted 1945, 1965, 1974, 1983).

Davenport, J.S. *European Crowns, 1484–1600*, Frankfurt am Main, 1977.

Davenport, John S. *European Crowns, 1600–1700*, Galesburg, 1974.

Davenport, John S. *European Crowns, 1700–1800*, London, 1964

Davenport, John S. *European Crowns and Talers Since 1800*, London, 1964.

Davenport, John S. *German Talers, 1500–1600*, Frankfurt am Main, 1979.

Davenport, John S. *German Secular Talers, 1600–1700*, Frankfurt am Main, 1976.

Davenport, John S. *German Church and City Talers, 1600–1700*, Galesburg, 1967.

Davenport, John S. *German Talers, 1700–1800*, London, 1965.

Davenport, John S. *The Dollars of Africa Asia and Oceania*, Galesburg, 1969.

Davenport, John S. *Silver Gulden, 1559–1763*, Frankfurt am Main, 1982.

Davenport, John S. *Eastern Baltic Regional Coinage, A. D. 1425–1581*, Dallas, 1996.

Davenport, John S., and Tyge Sondergaard. *Large Size Silver Coins of the World*, Iola, 1991.

Elizondo, C. *Eight Reales and Pesos of the New World* (second edition), San Antonio, 1971.

Friedberg, Arthur L. and Ira S. *Gold Coins of the World, from Ancient Times to the Present* (seventh edition). Clifton, 2002.

Krause, Chester L., and Clifford Mishler. *Standard Catalog of World Coins* (four volumes: 1901–Present; Nineteenth Century; Eighteenth Century; Seventeenth Century), Iola, 1999–2004.

Kritt, Brian. *Seleucid Coins of Bactria. Classical Numismatic Studies No. 1*, Lancaster, 1996.

Mattingly, Harold, et al. *The Roman Imperial Coinage*, volumes 1–10, London, 1923–1994.

Mitchiner, Michael. *Oriental Coins and Their Values. The Ancient & Classical World, 600 B.C.–A.D. 650*, London, 1978.

Munro-Hay, S.C., and Bent Jeul-Jensen. *Aksumite Coinage*, London, 1995.

Newman, Eric P., and Richard Doty. *Studies on Money in Early America*, New York, 1976.

North, J.J. *English Hammered Coinage* (two volumes), London, 1963, 1975.

Sear, David. *Roman Coins and Their Values*, volumes I–III, London, 2000–2005.

Spink. *Coins of England and the United Kingdom: Spink Standard Catalogue of British Coins*, 41st edition, London, 2006.